Mercosur:
Between Integration
and Democracy

Mercosur:
Between Integration and Democracy

Francisco Domínguez
Marcos Guedes de Oliveira
(eds)

PETER LANG
Oxford · Bern · Berlin · Bruxelles · Frankfurt am Main · New York · Wien

Bibliographic information published by Die Deutsche Bibliothek
Die Deutsche Bibliothek lists this publication in the Deutsche Nationalbibliografie;
detailed bibliographic data is available on the Internet at ‹http://dnb.ddb.de›.

British Library and Library of Congress Cataloguing-in-Publication Data:
A catalogue record for this book is available from The British Library, Great Britain,
and from The Library of Congress, USA

Cover design: Thomas Jaberg, Peter Lang AG

ISBN 3-906769-83-6
US-ISBN 0-8204-5920-8

© Peter Lang AG, European Academic Publishers, Bern 2004
Hochfeldstrasse 32, Postfach 746, CH-3000 Bern 9, Switzerland
info@peterlang.com, www.peterlang.com, www.peterlang.net

All rights reserved.
All parts of this publication are protected by copyright.
Any utilisation outside the strict limits of the copyright law, without the permission
of the publisher, is forbidden and liable to prosecution.
This applies in particular to reproductions, translations, microfilming, and
storage and processing in electronic retrieval systems.

Printed in Germany

Peter Lambert
Paraguay in Mercosur: *¿para qué?* 157

Suranjit Kumar Saha
Core-Periphery in the Americas: Understanding the Political
Economy of Mercosur and FTAA 181

Bibliography 205

About the Authors 215

Contents

Acknowledgements	7
Introduction	9
Basic Facts about Mercosur	11
Abbreviations and Glossary	13
Marcos Guedes de Oliveira Limitations on Democratic Transitions in Latin America and the Fate of Mercosur	17
Francisco Domínguez Democracy and Economic Integration: The Continental Context	29
Marcos Costa Lima Mercosur and the New Global Order: a Methodological Essay	57
Marcelo de Almeida Medeiros Multi Level Governance and the Problem of Balance within Mercosur	75
Tullo Vigevani, Karina Pasquariello Mariano and Marcelo Fernandes de Oliveira Mercosur: Democracy and Political Actors	97
Olivier Dabène Does Mercosur Still Have a Project?	141

Acknowledgements

The editors wish to thank all the referees who, in subjecting the original submission to rigorous criticism, helped us significantly to improve this contribution. Thanks also go to the authors whose resilience and determination to get this volume in print led them to endure going over several drafts, something they did with exemplary patience. Our recognition must be extended to the Centre for Brazilian Studies at Middlesex University, for providing the primary academic impetus and initiative that ended up being this book. Last but not least, our thanks to Anna Milsom for the painstaking and tedious but precious task of checking the final manuscript.

Introduction

This volume aims to contribute to the understanding of the process of regional integration currently underway in the South of the American continent in the form of Mercosur. Mercosur is a regional manifestation of the worldwide process of globalisation whose driving force is economic, but which is much more than that. In fact, it involves political, social and cultural processes, some of them barely at an embryonic stage, each advancing at uneven rates of progress.

A crucial but unavoidable dimension of any analysis of Mercosur is the economic policy framework, namely, neo-liberalism, within which it has been both conceived and implemented. As shown by the experience of the entire American continent, neo-liberalism takes the economic decision-making process outside the realm of politics, leaving social actors, especially large non-powerful majorities, with no mechanism to influence the integration process so that it addresses their urgent needs and demands. Thus if one regards Mercosur as a merely defensive reaction to the aggressive US policy to set up a Free Trade Area of the Americas threatening to descend from North America with the force of a flood that may engulf the continent right up to the icy Cape Horn, such a defence seems flawed insofar as it is structured around core principles of the neo-liberal agenda. The integration process underway benefits only a relatively small proportion of the population and few of the more developed regions and industries of the member and associated states, to the detriment of peripheral areas within the geographical space of Mercosur.

Marcos Guedes' 'Limitations on Democratic Transitions in Latin America and the Fate of Mercosur' looks at the post-dictatorship legacy in Brazil and examines how the bureaucratisation of the political decision-making process under Cardoso militates against democratic expansion, and conditions the fate of Mercosur. Francisco Domínguez advances a critique of 'neo-liberal democracy' in his 'Democracy and Economic Integration: the Continental Context', in which his contextualisation centres on the rivalry between the USA and the European Union over Mercosur and Latin America. Marcos Lima's 'Mercosur and the New Global Order: a Methodological Essay', supplies the volume with an analysis of how to understand theoretically Mercosur within the overall process of globalisation. Marcelo de Almeida Medeiros in 'Multi-Level Governance and the Problem of Balance within Mercosur' discusses the various layers of political decision-making in Mercosur, an analysis he places within a historical survey of the Latin American experience of state formation. Tullo Vigevani, Karina Pasquarello Mariano and Marcelo Fernandes de Oliveira, in 'Mercosur: Democracy and Political Actors', show how Mercosur operates at the level of its formal institutions and the extent to which social and political actors influence the political process in the member states. In 'Does Mercosur Still Have a Project?' Olivier Dabene puts forward a critical view of the inconsistencies and weaknesses of the establishment and consolidation of Mercosur as a vibrant regional process of integration. Peter Lambert, in 'Paraguay in Mercosur: ¿Para Qué?', offers an insightful analysis of Paraguay's relationship with Mercosur, in which this extremely poor, landlocked country has failed to benefit significantly from its membership of Mercosur, except in the crucial question of defending its ever-precarious democracy. Finally, Suranjit Kumar Saha, in 'Core-Periphery in the Americas: Understanding the Political Economy of Mercosur and the FTAA', looks at the core periphery relationship, at both continental as well as Mercosur levels, thus advancing our understanding of Mercosur in an area that has been generally neglected.

It is to be hoped that this volume will both help students of regional integration processes, globalisation, Mercosur and Latin America to gain a better understanding of the current reality of the effects of neo-liberalism and globalisation in the Americas and become an incentive for further research.

Basic Facts about Mercosur

MERCOSUR, the Mercado Común del Sur (in Spanish) or Mercado Comum do Sul (in Portuguese), is a process of integration between Brazil, Argentina, Paraguay and Uruguay begun in 1991 with the signature of the Asunción Treaty. The final objective is to establish a common market in South America. Mercosur has signed free trade agreements with Chile and Bolivia.

Mercosur and the European Union have also signed a free Trade Agreement, which is the first of this type in the world.

Mercosur has continental dimensions with a geographical area of about 12 million km^2 and with a potential market of over 200 million people and with an added GDP of about 1 trillion dollars, which makes it the fourth largest regional economy in the world after NAFTA, the European Union and Japan. Mercosur has become one of the major poles of attraction of investment worldwide.

MERCOSUR: BASIC INFRASTRUCTURE	
Railways	68,643 km
Motorways	2,114,923 km
Navigable rivers	65,000 km
Pipelines (oil)	12,794 km
Pipelines (gas)	11,013 km
Airports	6,083 units
Telephones	12,925,300 units

Source: ECLAC

MAIN INDICATORS OF MERCOSUR AND COMPARISON WITH OTHER REGIONS

GDP: 2000

	US$ bn	%
Mercosur	914.2	2.92
Mercosur, Chile and Bolivia	992.2	3.17
NAFTA	10,748.3	34.32
European Union	8,440.2	26.95
Asia (Selected) [1]	897.0	2.86
Other	10,237.3	32.69
World	31,315.0	100.00

(1) Includes South Korea, Hong-Kong, Malaysia, Singapore and Thailand.

Commercial Exchange: 2000[1]

	US$ bn	%	% GDPI[1]
Mercosur	174.5	1.34	19.09
Mercosur, Chile and Bolivia	212.6	1.64	21.43
NAFTA	2,865.1	22.07	26.66
European Union	4,579.5	35.27	54.26
Asia (Selected) [2]	1,331.4	10.25	148.43
Other	3,994.4	30.77	39.02
World	12,983.0	100.00	41.46

(1) Exports (FOB) plus imports (CIF).
(2) Includes South Korea, Hong-Kong, Malaysia, Singapore and Thailand.

Source: IMF – Direction of Trade Statistics.

Abbreviations and Glossary

AILA	Latin American Industries Association: regional association of industrialists in Mercosur.
ALADI	Asociación Latinoamericana de Integración: Latin American Integration Association – LAIA. Set up in 1980 to promote economic integration among the countries in the region.
ALALC	Asociación Latinoamericana de Libre Comercio: Latin American Free Trade Association – LAFTA. Set up in 1960 to promote free trade among the countries of the region.
Andean Pact	Regional agreement of economic coordination of the Andean countries set up in 1969 (Peru, Bolivia, Chile, Ecuador, Colombia and Venezuela; Chile used to be a member but withdrew during Pinochet's dictatorship. Post-Pinochet governments have not renewed the country's membership).
APEC	Asia-Pacific Economic Cooperation established in 1989 in response to the growing interdependence among Asia-Pacific economies. APEC has become the primary regional vehicle for promoting open trade and practical economic cooperation. Its goal is to advance Asia-Pacific economic dynamism and a sense of community. The GDP for APEC economies for the year 2000 was US$17,921 billion and its percentage of global trade for the same year was 46.76%.
ASEAN	Association of South East Asian Nations: body of economic cooperation among South East Asian nations (Japan, Brunei Darussalam, Cambodia, Indonesia, Laos, Malaysia, Myanmar, Philippines, Singapore, Thailand, and Vietnam).
CARICOM	The Caribbean Community and Common Market (CARICOM) was established by the Treaty of Chaguaramas, which was signed by Barbados, Jamaica, Guyana and Trinidad & Tobago and came into effect on 1 August 1973. Subsequently the other eight Caribbean territories joined CARICOM. The Bahamas became the 13th member state of the Community on 4 July 1983. In July

Abbreviations and Glossary

	1991 the British Virgin Islands and the Turks and Caicos became Associated Members. Twelve other states from Latin America and the Caribbean enjoy Observer Status in various institutions of the Community and CARICOM ministerial bodies. Suriname became its 14th Member State on 4 July 1995.
CCSCS	Coordinadora de Centrales Sindicales del Cono Sur (Southern Cone Confederation of Unions) which involve membership from trade union federations of all South America, not only from the Mercosur countries.
CMC	Mercosur's Common Market Council set up by the Ouro Preto Protocol, December 1994; responsible for the political conduct of the integration process, and made up of Economic and Foreign Ministers of the member states. The CMC operates by unanimous decisions, which are compulsory on all member states; its presidency rotates every six months.
CMG	Mercosur's Common Market Group set up by the Ouro Preto Protocol, December 1994. Executive body of Mercosur, responsible for making recommendations about projects to the Common Market Council. It operates by unanimous resolutions on subjects delegated by the CMC, which are obligatory on all member-states. The CMG is composed of four delegates representing the Foreign Ministry, Economy Ministry and Central Bank from each member state. It has additionally ten working groups.
Crecenea-Cedesul	Body that coordinates the North-East Argentine provinces and the Southern Brazilian states.
ECLAC	Economic Commission for Latin America and the Caribbean – United Nations agency devoted to the study of socio-economic trends in Latin America and responsible for the publication of the journal, *CEPAL Review*.
ESFC	Mercosur's Economic-Social Consultative Forum set up by the Ouro Preto Protocol, December 1994. It gathers representatives of various pressure and interest groups from all sides of the economy (trade unions and business) of all member countries to discuss issues relevant to the integration process. Its function is consultative.
EU	European Union: regional economic community comprising 15 Western European countries (Germany, France, Italy, Spain,

Abbreviations and Glossary

Portugal, Greece, United Kingdom, The Netherlands, Belgium, Luxembourg, Finland, Sweden, Denmark, Ireland, Austria).

FTAA — Free Trade Area of the Americas (also known in Spanish as ALCA, Area de Libre Comercio de las Américas). US policy aim, of creating a single free-trade area in the American continent from Canada to Tierra del Fuego. It explicitly excludes Cuba.

GATT — General Agreement of Tariffs and Trade: international body responsible for regulating international trade behaviour and disputes. Replaced by the World Trade Organisation.

ICM — Industrial Council of Mercosur: regional organisation of industrialists in Mercosur. Its main function is lobbying on behalf of the region's industrialists.

JMC — Mercosur's Joint Parliamentary Commission set up by the Ouro Preto Protocol, December 1994. It represents the member states in Mercosur through the same number of deputies and senators to the JMC from their national parliaments. Its principal role is to accelerate national parliamentary procedures for the adoption and implementation of Mercosur's decisions, resolutions and directives at the domestic level. Its function is strictly consultative, and it operates through recommendations to the Common Market Council.

MAS — Mercosur's Administrative Secretariat set up by the Ouro Preto Protocol, December 1994; charged with the administrative running of Mercosur and publishing Mercosur's official publiccation, *The Official Journal*.

Mercociudades — Network of cities of Mercosur.

Montevideo Group — Network of universities in Mercosur countries.

MTC — Mercosur Trade Commission set up by the Ouro Preto Protocol, December 1994; charged with helping the Common Market Group in trade policy matters. It oversees trade policy within Mercosur and between the latter and third countries. It operates on the basis of unanimous directives that are binding on all member states and considers complaints about trade conflicts. It is composed of ten technical committees.

NAFTA	North American Free Trade Agreement: regional economic community between the United States, Canada and Mexico.
OECD	Organisation of Economic Cooperation and Development – body of coordination of about thirty of the most industrially and economically developed countries in the world, which is committed to the market economy and free trade.
TEC	Common External Tariff. Mercosur's policy of gradual application of a 'customs unions' policy that affects a range of products.
Treaty of Asunción	Treaty signed in Asunción, capital of Paraguay, on March 26, 1991, by Brazil, Argentina, Uruguay and Paraguay and which gave birth to Mercosur.
WTO	World Trade Organisation: international body that replaced GATT with the function of policing adherence to free trade.

Marcos Guedes de Oliveira

Limitations on Democratic Transitions in Latin America and the Fate of Mercosur

The universal exercise of democracy has never been achieved in Latin America. The association between domestic oligarchies and foreign economic interests has traditionally thwarted repeated efforts to forge a political and social democracy in the region. Populism, clientelism and corporatism have been some of the political mechanisms used by these interests in order to secure political control, as well as the social and political exclusion of the lower classes.

From the early 1930s and up to the 1960s, the means to control the Latin American nations politically depended essentially on the role of the state as political actor. The state was the means to: (a) provide local, regional and national élites with the resources to perpetuate, via clientelism, their parasitic hold on power; (b) co-opt leading sectors and representative institutions of the middle and working classes in order to demobilise opposition; (c) repress any attempt to substantially alter or challenge its élitist and authoritarian rule; (d) use the police to control social organisations and the media in order to manipulate public perception of politics and government. The state in Latin America has been large and omnipresent in its authoritarianism, but small and absent in its democratic scope.

In order to modernise their countries, regional élites adopted a strategy of import-substitution industrialisation. The state promoted industrial growth by protecting internal production and creating state companies to invest in infrastructure. Though this policy was successful in boosting industrialisation and securing the association of national, foreign and state élite interests alongside the processes of urbanisation and modernisation, it failed to deal with the issue of democracy.

Paradoxically since the 1960s the state's failure has been due to its achievements in achieving substantial import substitution industrialisation by home manufacture. Within a period of about fifty years it produced a complex urban society that did not fit within the limits of the populist state model. The contradiction between an outdated form of statehood and a modern society led to pressure for social change generating both a strong reaction from the élites in the form of military dictatorships and an intensification in the struggle for democracy and social justice.

US support of military dictatorships all over Latin America was in part also a response to the Cuban revolution and advances of social reform throughout Central and South America. The region's potential for continent wide social protest and revolution led the US to identify it as a key threat to its national security. Resources were made available to produce more intelligence and finance overt intervention. One result of this was the proliferation of military coups. A long term policy that began in 1964 with the US-supported military coup against the centre-left government of President Goulart in Brazil, was followed by the 1966 coup in Argentina, and reached its peak with the 1973 Pinochet coup against Chilean socialist President Salvador Allende.

Military governments, expression of a new alliance involving foreign and national capital and top state bureaucrats, were the consequence of the failure of the populist state. Repression against the working class and a radicalised petty bourgeoisie plus strong governmental control of trades unions, wages and political rights, aimed at holding the new alliance together, signalled a more authoritarian and one-sided policy. Politically, however, the retreat from the populist state led to a reduction in its power for co-option and permitted the rise of new social movements outside state-controlled trades unions.

In Argentina, after waging an open war against the opposition and abolishing labour organisations, the military suffered a major setback in the Malvinas/Falklands conflict. The military invasion of the Malvinas/Falklands gathered nationalistic support around General Galtieri's feeble government. Nevertheless, the war ended in defeat for the generals. Britain's reaction and subsequent victory over numerically superior Argentine armed forces turned the population against the military. This permitted the emergence of democratic currents in the country.

Like the Sarney government in Brazil, the democratically elected Alfonsin government in Argentina struggled to overcome the economic crisis inherited from the military and pushed strongly for a democratic transition. Inflation coupled with the determination of key sections of the élite of both countries to stop their respective democratisation processes or at best keep them under their control, slowed and deflected a rapid restoration of full democracy.

During the interregnum between the end of military rule and the imposition of neo-liberalism – and for the first time in the country's history – the Brazilian working class was able to organise itself outside state-controlled or communist-controlled trades unions. Charged with being both subversive and conservative, the labour movement that sprang up in São Paulo grew to the point of furnishing the social basis for a new political party, the Partido dos Trabalhadores (PT) and a new national trade union organisation, the Central Unica dos Trabalhadores (CUT). These two organisations have changed the face of politics in Brazil.

The upsurge generated by the struggle for democracy in South America cannot be associated exclusively with the emergence of these new social actors into the political arena. Nevertheless, in most countries in the region, a movement aimed at creating an alliance of diverse opposition forces around a project of democracy, included the guarantee of civil, social and human rights. This meant a radical change in the way of doing politics in the region. Unfortunately, the high expectations of this short-lived phase died out with the sharp decline of social democracy in Europe and the global imposition of new neo-liberalism.

The élite's response to this emerging social democratic project was an enthusiastic embrace of neo-liberalism. Chile was to be the first Latin American country unequivocally to take this road. After consolidating his hold on power, General Pinochet, under the guidance of monetarist technocrats, adopted an economic policy oriented towards market forces and privatisation. Governmental intervention in the economy was drastically reduced, and so was tariff protection. Government companies were sold off and the social state minimised. The economy was directed towards attracting foreign investments and producing goods for export. These central pillars of neo-liberal economic policy meant a shift in the relations between national and foreign élites. Now international, mainly banking and corporate foreign interests became overwhelmingly dominant.

In Argentina with Menem, and in Brazil with Collor, neo-liberalism was introduced after a presidential electoral campaign conducted around the rhetoric of social reform and the struggle against corruption. On coming to office Menem started a programme that involved privatising state companies, reducing inflation by means of recession and the dollarisation of the Argentine peso. This increased unemployment dramatically and provoked open rebellion from the government-supporting Peronist trades unions. Menem eased pressure on human rights trials and pardoned army officers who had been involved in human rights violations.

Collor came to power in Brazil late in 1989 and embarked upon a programme of privatisation and the opening up of the economy to international investment. Ousted from power amid accusations of corruption, Collor was succeeded by Itamar Franco who resisted neo-liberalism. However, Cardoso, Franco's successor, adopted the same rhetoric of social reforms that had brought Collor to office but reintroduced neo-liberal economic policies modelled on other regional experiences.

A decade of neo-liberalism in Latin America from 1992 to 2002 has brought about substantial change. Politically, the drive towards a democratic society has become twisted. Human rights issues remain unresolved, political parties continue to be weak and media manipulation and indifference towards electoral processes have increased. The reduction of already poor state services, the growth of poverty, and the rise of unemployment and low-paid employment predominate. This has resulted in acute political conflicts and doubts about the consolidation of democracy. The illusion that the Latin American economies would benefit by selling to a global and competitive open market became obvious when the region realised that the forces in favour of trade protectionism in both the European Union and the United States were predominant, and that their actions were jeopardising Latin America's comparative advantages.

Perhaps the most striking aspect of neo-liberal ideology in Latin America is the contradiction between the democratic discourse of its agents and the growth of social exclusion and political authoritarian mechanisms that have resulted from their practices.

For neo-liberals the sum total of democratic goals is changing the way presidents and political leaders in the region are chosen, ending political torture and state terrorism, and the freedom to organise political parties. Formal democracy and the freedom of political organisation are obviously of vital importance when compared to the situation Latin America experienced before. Nevertheless, this is a far cry from the democratic outcome many Latin Americans opposed to military regimes and traditional oligarchic alliances that dominate politics in the region, were seeking.

Traditionally democracy has been considered a means to broaden citizenship, not to increase social and political exclusion; a way to transform clientelistic and corrupt state structures into effective, transparent, socially functional ones. Overall, democracy has been defined as the search for equality and justice and political freedoms and the state were to be the means by which to achieve them. Conversely, neo-liberal democracy is defined from the perspective of international market interests. The solution to society's problems, such as, human rights issues and social exclusion result from the successful application of liberal economic reforms.

According to Pereira, neo-liberalism has presented itself in quite a sophisticated form in Brazil. It is associating its objectives with the long-established debate on the need to reform the Brazilian state around key ideological tenets, namely, limitation of its size; redefinition of its role as regulator; recovery of its financial and administrative capability; and enhancement of its ability to govern.[1]

The first two refer explicitly to the need for privatising state companies and for the state to retreat from economic and social activities into becoming just a regulatory and supervisory body. The recovery of the state's financial capability has been practically understood as an attempt to reduce the public deficit by increasing taxation on the middle class and laying off civil servants, while no reference is made to the payment of high interest on the external debt. In this context, the ability to govern is nothing but a rhetorical device. What has actually happened in Brazil and in Latin America as a whole is that, as neo-liberalism gathers pace, the inability to govern has spread.

---

1   Luis Carlos Bresser Pereira, *Reforming the State: Managerial Public Administration in Latin America*, London: Lynne Rienner Publishers, 1998.

Pereira's conclusion, that the new state would be directed towards fostering competition, not protectionism, towards subcontracting hiring social services rather than supporting institutions in order to fulfil its social obligations, sums up the main objectives of Latin American neo-liberalism. Instead of substituting the elitist bureaucratic state for a social democratic one, he proposes what he calls a social liberal state.

A less blunt argument in favour of a neo-liberal state in Brazil has developed out of the debate on its democratic transition, particularly the discussion on governability and accountability.[2] The debate on the latter focused on the problems arising from the democratisation process. These were the sharp increase in social and political demands from various sectors of society – mainly those marginalised during the military regime – that paralysed governmental capacity to act and respond. This revealed the existence of a strong state in terms of political decision-making and, at the same time, a weak one where its capacity for action was concerned. This weakness enhanced the power of the executive and the president to the detriment of congress and the judiciary. In order to resolve these tensions, accountability and state reforms should occur, so as to develop governability.[3]

The overall perspective of this view is essentially correct. The state in Brazil has been controlled and used by the élite and its policies have not been directed towards the interests of civil society. Democratisation has posed a major challenge, namely, the transformation of the state into a modern social democratic apparatus. The lack of governability results from the conflict between the social pressure to democratise the state and the resistance of the ruling élite. Governability would be possible only where either the popular classes or the élite obtain hegemony. The political ups and downs of the 1980s and 1990s in Brazil were precisely the outcome of a situation of this type

---

2   'Governability', term used by social scientists to denote the ability of governments to achieve broad social consensus on the implementation of, usually, neo-liberal policies.

3   Eli Diniz, *Crise, reforma do Estado e governabilidade: Brasil, 1985–95*, Rio de Janeiro: Fundação Getulio Vargas, Editora, 1997.

of conflict, where civil society's rejection of traditional state structures was insufficient to bring about substantial change in them.

While working class élites were unable to foster a broader alliance against traditional right-wing rule, the Brazilian élite attempted to redefine itself within the wave of neo-liberalism by changing its image cosmetically and by associating its interests more closely with global capitalism. This was epitomised in Collor de Mello's campaign for the presidency. A young aristocrat, politically associated with the most backward aspects of Brazilian politics, he was magically transformed into the perfect, upright leader to modernise Brazil. Basing his campaign on the need to open the economy, privatise, and reduce the size of the state, Collor laid out a new basis for the restructured political alliance between the national élite and international capital. His downfall was, above all, due to his inability to lead this emerging alliance in the face of growing popular pressure.

Itamar Franco's government slowed down the shift towards neo-liberalism but was unable to put forward an alternative set of policies. By then, the new right wing alliance had managed to articulate traditional élites around its São Paulo's business associates and co-opt a considerable proportion of the Brazilian intelligentsia in favour of presidential candidate Fernando Henrique Cardoso. The shift in the balance of power in favour of neo-liberalism was now accentuated. After the success of Cardoso's monetary stabilisation policy as Franco's economy minister, he gained enough electoral support to be voted president. In 1995 he won 54% of the votes on a platform of attacking social problems and enhancing democracy. Needless to say, Cardoso's first government was marked by the resumption of privatisation and neo-liberal policies. Electoral promises of social policies were forgotten.

Despite its political weaknesses, Cardoso's government was the best attempt by the élite to create a limited hegemonic project in order to consolidate its new alliance and maintain a state based on social exclusion.

Within this context governability is opposed to democracy. The idea of enhancing governmental links with civil society in a situation of growing social exclusion can be achieved only by traditional authoritarian methods such as co-option and corruption. True ability to govern in Brazil can only emerge from a social democratic state constructed around the concept of citizenship. Cardoso's attempt to forge democracy and the ability to govern within a neo-liberal framework had disappointing results.

The unrealistic nature of neo-liberal ideology in Brazil becomes evident when we confront the actual changes that have taken place in Brazilian politics and economics since Collor de Mello's presidency. An increasing concentration of power in the executive at the expense of the legislature and judiciary; the consequences of the privatisation programme; the reform of state and public administration; and the growth of violence and social exclusion.

If during the military regime Brazil was ruled from the executive by so-called *decretos-lei* and *atos-institucionais*, during the Sarney government they were substituted by rather similar instruments called *decreto-lei* and *medida provisoria*, tools conceived by the 1988 Constitution to be used in exceptional circumstances. Many neo-liberal policies have never passed through congress instead they have been imposed by the presidential use of these mechanisms. These tools have been employed on a daily basis and in nearly all issues concerning government, particularly those associated with fostering neo-liberalism.

During his government Sarney issued 147 *medidas provisorias*; Collor issued 157 in his three years in power; and Franco, 508. In the period from 1994 up to 2002, Cardoso issued more than 2,000.

The executive determines the key issues of debate in congress. Between 1989 and 1993, 78% of approved legislation originated within the executive.[4] The executive controlled the congressional majority by means of clientelism and co-option. The coalition in power was thus an ensemble of contradictory individuals and interest groups that conspired against the emergence of a party system.

The judiciary was even more firmly under the influence of the executive. Its highest echelons were filled with judges appointed by the president. And although from time to time the judiciary was involved in scandals involving nepotism and corruption, judiciary

4   Argelina Figuereido and Fernando Limongi, 'As medidas provisórias: delegação ou abdicação?', *Novos Estudos CEBRAP*, No. 47: 127–54, 1997.

structures were both incapable of guaranteeing justice – there is one judge for every 17,500 inhabitants in Brazil where double that number would be needed – and were continually under political pressure from congress and the executive.

The privatisation programme has been another key aspect of neo-liberal reforms. It is associated with opening the internal market to international competition and with the idea that the road to economic growth in the global economy is through foreign investment. The policy of privatisation has been sold using the arguments that it diminishes the burden on state expenditure and therefore helps reduce the deficit, and that it brings in new external investments and modernises services. The state is to continue its withdrawal from the economy, and foreign capital is to play the role of boosting domestic growth.

So far, privatisation has had a modest impact on reducing the deficit.[5] The ongoing energy crisis in Brazil demonstrates that investments in infrastructure cannot be left solely in the hands of private companies. The same can be argued for other privatised sectors, such as the rail system.

The growing interests rates levied on the Brazilian debt, associated with the international crises in Asia and Latin America, have been the principal drain on Brazil's resources. Though the country reached a certain level of fiscal stability it relied on budgetary restrictions in order to pay very high interest rates. The rapid modernisation process evident in industry and the service sector is swelling the number of the unemployed. Since they are not assisted by a shrinking state, they have swelled the already huge mass of the socially and economically excluded.

Since Collor de Mello, the government has managed to change the legislation that permitted foreign capital to control up to 40% of former state companies, as well as to penetrate areas such as the media, deemed strategic. From 1991 to 1996 the sale of state

---

5 Pinheiro and Giambiagi, 'Lucratividade, dividendos e investimentos das empresas estatais: uma contribuição para o debate sobre a privatização no Brasil', in *Revista brasileira de economia*, 51(1), January–March 1997: 93–132.

companies produced US$24.7 billion revenues. In 1997 alone, it produced US$23.7 billion.[6]

Accusations by the opposition of undervaluing state assets prior to privatisation have coincided with governmental overestimates of revenues from privatisation programmes. The privatisation of Telebras, Brazil's telephone company is a good example of this. At first it was valued at US$80 billion;[7] later the figure dropped to US$60 billion. It was actually sold for US$19 billion.[8] Nobody dares declare its actual value.

At its core, the idea of a new public administration through a discourse of efficiency brings in not only measures to reduce expenditure on the civil service and the already inadequate assistance given to the have-nots. Additionally, it aims to restructure most of the public sector, such as higher education and health, making it rely on ever-growing private funding in order to subsequently privatise it.

Despite the rhetoric that neo-liberal reforms will reduce poverty, generate jobs and spur on economic growth, in the decade since these changes were introduced, Brazil and South America as a whole have experienced quite the opposite. Economic growth has been weak, there has been a sharp drop in the quality of social services, and unemployment, social exclusion and poverty have reached new levels.

Although the second Cardoso government declared its intention to address social problems, neo-liberal views and policies continued to be dominant, therefore, its administration began to face the consequences of such policies. The expected boost in exports never materialised. Privatisation did not produce extra foreign revenue nor did it prove able to respond to internal consumption demand. Despite the many social programmes created by Cardoso, social exclusion and the increase of social violence, together with unemployment, remained as prevalent social scourges.

---

6 Andrews and Kouzmin, 'Re-legitimating "voice" and "loyalty" within economic theories of democracy and accountability: Brazilian exemplars', *International Review of Administrative Sciences*, 65(3), 1999: 395–409.
7 *Gazeta Mercantil*, 13 May 1998.
8 *Financial Times*, 30 July 1998.

On foreign policy, despite some important aspects of Cardoso's policies, he was unable to relaunch Mercosur as a strategic project for Brazil and South America. The idea of Mercosur had emerged with the onset of military regimes as a regional arrangement to be constructed in order to favour regional economic and political cooperation and protect the countries of the region in the face of European and North American regionalisms.

Mercosur was forged during the Alfonsin and Sarney governments. Its aim was to go far beyond a free trade area agreement and, in about a decade, create a common market between Brazil, Argentina, Uruguay and Paraguay. For many in South America, the European Union provided the model for Mercosur. Hopes that historical deficits in democracy, and social and economic development could be addressed in the process of building a common market were high, and the rapid increase in trade, particularly between Brazil and Argentina, suggested that this dream could become reality.

But the wave of neo-liberalism hit the regionalist vision of Mercosur hard. There was no longer any place for protectionism or state policies aimed at boosting the economy or guiding a process of regional integration. The attempt to create strong institutions in Mercosur degenerated into nothing but wishful thinking. The discourse of trade liberalisation dominated the debate on regional integration. Of course, part of this failure is to be credited to the traditional élites that feared that Mercosur might bring about their demise. The populist and undecided Menem government represented this trend well.

The success of Mercosur depended on (a) the reduction of regional economic, cultural and social distances; (b) the common enhancement of citizenship, human rights and democratic mechanisms; (c) the enlargement of regional economic and social élites; (d) the capacity of governments and states to support common macro-economic policies and development programmes; and last but not least, (e) a growth in interregional trade and investments.

Only the last condition was successfully fulfilled during the 1990s. The historic mutual economic isolation between Brazil and Argentina was overcome and both countries became key trade partners. However, the establishment of a common market between Brazil, Argentina, Uruguay and Paraguay, as intended by the

Mercosur agreements, did not replicate the trade success of its two larger partners.

The reduction of the state's role in the economy made co-ordinated governmental investment in infrastructure and in favour of small and middle-sized enterprises, impossible. The continuous concentration of wealth, power and knowledge has deepened divisions in the societies of the region and accelerated the vicious circle of social conflict and exclusion. Thus neo-liberalism has jeopardised the development of the basic conditions that would have guaranteed the progressive organisation of Mercosur. The forces supporting it have frozen the process of creating a common market, just as they have frozen the increasing democratisation of the region.

More than ten years after the creation of Mercosur, we still do not know if this is destined to become a serious intergovernmental strategic project for Brazil and Argentina, or if it has been just a tactic to help these countries in the negotiations to create the Free Trade Area of the Americas.

The year 2002 began by exposing some of the terrible consequences of neo-liberalism in Argentina and Brazil. Economic growth and stability continue to be central problems. Dependence on international finances has increased dramatically, while social exclusion and violence dominate the political agenda. Neo-liberal promises have failed to materialise and if, with the newly elected administrations in both Brazil and Argentina, the era of neo-liberalism comes to an end, then – perhaps – policy makers may consider the solution to social exclusion and the promotion of democracy and citizenship as equally important as fiscal and economic policies. Mercosur can re-emerge as an original scheme to help foster strong regional economic and democratic mechanisms, as well as consolidating South America's ambition to become a key global player in international politics.

Francisco Domínguez

Democracy and Economic Integration: The Continental Context

Introduction

Since the mid 1980s Latin America has experienced the combined effects of globalisation, economic integration and democratisation all rolled into one. However, post-dictatorship democracy in Latin America operates within a very strict neo-liberal matrix. Regardless of which party has come into office and despite the arduous social and political battles waged against repression, dictatorship and neo-liberalism in countries such as Chile, Argentina and Uruguay, neo-liberal economic policy is the one persistent legacy that has remained an immutable feature of every democratic administration in the region. At the time, Chicago Boys-inspired economic policies were seen as inherent in military rule but those who fought hard against them – thousands risking and losing their lives in the process – were to be thoroughly disappointed when democracy arrived.

> Democracy, free market economics, and pro-American outpourings of sentiment and policy dot the landscape of a region where until recently left-right confrontation and the potential for social revolution and progressive reform were widespread. Today, conservative, pro-business, often democratically elected pro-US technocrats hold office around the hemisphere.[1]

This reality was confirmed at the end of the year 2000. After a tense electoral process, Ricardo Lagos was elected to office in Chile as the first 'socialist' president since Salvador Allende. Lagos, is a socialist with a difference, he stands for neo-liberalism. In Brazil, Fernando Henrique Cardoso was the neo-liberal president for two

---

1   Jorge Castañeda, *Utopia Unarmed*, New York: Vintage Books, 1994: 3.

presidential periods. In addition, Argentina confirmed this trend by electing Fernando De La Rua whose neo-liberal economic policy is simply a continuation of that of his predecessor, Carlos Menem, a Peronist turned neo-liberal. Thus from Mexico all the way down to Tierra del Fuego there were elected administrations committed to neo-liberalism.[2] Even where strong social resistance against the neo-liberal dollarisation of the economy had taken place, such as in Ecuador where a semi-insurrection of indigenous communities supported by army officers led to the ousting of the government, the crisis was eventually settled by the vigorous political intervention of the US, and the appointment of the vice-president as a president committed to – dollarisation and neo-liberal economic policies.

The military coup in Brazil in 1964 inaugurated a period characterised by dictatorship, military regimes and authoritarianism in Latin America that was to last for nearly 30 years. Regimes such as those of Pinochet in Chile or Videla in Argentina were two of the most obvious examples of a more generalised trend. This is not to suggest that democracy in Latin America up to 1964 had been a prevailing trend abruptly brought to an end by *coups d'état*. In fact, with few exceptions, democratic rule, elections and political freedoms had not been the norm in the region; quite the opposite. Although this article proposes neither to chart the history of democratic rule in the region nor to recount the horrors endured by people during the terrible years of military rule, reference to both is obligatory background in order to understand the political arrangements stemming from the end of military dictatorship. In the 1980s, in different ways, with diverse rhythms but more or less contemporaneously, all countries in the continent under authoritarian or dictatorial regimes began upon the painful road out of military dictatorship and into democratic rule. Although some dictatorships collapsed early on (Argentina in 1982), most countries, as if responding to a single stimulus, began to take timid steps towards the restoration of political freedoms by the end of that decade. Purportedly, the stimulus came out of the democratic wave that swept

---

2   The exceptions to this trend are Cuba, a very special case anyway, and recently, Venezuela's election of Hugo Chavez; a man committed to anti-neo-liberal economic policies.

the world at the time, particularly in Stalinist, pro-Soviet Eastern European governments, including that of the Soviet Union itself. Some became so excited with the process of the restoration of capitalism, almost invariably equated with the advent of democracy that went as far as to proclaim 'the end of history'.[3] Simultaneously with this democratic wave, and because of the collapse of communism, the globalisation of capitalist processes was given an unprecedented impetus, most notably in two decisive areas: economic integration and financial transactions in 'emerging markets'.

The international context for the last two decades has been dominated by the reorganisation of the world economy into economic blocs. With the launching of the Euro – whatever its temporary ups and downs – the European Union took a giant stride towards the economic union of Western Europe. By proclaiming the Initiative for the Americas in 1991 and then by signing the North American Free Trade Agreement (NAFTA) in 1994, effectively integrating the economies of Canada, the United States and Mexico, George Bush Sr. ostensibly heralded a new era of political and economic relations in the American continent. NAFTA was to be the forerunner of the strategic objectives announced by the Bush Sr. July 1991 speech, the final aim of which was the creation of a Free Trade Area of the Americas. President Clinton sought, but failed to obtain, congressional fast-track authority to set it up. In Latin America itself, economic integration and the return to democratic rule acquired the form of Mercosur, the most advanced experience of economic integration ever to involve nations south of the Rio Grande. Despite facing difficulties, and sometimes intractable, obstacles there does not seem to be any question that Mercosur is here to stay. Not only is there a deepening – albeit uneven – process of economic integration between the four member countries (Brazil, Argentina, Uruguay and Paraguay), Mercosur is also attracting new

---

3 I am referring here to Francis Fukuyama's book, which contains much more intellectual complexity that one sentence here can convey, nevertheless, his essential message was the end of political and, therefore, social conflict because the collapse of communism had brought the East West ideological confrontation to an end. See Francis Fukuyama, *The End of History and the Last Man*, Harmondsworth: Penguin, 1992.

partners such as Chile and Bolivia, which, although associate members, have been gravitating towards Mercosur.[4]

Like other dependent regions in the world, Latin America has been subjected to the internationalisation and transnationalisation of economic processes, which have given rise to supranational political institutions, but, as elsewhere, this has not involved a concomitant development of equivalent democratic procedures or institutions which would enable citizens of the newly-created geographical-economic spaces to exert their rights *qua* citizens in order to influence the economic decision-making process. Nor can citizens – within the existing political systems – modify or limit the impact multinational agents have over the national sphere.[5] Furthermore, the economic weight in the world economy of poor and middle-income countries has declined substantially. Between 1980 and 1994 the developed countries increased their share of world output from 70% to 79%; that of middle-income nations went down from 23% to 16% whilst that of poor nations also declined, from 7% to 5%.[6]

In addition, the bitter medicine imposed upon peripheral countries (trade liberalisation, industrial protectionist policies, elimination of agricultural subsidies, no state intervention and such like) is in fact not practised by the central nations, since they do exactly the opposite against the former. The actual increase in agricultural subsidies in some of the key industrialised nations is as follows: EU, 49%; USA, 30%; Japan, 66%; Canada, 45%; and they are just some of the worst

4 Venezuela has also formally applied to join Mercosur, and there is an agreement in principle to intensify economic relations between Mercosur and the Andean Pact countries (Peru, Bolivia, Ecuador, Colombia and Venezuela). In fact, recently Peru has also formally applied to join Mercosur. Furthermore, there is an ongoing process of economic integration between Venezuela and Colombia. In this connection, the intense activity deployed by the CARICOM countries, and to a lesser extent by the Central American Common Market plus the recent free trade agreement signed between Mexico and the European Union should also be mentioned.
5 Edgardo Lander, *Neoliberalismo, sociedad civil y democracia*, Universidad Central de Venezuela, 1995: 160.
6 Carlos Vilas, 'Estado, mercado y globalización', paper presented to the *I Interoceanic Congress of Latin American Studies*, National University of Cuyo, 10–12 March, Mendoza, 1999.

offenders.[7] The ability of central countries to get away with such blatant inconsistency has been enhanced significantly by the sheer volume of Latin America's external debt. By the end of the 1990s, the external debt of Latin America reached the staggering figure of US$750 billion, up from US$69 billion in 1975, the year petrodollars began to be recycled through the Third World. That is, the external debt of the region increased eleven-fold in 30 years.[8] It also so happens that the most heavily indebted countries are precisely those most deeply involved in processes of regional economic integration – Brazil, Argentina and Mexico – together responsible for over 60% of the total external debt of the region. In 1999, for the region as a whole, the service of the external debt represented an annual disbursement of US$340 billion, a sharp increase from US$140 billion in 1991[9], thus significantly reducing the affected nations' bargaining position when seeking free trade agreements.

All this means that, increasingly, decisions with a massive significance on the Latin American countries' social order are taken outside the geographical space where these very nations exist, and, more importantly, they are arrived at outside the realm of democratic procedures. This applies crucially to economic policy. Furthermore, the dominant discourse concerning the restoration of democracy in the region is no longer about the expansion of the democratic gains resulting from defeating dictatorships, but how to make democratic procedures and norms functional to the workings of neo-liberalism. In short, 'democratisation' is not about democracy, as it was traditionally understood in Latin America before the advent of neo-liberalism. The source of such a qualitative leap backward largely stems from the arrangements, concessions and pragmatism that have pervaded the transitions to democracy especially in the Southern Cone nations.

The neo-liberal reorganisation of Latin America has had devastating social consequences. Ever growing sections of Latin American

---

7   Edgardo Lander, op. cit.: 165. The percentages are for 1992.
8   Eduardo Mayobre, 'El sistema financiero internacional, su impacto sobre América Latina y el Caribe', www.lanic.utexas.edu/~sela/ponencias/ponen18.htm, 12 May 2000: 5.
9   Ibid: 11.

humanity are being *de facto* excluded from even the existing restricted democratic procedures. With few exceptions, absolute poverty has increased absolutely in most countries in the region, with large sections of the population being chronically marginalised from economic and political circuits. Likewise, the gap between rich and poor has never been wider. The population's economic situation, relatively better aggregate figures notwithstanding, has never been so precarious in terms of job security, casualisation of labour, trade unions rights and bargaining power, and the continuous turmoil that people are subjected to due to the cyclical economic crises that plague 'globalised capitalism'. Finally, democracy and economic integration in Latin America take place in the context of the steady growth of the rivalry between the United States and the European Union. Contrary to the situation throughout most of the previous century, and despite currently benefiting from the status of being *the* superpower, the United States no longer enjoys unbounded economic and political hegemony.

The Hayekan and Friedmanite views of Latin American intellectuals

The Washington Consensus and its ideological trappings weigh as heavily over the newly emerging Latin American democracies as they did over their authoritarian predecessors. An examination of this dimension is essential in any discussion of democracy and democratisation in Latin America in general and Mercosur in particular.

The prevalent idea that democracy is 'coterminous with the mere establishment of adequate representative and governmental institutions,'[10] is a theoretical fallacy. To conceive democracy as a set of abstract rules and procedures that pose only technical, not political or ethical problems unrelated to the social context and values associated with its historic rise would amount to the divorcing of society from the

10   Atilio Boron, 'State Decay and Democratic Decadence in Latin America', *The Socialist Register*, 1999: 210.

socio-economic context on which it rests ('an operation worthy of an ostrich'[11]). Nevertheless, the dominant discourse on democracy in Latin America is riddled with these theoretical limitations and what passes for democracy is but a reflection of that discourse. Thus unsurprisingly, democracy is being redefined to suit neo-liberalism and has led many an intellectual or politician (in some cases they happen to be both) to seek intellectual shelter in the coherence of the ideological views posited primarily by Frederick Hayek and, to a lesser extent, by Milton Friedmann. Hayek – one of the intellectual fathers of neo-liberal economics and politics – disliked democracy and preferred a system of selective electoral rights for those sections of the population unlikely to develop a 'tribal' mentality as a result of being 'temporarily' disadvantaged by the process of 'creative destruction' intrinsic to capitalism.[12] Hayek's views have at least the merit of honestly identifying what he believes to be the ideal political system for unbridled capitalist accumulation. For him, the set of abstract procedures and institutions consonant with his definition of the ethical society and human liberty is not democracy but 'demarchy'; a type of hierarchical voting system to elect a parliament of sorts, but one which remains under the constitutional watchful eye of a non-elected upper chamber whose members are appointed for their commitment to the defence of the free operation of the market. Under demarchy the vote of the 'temporarily disadvantaged' is thus rendered ineffectual and, if necessary, Hayek suggests, it could be abolished altogether. The overriding Hayekian principle is not to champion people's rights but human liberty, defined as the individual right to unimpeded capital accumulation.

Perhaps the most disturbing feature of Latin America's neo-liberalism is the dramatic shift in the intellectual argument regarding societal objectives put forward by politicians of the right, centre and 'renovated' left.[13] Their thinking is dominated by what *Le Monde Diplomatique* calls *la penseé unique*. There is a frightening degree of

11   Cited in Boron, op. cit.: 212.
12   Frederick Von Hayek, *The Road to Serfdom*, London: Routledge, 1944.
13   For a comprehensive analysis and discussion of this intellectual shift in the Latin American left see, James Petras, 'The Retreat of the Intellectuals', in James Petras and Morris Morley, *Latin America in the Time of the Cholera*, London: Routledge, 1992.

consensus among these political currents as to the inevitability and/or desirability of neo-liberal economic policies. Jorge Castañeda in *Utopia Unarmed*[14] has put forward one of the most articulate arguments in favour of accepting the neo-liberal status quo which can only be reformed from within on the grounds that the overriding opposition between socialism and the market has virtually disappeared. The main difficulty with Castañeda's contention is that because neo-liberalism brings about such gross socio-economic inequalities and has such a grip on economic policy, its acceptance – out of expediency or conviction – strengthens, perpetuates and legitimises the very inequalities that make neo-liberalism and democracy incompatible. The casualties of such a strategy will be democracy and social justice reality which inexorably turns pragmatic tacticians of the Castañeda-type into apologists for neo-liberalism.

At present, key Latin American countries (Mexico, Argentina, Chile, Brazil, etc.) are governed by administrations that accept the logic of neo-liberalism despite their proclaimed concern for the poor.[15] Thus

> As a matter of principle, neo-liberal economics does not concern itself with social policy. A strong economy, it is argued, will make permanent social policies unnecessary. Social issues are considered a government expense, not an investment; the concept of social development gives way to that of social compensation. With the drastic cuts in social spending, however, only minimal compensatory mechanisms can be sustained. As a result, social policy has contracted, and its two traditional functions – accumulation and legitimisation – have experienced severe adaptations.[16]

It follows that access to social services is no longer considered one's rights as a citizen, but is based on one's ability to pay. The commodification of social services, especially health and education, has led one commentator to exclaim:

---

14 Castañeda, op. cit., see especially chapter 'A Grand Bargain for the Millennium': 427–76.
15 Suffice it to mention in this connection the principle espoused by the Chilean governments since the departure of the military from office: 'growth with equity'; yet Chile has the dubious merit of being a nation with one of the most unequal income distributions on earth.
16 Carlos Vilas, 'Rhetoric and reality. The World Bank's new concern for the poor', *NACLA, Report on the Americas*, XXIX(6), May June 1996: 18.

> They [education and health] are luxuries or, at least, pieces of merchandise to be bought and sold in the marketplace. If you cannot afford the merchandise, don't buy it. In other words, if you can't afford medical care, die. If you can't pay for education, stay illiterate and sell chewing gum on the street corner.[17]

Moreover, although some residue of social democratic spirit may still dot official pronouncements, at bottom, most Latin American administrations agree with the Hayekian principle that inequality, by permitting the rich to increase savings and, therefore, invest – which is key to increase overall wealth – benefits the poor.[18] In fact, according to Hayek, economic progress is impossible without economic inequality.[19]

The neo-liberal restructuring of Latin America – and of the rest of the world – is a political project aimed at bringing about a utopia based on the total and absolute separation of politics and economics and in which the procedures for electing governments not only do not in the least diminish but actually perpetuate the supremacy of the market.[20] This is what the much coveted and much talked about governability actually means; a rather frail foundation on which to base the political consensus for neo-liberalism.

Capitalism, neo-liberalism and democracy

In the 1980s the non-feasibility of maintaining stable military dictatorships led to negotiated transitions to democracy, which aimed at the depoliticisation of society by means of autonomising the economic sphere so as to protect it from the ups and downs of politics. Consequently, democratic politics (elections at every level of the state, the free operation of political parties, freedom of the press and of

---

17 Ibid: 19–20.
18 This is the gist of the by now thoroughly discredited 'trickle down' theory. In fact, most countries in Latin America can be described as applying 'trickle up' fiscal and economic policies.
19 Lander, op. cit.: 153.
20 Ibid: 167.

speech, etc.) has, at least temporarily, lost its capacity to influence economic policy, hence the widespread perception among ordinary voters that politics does not matter any longer.[21] One observer has rightly noted that 'one of the most striking features of the new democracies has been the growing depoliticisation of society and the marked absence of national political debates'.[22] Among growing sections of the electorate there is a sense that economic policies are indeed imposed from outside by supranational bodies such as the IMF and the World Bank. Many voters, having internalised the consumerist ideology of neo-liberalism, see themselves as consumers not citizens, with the attendant negative consequences for participatory democracy. And, last but not least, the record of post-dictatorship democratic administrations on righting the huge human rights debt as well as rectifying (or alleviating) the massive chasm between rich and poor is hugely disappointing, thus leading many people to shun politics altogether. Two key factors that have facilitated this have been the deliberate policy of political demobilization effected by post-dictatorial democratic administrations and the virtual disappearance or massive weakening of social and political forces that in the past had effectively opposed right wing, monetarist-type, economic policies.[23]

In this way the Washington Consensus finds its reflection in the internal political make-up of most Latin American countries where 'electable' political parties (or electoral alliances) competing for office are firmly committed to neo-liberal policies. For the electorate there seems to be no alternative but to vote for different varieties of neo-liberalism. Thus, on the surface it appears as though Latin American society is witnessing not the end of history but the end of ideology in the sense of the disappearance of competing global socio-economic and politico-ideological alternatives. Furthermore, as the end of history should logically lead to the end of ideology, it should also inexorably lead to the end of politics. Its corollary would be govern-

---

21   See discussion of this by Jorge Larraín, 'Modernity and Identity: Cultural Change in Latin America', in Robert N. Gwynne and Cristobal Kay (eds), *Latin America Transformed, Globalization and Modernity*, London: Arnold, 1999: 200.
22   Patricio Silva, idem: 54.
23   Ibid: 51–65.

Economic Integration: the Continental Context

ments exclusively concerned with the technical administration of the operation of the market, thus reducing electoral competition to political parties demonstrating or convincing the electorate that they are the most efficient administrators of neo-liberalism.

Neo-liberalism is a 'non-ideological' ideology, since it contains no socio-ethical project, except generalities regarding the best-supposed conditions for capital accumulation and economic growth. In this sense, the politics of neo-liberalism 'is the absolute petrifaction of what exists', consequently, a political contest within the current intellectual framework that offers no prospects of socio-economic change and that propounds the impossibility of such a change can arouse no interest in a demoralised, powerless, irrelevant electorate. Similarly, if what the future holds is the incessant repetition of the present, electoral antagonisms must perforce be just simulations since they avoid discussing the essentials of the current mode of capital accumulation and its concomitant model of society.[24] As it is becoming harder to get Latin American electorates to be interested in electoral contests this is resulting in low turnouts at elections. The paradox of the situation is that most parties or coalitions committed to neo-liberalism conceal their allegiance to it during election time, presenting themselves as anti-neo-liberal, only to perform the most acrobatic of somersaults in adopting it almost the moment they are inaugurated in office.[25]

Neo-liberalism in Latin America has generated unprecedented levels of socio-economic inequality. According to CEPAL, extreme poverty in Latin America and the Caribbean in the 1980s grew from affecting 130 to 196 million people and in 'the countries with the more concentrated income distribution, the richest 10% of the households receive 40% of the total income'.[26] In 1991 a survey found that 80% of households in Peru lived below the poverty line, whilst in Bolivia it was about 50%. According to a United Nations Human Development

---

24 The quote and the questions come from Tomás Moulián, *Chile Actual. Anatomía de un Mito*, Chile: Lom – Arcis, 1997: 58.
25 Fujimori and Menem are just two examples of a more generalised behaviour pattern; the latest is Argentina's president De La Rua who, having come to office as a Third Way politician [promising to alleviate people's poverty], went on to implement one of the most savage austerity packages.
26 Cited by Boron, op. cit.: 216.

Report, Brazil tops the inequality league by being the second most unequal nation on earth, 'where the richest 20% of the population earn more than 32 times the income of the poorest'.[27] In 1997, the number of billionaires in Latin America making it to the Forbes' list was 39, up from 8 in 1991. In 1994, in Mexico, 'a group of 182,000 individuals – 0.2% of the population – held capital equivalent to 51% of total GNP'.[28] Chile, the showcase of neo-liberalism, has a similar income distribution to Brazil and 15% of its population receive 54% of national income whilst the poorest 58% has to survive on a paltry 21% of the nation's total income.[29] In addition, Chile is one of the few countries where the income of the top 20% has actually gone up in the period between the 1960s and 1994, 'from 36.6% of national income to 45.8%'.[30] Most of the figures above relate to the early 1990s. Since then, Latin America has gone through the devaluation of the Mexican peso and the subsequent 'tequila effect', the devastating consequences of the South East Asia crisis, the massive devaluation of the Brazilian real, the Argentine economic meltdown, and the corresponding negative impact of these economic events on social indicators such as income distribution, access to welfare and so forth. As early as 1995, an author had already diagnosed that 'Latin America is left trying to find its way in a cut-throat global economy, saddled with a population weakened by poverty and ignorance.'[31]

Neo-liberalism, social fragmentation and political consensus

Ever since the military came to power in Latin America in the early 1970s, the economies of the continent have been subjected to profound restructuring. Belying neo-liberal dogma that a market-domina-

27 Duncan Green, *Silent Revolution*, London: Latin American Bureau, 1995: 93.
28 NACLA, Report on the Americas, XXX(6), May/June 1997: 19.
29 José Cademartori, *Chile. El Modelo Neoliberal*, Santiago: Ediciones Chile America CESOC, 1998: 47.
30 Cited in Boron, op. cit.: 214
31 Green, op. cit.: 111.

ted society is spontaneous, through a combination of authoritarianism, dictatorship and IMF-inspired adjustment packages and, ultimately, the integration of the economies of the region to the circuits of global capital (mainly by forcing them to abandon inward-oriented economic development and instead adopt export-oriented strategies), the supremacy of the market was dramatically ensured. The social consequences of this strategic shift in economic policies were catastrophic: whatever little social provision there was in areas such as health, education, housing, and subsidies, was simply obliterated. As a result, and with very few exceptions, the general trend has been towards a substantial increase in the 'diseases of poverty' commonly associated with acute poverty (dengue, cholera, hepatitis, typhoid and tuberculosis, for example)'.[32] Drastic cutbacks in state employment, the elimination of state protection of national industry and the rise of privatisation have brought about one of the most dramatic increases in unemployment and underemployment of the region in modern times. Thus, for example, between 1980 and 1985 underemployment grew by 48% whilst unemployment affected 14% of the economically active population compared to 6% about ten years earlier.[33] In addition, although the situation improved slightly in the 1990s, unemployment and underemployment figures, particularly in relation to the young, remained very high indeed. These structural reforms have also led to a sharp decline in people's real earnings, thus between 1980 and 1991 'the average industrial wage in Latin America fell by 17.5 per cent', and the 'average minimum wage by 35 per cent.'[34] Additionally, there has also been an increase in the informal sector of the economy: from an average of 25.6% to 30% for the 1980–1990 period.[35] The average monthly income of the 200 million poor in Latin America is US$60 or

---

32   Sylvia Chant, 'Population, migration, employment and gender', in Gwynne and Kay (eds), *Latin America Transformed. Globalization and Modernity*, London: Arnold, 2000: 233. The most notorious example of this trend is the re-emergence of cholera in Peru, where it had been eradicated in the first decade of the 20th century.
33   Ibid: 251.
34   Ibid: 253.
35   Ibid: 255.

less.³⁶ Lastly, a central tenet of the neo-liberal agenda has been the increased flexibility of labour markets, euphemistically referred to by international organisations such as the IMF and the World Bank as 'reducing structural rigidities'. Labour legislation in most Latin American countries has undergone a visible weakening, leaving most workers and employees in a precarious position. There is virtually no security of employment. So 'of the 15.7 million jobs created in all of Latin America over the last 15 years [1980–1995], 13.6 million of these came from the informal sector.'³⁷ The model guarantees nothing but the certainty of the expanded reproduction of capital. The predominant view seems to be that labour reproduces itself – somehow, and there are large pools of it cheaply available, in any case. In fact, about a third of Latin America's population 'has been progressively excluded from the benefits of material progress, doomed to become an underclass or a decaying segment in modern society.'³⁸ The level of social exclusion has reached such proportions that for 'growing sections of Latin American societies class exploitation is not their immediate problem. Their handicap is precisely their inability to become exploited.'³⁹ The creation of these obscene social ills has brought about an unprecedented social phenomenon: 'rich and poor increasingly tend to live socially, culturally and ecologically in worlds apart.'⁴⁰

Because of the social consequences of neo-liberalism, large sections of the Latin American population have been browbeaten into a grudging acceptance of a political consensus whose justification rests on the fatalistic notion of the inevitability of current economic policy. In other words, what exists does so because nothing else can. During neo-liberalism's dictatorial phase, activists risked life and limb to oppose the military regimes that were implementing it. Under its non-dictatorial phase, opposition to it is very difficult to organise, for trade union activists face the prospect of dismissal and risk being

36   NACLA, op. cit.: 15.
37   Vilas, op. cit.: 25.
38   Boron, op. cit.: 221.
39   Ibid: 223.
40   Ibid: 222.

pushed, along with their families, into the dreaded informal sector. Furthermore, the almost religious devotion of intellectuals to 'civil society' during the 1980s facilitated the task of military and authoritarian regimes in rolling back the boundaries of the state, a key neo-liberal tenet. Most, genuinely believed that a reduction in the power of the state would automatically lead to an expansion of democracy. Actually, the weakening of the collective organisations of the people who find themselves at the wrong end of neo-liberal restructuring, the great majority of society no less, *does* lead to an almost automatic strengthening of the power of the business élite.[41]

As stated earlier, this consensus has been substantially buttressed by the ideological conversion of many Latin American left-wing intellectuals to the 'wisdom' of neo-liberalism. Such conversion seems to have been vindicated by the collapse of Eastern European socialism thus making neo-liberalism appear politically unavoidable and ideologically unassailable. That is, neo-liberalism seems to enjoy not only uncontested world political supremacy but has had the status of science bestowed upon it by a substantial part of the intellectual community. In effect, a large section of the intelligentsia previously committed to radical or progressive social change, has for all practical purposes, embraced a Hayekian model of democracy. Although many of them do not articulate it as Hayek himself would have done, there is a deliberate refusal on their part to challenge the theoretical premises on which this notion of democracy rests. Castañeda epitomises this by suggesting that – in the current reality – all that is left to do is 'bending and moulding existing [models of capitalism] into something new, yet not totally opposed to the status quo'. And, given the socially explosive potential of the huge income disparities brought about by neo-liberalism, the Left can enhance its 'only true leverage: being a lesser evil'.[42]

In Hayek, the dominance of the market is presented as inevitable in the sense of being natural, i.e. the spontaneous result of centuries of human action, and the social order it gives rise to is assumed to be moral. In such an ideological construct, social justice is not only impossible but also an obstacle to the workings of the only possible

41 Lander, op. cit.: 167.
42 Castañeda, op. cit.: 428.

economic system – all the others having failed – that humanity can give itself: the market.[43] Therefore, for Hayek the most dangerous threat to human liberty comes from state intervention designed to rectify the inequalities brought about by the operation of the market. The urge for such state action originates with social groups negatively affected by the market and who, by using their vote, force governments to embark on the road to social equality, thus unwittingly taking society down the path of totalitarianism.

Under the democratic phase of neo-liberalism the fact remains that the vote of the poor and the disadvantaged presents no danger to the process of capital accumulation or that the workings of the market is not a major issue for 'democratic' governments in the region, nor for most 'renovated' intellectuals. In the transition from military to civilian rule, the flagrant conflict between democratisation and neo-liberalism was 'resolved' by a number of subterfuges, which we shall now discuss.

Democratic transitions in Latin America

From the early eighties (Argentina) and then the early nineties (Chile, followed by other countries), Latin America embarked on what was ostensibly democracy. The changes wrought by these newly democratised societies were indeed substantial. Among others there was a return to civilian rule, elections, a significant assertion of the right to free expression, the legalisation of outlawed political parties, movements and social organisations and, in some cases, even the bringing to trial of some of the culprits responsible for human rights violations. However, in some countries the military have been able to secure for themselves the position of (formal and informal) institutionalised guardians of the economic model developed under their rule. In addition, civilian politicians of almost every hue have been quick to

---

43 See a competent discussion of the Hayekan views of democracy in Lander, op. cit.

Economic Integration: the Continental Context

swear allegiance to neo-liberalism. This has resulted in serious limitations to the democratic impulse that led to the demise of dictatorships and the restoration of civilian rule.[44] At the structural level the main limitations are of two types: regardless of electoral outcomes, the basic elements of neo-liberalism are preserved by various institutional and constitutional arrangements[45] and, the granting to the military of special constitutional privileges resulting from compromises with them, justified as necessary to ensure the process of democratisation.[46] These limitations have produced authoritarian enclaves, i.e. bodies of the state and key government institutions unaffected by the democratising process. Secondly, concerning economic policy and the yawning gap between rich and poor, the 'depoliticisation' of economic decision-making has rendered electoral events ineffectual. It does not matter who citizens vote for, neo-liberalism is here to stay and the democratisation process is unlikely to progress to the point of harnessing the market to social need, or completely subordinating the military to the democratic accountability of the justice system, nor to the civilian political authorities.[47]

44   It is common to present what has been achieved as the result of the cerebral prowess of intellectuals who purportedly managed to articulate the politics of the very difficult transitions they led, through a combination of reassuring the military they would be immune to the rule of law for the atrocities committed during their regimes and simultaneously blunting the most 'excessive' demands emanating from anti-dictatorial mass movements (Jeffrey Puryear, *Thinking Politics: Intellectuals and Democracy in Chile, 1973–1988*, Baltimore: Johns Hopkins University Press, 1994 and Pamela Constable and Arturo Valenzuela, *A Nation of Enemies: Chile under Pinochet*, London: W.W. Norton, 1991). In this interpretation democratic transitions have actually occurred thanks to the delicate balance struck by these intellectuals in terms of discourse, demands and compromise.

45   Essentially these arrangements manifest themselves in the 'autonomy' of the Central Bank, where the fixing of interest and exchange rates are outside the purview of the government.

46   Thus, for example, the Chilean constitution stipulates that the military are the ultimate guardians of the socio-economic model developed under Pinochet. Civilian administrations have largely accepted and defended the impunity the military granted themselves.

47   If there were any need of proof, during recent events surrounding the extradition case of Pinochet in Britain, the Chilean military have acted throughout as a law unto themselves with complete disregard for the views of the

An important aspect of the incompleteness of the democratisation process is usually attributed to pragmatism: democratisation could be put in jeopardy if the military were brought completely to account and made to pay for their crimes. No doubt this dimension is a real one, irrespective of whether the anti-dictatorial mass democratic impulse of the 1980s could have produced more fruitful democratic outcomes. However, a more crucial aspect has been neglected. Neo-liberal governability necessitates these arrangements. On governability, neo-liberal governments (or governments forced to adopt neo-liberal policies) face an intractable dilemma: 'how can a party hope to be elected if its policies are guaranteed to inflict an instant and devastating blow to the standard of living of the population?'[48] It is now universally accepted that the income distribution of societies under the grip of neo-liberalism grows increasingly unequal and that the much-publicised trickle-down effect is more an illusion than a fact (illusion perpetuated in some cases by a massively irresponsible expansion of credit).

> The class selectivity of the neo-liberal state is blatant: strong to promote the market forces and to advance the interests of big capital, weak to defend the public interest or to be responsive to the needs of the poor.[49]

Thus, the redemocratisation of Latin America suffers from a serious handicap. For as long as the market reigns supreme there can be no full democracy and there could be no market supremacy if the democratic aspirations of the majority of the population were to be addressed, let alone resolved. The logic of this reality is indeed diabolical. Neo-liberalism deals with such a glaring contradiction making the overwhelming majority of the people so extraordinarily vulnerable that they are willing to forsake their democratic and social rights for the sake of not being totally marginalised.

Concertacion government, a situation which at points led many to wonder who really ruled in Chile.
48 Green, op. cit.: 157.
49 Boron, op. cit.: 219.

The international context

Perhaps the most decisive feature of the current situation in Latin America is the international context in which it is taking place. This has changed greatly since the early 1970s when, after having crushed any political or economic experiments undertaken by Latin American regimes that were perceived as a threat to that very hegemony, the US was almost completely hegemonic. Paradoxically, since the collapse of communism in Eastern Europe, which turned the US into the world Supremo, its grip on the countries south of the Rio Grande has somewhat weakened. Not only have key Latin American nations embarked on a process of economic integration – notably the nation members of Mercosur – thus giving them a greater degree of economic – and political – autonomy vis-à-vis Washington, but the US has also had to face stiff competition from the European Union in its own backyard. The EU has signed a free trade agreement with Mercosur, is strengthening links at every level and in every field with many Latin American nations and has even managed to sign a free trade agreement with Mexico, a country that was being separated from the rest of Latin America by its membership of NAFTA.[50] The point here is not to suggest that we are witnessing the economic defeat of the US at the hands of the European Union in Latin American markets, but to register the end of its *absolute* hegemony in the region. This can be confirmed by the fact that the US is increasingly resorting to political, as opposed to economic, means to secure its position in the continent. An illustration of this was US President Clinton's visit to Latin America during the second week of October 1997, when he paid a surprising six-day visit to Venezuela, Brazil and Argentina. Its purpose was to secure support among the three biggest and strongest Latin American economies for his Free Trade Area of the Americas, that is, to turn the whole of Latin America into a bigger and broader version of NAFTA, the treaty that allowed the US to use Mexico for its own

---

50   For a detailed analysis and discussion of the EU/US rivalry in Latin America see Francisco Domínguez, 'Latin America, Spain, the European Union and the United States', in Francisco Domínguez (ed.), *Identity and Discursive Practices: Spain and Latin America*, Oxford: Peter Lang, 2000.

economic ends as a source of cheap raw materials, cheaper labour and a dumping ground for exports of manufactured goods and foodstuffs.

Latin American leaders have been wary of US intentions ever since George Bush Sr's *Initiative for the Americas* speech. This wariness intensified in 1995–96 with the Mexican economic crash, which led to the collapse of the peso and the 'tequila' effect that threw most Latin American economies out of balance. Clinton's US$50 billion rescue package – mainly to bail out Wall Street investors – left Mexico more or less at the total mercy of the Federal Reserve Bank. One Latin American response to the irresistible embrace of US free trade has been the development of intra-Latin American trade and the strengthening of regional common markets. Since the early 1990s Latin America has witnessed a spate of regional Trade Agreements [22 between 1990 and 1994 alone] largely driven by the fear of being 'frozen out of the main trade and investment flows of the world economy, like much of Africa'.[51] Additionally, there is a much less well-known, but no less intense, process of economic integration between Colombia and Venezuela.[52] Mercosur is the most important of these regional integrations.

Mercosur includes two of the largest Latin American economies (Brazil and Argentina), which with the addition of Chile makes it a hugely attractive market comprising about 220 million people. The levels of integration within Mercosur are indeed impressive and, with the exception of Chile, the other member nations have reduced tariffs on intra-trade imports to unprecedented low levels. Additionally, Mercosur countries have displayed an unusual degree of political independence vis-à-vis their powerful northern neighbour, specifically on knotty issues such as the US blockade against Cuba and the extra-territorial Helms–Burton Law.

Ostensibly, most Latin American nations are committed to the US project of the creation of a Free Trade Area of the Americas;

---

51 Green, op. cit.: 143.
52 See details in the special edition of *Análisis Político*, 1999, 'Análisis de la agenda del siglo XXI', published by the *Instituto de Estudios Políticos y Relaciones Internacionales and the Universidad Nacional de Colombia*, Colombia, Venezuela.

however, Clinton was unable to obtain special fast track legislation to speed up the process of continental integration. Chile, for example, which was next in line after Mexico, waited for several years for some progress to be made. Negotiations between the president and the US Congress produced no practical results. The uncertainties about the FTAA have given extra impetus to the prospect of a vast commercial alliance among South American countries centred on Mercosur, and for whom a decisive external economic partner could be the EU.[53]

Furthermore, trade between Mercosur and the EU has grown significantly in recent years. Currently 52% of exports and 51% of imports to and from the European Union's total trade with Latin America is with Mercosur. Moreover, the six largest economies in Latin America (Argentina, Brazil, Colombia, Chile, Mexico, and Venezuela) account for more than 80% of Latin American trade with the European Union. Furthermore, six EU members (France, Germany, Italy, The Netherlands, Spain and the UK) account for more than 80% of European imports from Latin American and almost 90% of sales to the region.[54] With respect to Foreign Direct Investment, 30% of the EU's total FDI outside the Organisation for Economic Cooperation and Development countries went to Latin American in the 1990s, whilst for the US the figure was 64%. That is to say, despite the huge advances made by the EU in Latin America, the Northern giant remains a giant. What has changed, however, is the distribution of US imports, exports and FDI towards Latin America, which are heavily skewed towards Mexico (although there is still a major US economic presence in Brazil and Venezuela), whilst those of the EU are heavily skewed towards Mercosur.

The EU has been building political and cooperation links with Latin America as a deliberate policy to facilitate its penetration of such an interesting market. Thus the EU's official development assistance to Latin America went up from 46.6% of total bilateral aid in

---

53 Trade between the EU and Latin America is still growing and even Chile, which is the process of joining NAFTA, will soon sign a free trade agreement with the EU (*The Economist*, May 18 2002).
54 IRELA Briefing, 'European Union–Latin American economic relations. Statistical profile', *Instituto de Relaciones Europeo-Latinoamericanas*, November 15 1996: 1.

1990 to 52.7% in 1995; whilst that of the US, which was 32.5% in 1990, was a paltry 17.2% in 1995. The EU is the biggest provider of official development assistance to Latin America, contributing about three times more than the US.[55] In the tough world of cut-throat global competition, such initiatives cannot be purely altruistic.

In this context, all of the EU's diplomatic initiatives in the region are aimed at obtaining better bases from which to challenge the traditional hegemony of the US in Latin America. In March 1997, French President Jacques Chirac visited four Latin American countries and heaped praised on Mercosur on more than 20 occasions. Chirac then proposed a summit at the highest level between the EU and Mercosur to be held in 1998. The response from Brazil and other Southern American countries was positively supportive. At present, Mercosur and the EU are negotiating the signature of an economic cooperation agreement as well as a free trade agreement. The thinking in leading circles of the EU seems to be that formalisation at the political level of their growing trading links with Latin American nations is part of the process of common resistance to the consolidation of a US-dominated unipolar post-Cold War world. In short, the EU is busily challenging US hegemony in a crucial region of the world.

This background explains Clinton's energetic diplomatic initiatives in Latin America in 1997. In typical fashion, the US is resorting to political rather than economic means to maintain its hegemony in Latin America. A series of US proposals to individual Latin American countries were clearly aimed at destroying the internal unity of Mercosur. First, the US lifted the ban on sales of advanced weapons to Chile, allowing it to buy F-16 fighters, thus breaking the military balance between Chile and Argentina. Argentina protested immediately. Next, in order to ostensibly 'assuage' Argentina, Clinton offered Buenos Aires the status of a special military ally as non-NATO member, eliciting a prompt protest from Chile whose spokespeople claimed that such a move would upset the strategic balance in the region. Finally, in a move that appeared to be designed to stir up maximum internal division within Mercosur, Clinton proposed to make

---

55   Ibid: 7–8.

Brazil a permanent member of the UN Security Council, prompting a predictably strong reaction from Argentina and Chile.

Leading US politicians are drawing the conclusion that Mercosur, and particularly its expansion, cannot be allowed to continue. In their view, matters are made worse by the strategic commercial alliance being built between Mercosur and the US's main economic rival in the world, namely, the EU. And although Clinton did succeed in creating internal difficulties within Mercosur, his trip to Latin America in 1997 was received with a mixture of empty rhetoric about the creation the FTAA, scepticism, and even opposition to the opening of the economies in the region to further US trade and investment. And as for his aim of sowing division among the South American nations in question, the actual divisions (which do reflect genuine rifts) were neither insurmountable nor long-term. As was aptly pointed out by *The Economist*, 'his visit underlines that the days when his country's policy in Latin America was limited to finding reliable strongmen to crush communism were over.'[56] Even regarding 'communism' the US is not being very successful, for it faces unprecedented united Latin American–EU opposition to the Helms–Burton Law; a law designed to crush Cuba, almost the only communist state left in the world.[57]

The structure of EU–LA trade relations reflects Europe's strategy towards the region, since it privileges Mercosur, Chile and, more recently, Mexico while it simultaneously de-emphasises trade with Central America, the Caribbean and the Andean Pact nations. Nevertheless, the European Union is the second largest commercial partner of Latin America as a whole with the United States still occupying first position. The exceptions to this ranking are Mercosur, Chile and Cuba where the EU outranks the US.[58] What is novel and surprising is the

---

56 *The Economist*, 'Partners or just neighbours?,' October 11 1997.
57 Even more poignantly, the Latin American nations collectively condemned the short-lived US-supported (if not US-organised) *coup d'état* against Venezuelan president Hugo Chavez through hitherto US-controlled Organization of American States.
58 EU–LA trade relations do not grow further mainly due to the former's Common Agricultural Policy which erects protectionist barriers against the latter's agricultural goods; it is estimated that the EU would have to indemnify its farmers to the tune of between 5,700 to 14,300 million euros annually should European

EU–Mexico free trade agreement. After the 'tequila' financial hangover of 1995, Mexico is seeking new commercial partners in order to counteract NAFTA, while for the EU this is a way into NAFTA (mainly the US market).[59] It is not only interesting that Mexico has actually signed such a free trade accord with Europe, but that it is also the first Latin American nation to do so. The EU free trade agreement with Chile has already been mentioned. Moreover, and crucially, next in line is Mercosur. An EU–Mercosur free trade agreement would be the first of its type between two customs unions, giving Europe the bases for permanent influence in South America. Thus, an EU–Mercosur FTA is objectively an alternative to the US-inspired FTAA. Furthermore, in July 1999 Brazil signed an agreement with the Andean Pact nations in order to lure them towards Mercosur so as to strengthen South America's position for the negotiations on the FTAA as well as to seek the creation of a Free Trade Area of South America (including Chile). Thus, an EU–Mercosur free trade agreement would enhance the EU's position in South America enormously. Some estimates indicate that trade liberalization between the EU and Mercosur would lead to an additional economic growth of about 5% in Brazil and 6% in Argentina, whilst a similar liberalization between Mercosur and the US would lead only to an additional economic growth of 2% in Brazil and 1% in Argentina.[60]

With the onset of the new century, Latin America finds itself in the grip of a widespread economic crisis that refuses to subside. The effects of the 'tequilazo' of the mid 1990s can still be felt and its political consequences have made stability a rare commodity indeed. Despite the high-flown proposals to instil democracy in Mexico, the Fox administration has made no visible progress, nor has its legislation to grant ethnic rights to its indigenous population passed Congress. Growing social marginalisation continues to be the country's

protectionism be abolished for Mercosur agricultural goods. (Susanne Gratius, 'Las relaciones comerciales entre la Unión Europea y Mercosur en el actual contexto internacional', www.lanic.utexas.edu/~sela/docs/spstncmdi4-2000-1.htm, May 2000: 4–5 and www.lanic.utexas.edu/~sela/docs/spstncmdi4-2000-2.htm, May 2000: 5).
59   Gratius, ibid: 1.htm: 10.
60   Ibid, 2.htm: 8–9.

central feature. Central America has not recovered from the harsh social consequences of displacement and the physical and human destruction resulting from the civil wars of the 1980s. Colombia, however special a case it may be, is still in the midst of a peace process that looks increasingly like all-out war, plus facing massive US military intervention. Brazil confronts almost permanent political and economic crisis. Argentina is under the powerful grip of an economic meltdown and an acute political crisis. Even Chile is feeling the pinch of world economic slowdown. The few remaining countries such as Paraguay, Uruguay, Peru, Ecuador, etc., are faring no better, but rather worse.

Perhaps the most worrying aspect of the region's economic woes is that 'support for democracy has suffered steep falls across the region'.[61] Most people in Latin America seem to be 'dissatisfied with the way democracy is operating in practice' and although they broadly seem not to wish to oppose the market economy, they are growing increasingly wary of privatisation.[62] The truth of the matter is that neo-liberalism constantly undermines the political stability of regimes that apply neo-liberal policies, which, in response, have a tendency to flout democratic procedures in order to maintain the predominance of the market over social considerations. Fujimori's sinister shenanigans are just one of the most recent examples of this.

Conclusion

The main problem is that the current neo-liberal regimes in Latin America realize the contradictions and tensions intrinsic in their relations with the US but do not have the politics to be successful in the battle that is looming in the horizon. They are most likely to capitulate and sell out when the real crunch comes. Enhancing the region's economic autonomy with any prospect of success requires both an

61   *The Economist*, 28 July 2001, 360 (8232): 15.
62   Ibid: 51.

economic policy congruent with such an objective, not neo-liberalism, and, therefore, necessitates governments based on different social alliances, obtainable only through opposition to neo-liberalism. Current trends do not point in the right direction, however. According to an ECLAC report *(The Equity Gap: Latin America, the Caribbean and the Social Summit)*, presented to the First Regional Conference in a follow-up to the World Summit for Social Development held in São Paulo in April 2000, 'the richest 10% of households held onto or increased their share while the poorest 40% just managed to maintain theirs, or suffered a decline'.[63] By the end of the decade it was forecast that

> The region's economic performance will not be strong enough to sweep away the creeping disillusion with market economics. But neither will the broad liberal reforms of the past decade be abandoned wholesale [...][64]

In other words, international capital is aware of the difficulties ahead but confident that current and future Latin American administrations will stick to la *penseé unique*.

Neo-liberalism is paradoxically both the driving force pushing regional economic integration and its main obstacle. When Brazil devalued the real after the South East Asia crisis, its trading relations with Argentina, its main intra regional trade partner, reached a low ebb when Argentina resorted to restrictions on the importation of Brazilian goods such as shoes and textiles. Both nations, have as a result, agreed to seek macroeconomic harmonization via a mechanism similar to the Maastricht treaty and committed themselves to adopting a single currency. Such a development would institutionalise neo-liberal polices at a supranational level but would undermine the legitimacy of the integration project itself. In Europe the losers in the implementation of Maastricht criteria have been pensioners, industrial workers, public employees, women, farmers, small enterprises, the disabled and wage earners in general. There is no doubt that macro-economic harmonization would enhance Mercosur's bargaining position at FTA negotiations with either the EU or the US. However, if the administrations involved in the bargaining process have a precarious

63 http://www.cepal.org
64 *The Economist*, 'The World in 2000': 88.

Economic Integration: the Continental Context 55

electoral base it is doubtful that they could claim a mandate for a Maastricht-type economic integration that largely benefits capital and is detrimental to everyone else. This would pose two possible alternatives: either, because of electoral pressures at home, a Maastricht-type economic integration could be seriously modified to take account of the interests of other social actors, or governments could press on regardless, including the adoption of authoritarian or dictatorial forms of political rule.

With regards to the EU–US rivalry in the region, a countervailing factor that is reducing the EU's possibilities for expanding its influence in the region is the urge for dollarisation. No doubt, this gives the US an extraordinary lever with which to influence economic policy, investment and the strategic economic orientations to be pursued by the countries of the region. Nevertheless, Latin America will continue to be a terrain of rivalry between these two giants: the European Union and the United States. If EU–US competition continues to express itself in the form of courting Latin Americans with better deals than those offered by their rival, then that should, all other things being equal, furnish the countries of the continent with vital breathing space to develop their own domestic economies and offer a better deal to their populations. The benefits of this extra room for manoeuvre can be maximised if done collectively, hence not only the importance but also the significance of Latin American regional integration. Mercosur is weighty and attractive because it includes two of the largest regional economies, Brazil and Argentina.[65] Furthermore, Mercosur has enhanced its position vis-à-vis the US and the EU by pulling Bolivia and Chile towards itself as associate members and by seeking economic arrangements with the Andean Pact countries. It is becoming increasingly apparent that Brazil is rising to become the regional leader of the whole of Latin America.

Finally, a worrying trend has begun to assert itself, namely, a return to authoritarian methods of political rule. The case in point here is that of Fujimori who flouted every democratic procedure in the book in order to obtain a third term in office. The US-assisted attempt

---

65 In the period 1990–1993, Mercosur countries accounted for 51.9% of Latin America's output (Green, op. cit.: 144).

to overthrow Chavez is another such example. The amount of national and international vested interests that Peruvian neo-liberalism developed during Fujimori's tenure of office could no longer be sustained by electoral legitimacy,[66] hence the electoral fraud. Likewise, the contemptuous disregard for public opinion in Ecuador and the pursuit of the dollarisation of the economy regardless of a phenomenal social explosion appears to be a symptom of the same malaise. In the same vein, US hostility to Chavez's anti-neo-liberal programme and his strong popularity led high US officials, the Venezuelan economic élite and sections of the country's top brass to brush democratic niceties aside and wage a military *coup de main*. Furthermore, a strong undercurrent that furnishes Chavez with mass political support seems to be the belief among large sections of the *de facto* disenfranchised poor that nothing can really be changed by traditional, electoral methods.[67] Thus it would appear that the restricted democratic system developed in order to secure neo-liberal policies fails to give citizens a sense that they can rectify the gross inequalities and disadvantages they endure via the ballot box but, likewise, when they do exert their right and unwittingly threaten the unprecedented privileges that national and international capital enjoy, their democratic aspirations are simply quashed by means of authoritarian solutions.

66 See in this connection Aznar's highly ambiguous statements when commenting on the massive electoral fraud carried out by the fujimoristas; this is not surprising when one looks at the vast amount of Spanish capital tied up in the Peruvian economy.
67 In this connection, it is symptomatic that the very same social constituency was highly sympathetic to the attempted coup led by Chavez in 1992.

Marcos Costa Lima

Mercosur and the New Global Order: A Methodological Essay

The study of the formation, development and prospects of a regional trade bloc like Mercosur is, in many ways, a complex task. Firstly, several theoretical questions have to be dealt with at the centre of which is the degree and nature of the transformations in the capitalist system of production. Secondly, there is the need to consider the relevance of the question of territoriality. Thirdly, there are issues of identity, cultural heritage and the distinctiveness of cultural capital. Finally, we have to examine the feasibility of the region sharing a common sovereignty and its implications for the nation-state.[1]

A whole set of practical questions are also involved. Important among these are: the relative position of the countries of the periphery in the new world order; the role of the state in this process; the redevelopment of derelict areas into industrial parks and how can this help in achieving greater levels of competitiveness; the struggles and shifting balances of power within each of the member states participating in the world order; the politics of work; and the role of multinational companies in creating cross-border structures of economic integration. These issues have a bearing on the strategies for regional integration in the Southern Cone of the American continent.

Dealing with these issues requires transcending the frontiers of academic disciplines. We have to enter not only the realm of economics, but also politics and sociology, even though, economics has perhaps played the strongest role in studying earlier phases of regional integration and cross-border trade.

---

1   Jurgen Habermas, 'O Estado-Naçao Europeu Frente aos Desafios da Globalizaçao', *Novos Etudos*, No. 43, Novembro 1995: 87–101.

National governments often relegate cultural matters to the realm of the 'traditional' invoking them only in rhetorically or at worst treating them as superfluous. They tend to associate culture with folklore, something of only limited historical value, lacking in precision and concrete definition. A more comprehensive understanding of culture must consider the distinctive identity of a nation, its historical roots, language, idiosyncrasy, religious beliefs and indeed, creativity. Culture is what determines the identity of a specific group and allows for greater cohesion; it is capable of linking with the inner self of a specific group. In a world of all-pervasive homogeneity and sameness, which is pasteurised and bureaucratic, the cultural dimension turns out to be the background to the predominance of instrumental reasoning which affronts the Weberian world of disenchantment.[2]

There are many themes that can be invoked to strengthen the cultural cohesion among the countries of the Mercosur area. These often relate to aspects which are imaginary and symbolic. How do Brazilians, Argentinians, Uruguayans and Paraguayans see themselves as citizens of Mercosur? How do the citizens of each of these countries understand their own and each others' historical specificities and common problems? How do the member states deal with problems of regional fragmentation within their own territories, such as, for instance the underdevelopment of interior areas like Patagonia in Argentina and the Northeast in Brazil? How is this problem related to global processes? After all, it is impossible to deny that the regional integration currently being developed by Mercosur is focused on a territorial synergy which only extends from Buenos Aires in Argentina to the so-called Bermuda Triangle in Brazil.

An excessive emphasis on economic matters in the Mercosur project has led to neglect cultural policies. The only issues taken up so far in this area relate to educational matters, such as curriculum compatibility and diploma revalidation. This is not much. Some universities have, no doubt, made significant research efforts in the general area of common market processes. But even here the implications of these processes for education, the environment, health and

---

2   Jurgen Habermas, *O Discurso Filosófico da Modernidade*, Lisboa: Publicações Don Quixote, 1990.

employment have not been explored.[3] The mass media too, has done little in terms of bringing the four partners together, even though, because they joined Mercosur, each one of them has experienced significant economic growth in recent years.[4]

The Treaty of Asunción of 26 March 1991, clearly states that member states are 'convinced of the necessity of promoting the scientific and technological aspects of cooperation.' These are decisive elements of culture in the global context and are essential to achieve global competitiveness. There has, however, been very little evidence of this conviction in practical terms – whether in relation to budgetary allocations, capacity building efforts or the launching of collaborative projects.[5]

Mercosur guidelines notwithstanding, the disparities in the scale of the volume of trade when compared with other trading blocs[6] reflect the same norms and are built on the same free trade premises as

3   In 1993 CAPES – government Agency for Higher Education – carried out a survey on public universities, aimed at identifying the modalities of exchange and the structures being used for that. They discovered that cooperation on this specific matter between Mercosur countries was conducted in an informal way and very unsystematically, without any formal mechanism of support.

4   Hugo Achugar e Gerardo Caetano, 'Mundo, region y aldea. Identidades, políticas culturales e Integración regional', Montevideo: *Colóquio sobre Identidades Políticas Culturales e Integración Regional*, 21–23 Julho, 1993; Guy de Almeida, 'Mercosul nas universidades', *Promer Site mercobol@pucminas.br*, Belo Horizonte: PUC Minas, 1998.

5   An ECLAC study in 1992 points out the very low index of science and technology development compared to OECD countries, to East Asia and also to Southern European nations, such as Portugal and Spain. In terms of dollar/inhabitant ratios for R&D, Latin America spent 10, the OECD 448, Asia 23 and Southern Europe 44. Related to R&D expenditure *vis-à-vis* GDP: Latin America has 0.5%, OECD 2.5%, Asia 1.4% and Southern Europe 1%. The number of college graduations per 100,000 inhabitants was: Latin America 156, OECD 592, Asia 478 and South Europe 191 (CEPAL and UNESCO, *Educación y Conocimiento: Eje de Transformation Productiva con Equidad*, Santiago de Chile: CEPAL, 1992).

6   The European Union has a GDP of US$8,219.5 trillion and a population of 371.9 million, NAFTA has a GDP of US$8,061.4 trillion and a consumer market of 387.4 million, and MERCOSUR has a GDP of US$971.5 billion and a population of 204 million (*Mercosul: Informações Selecionadas*, set–dez, 1996, No. 19, Banco Central do Brasil).

elsewhere in the industrialised world. This presents a theoretical contradiction which this paper intends to examine. Are ongoing efforts towards building regional alliances indicative of the forging of strategic defence mechanisms by specific groups of countries seeking shelter from the turbulence of ever growing global financial anarchy? Furthermore, in the context of increasing economic globalisation across the world, not only in terms of the control of technology and production, but also in terms of political control, is Raul Prebisch's idea of regional trading blocs, developed in the fifties, relevant any more? At the time he formulated the matter thus:

> It is not only a question of productivity, though important in itself. There is another aspect which I would like to emphasise – it is the economic vulnerability of the Latin American countries. I do not see any solution to this problem nor to that of the high costs of imports other than to break away from this anachronistic model through the gradual and progressive formation of a common market and increasing diversification of trade.[7]

Forty years separate us from this pronouncement by the architect of ECLA. During this period, Latin America has witnessed several attempts to consolidate and enlarge regional markets and develop common industrialisation strategies with a view to overcoming the disadvantages of unequal trade or deteriorating terms of trade which characterise core-periphery relationships. These attempts did not succeed, possibly because of the hegemonic and nationalistic ambitions of individual countries, or because, as Prebisch pointed out in 1968, the region's industrial development itself was founded on protected and compartmentalised markets which would have made mutual reciprocity between countries extremely difficult. Another reason for the failure was, of course, the region's endemic political and institutional instability.

It is important to understand the prehistory of Mercosur from the early days up to the beginning of 1999 when, because of the sharp deterioration in the exchange rates suffered by most Latin American countries, the idea of integration itself was threatened. For analytical purposes one can divide this into periods in the following way:

---

7   Raúl Prebish, *El Mercado Común Latinoamericano*, México, D.F.: Publicación de las Naciones Unidas, 1959.

- Antecedents: from ALALC to ALADI (1960–1980);
- Formulation: from the return to democracy to the Treaty of Asunción (1985–1991);
- Transition: from the Las Leñas development to the establishment of external common tariffs at the Buenos Aires negotiations (1992–1994);
- Constitution: the institution of the Free Trade Area and the Complete Customs Union – covering 85% of the items on a list of products (1995–1998);
- Consolidation: rapid growth in the volume and value of trade (1995–1998);
- Macroeconomic crises (January, 1999).

The shifts and adjustments which have been shaping the configuration of international relations since the beginning of the sixties, and more profoundly, since the oil crisis of 1973, referred to by economic journalists as globalisation, have been unprecedented as well as complex in character. The term globalisation has a strong ideological emphasis. It signifies an unstoppable process to be imposed on continents, countries and peoples giving rise to a frontierless world and setting in motion trends which are not only irreversible but also supposedly beneficial for all. This perception was given wide currency by the American Business School, particularly through the widely read works of Kenichi Ohmae[8] and Michael Porter.[9] Even though a dubious and imprecise term, 'globalisation' has become the subject matter of a great number of studies, not only in economics but also in geography, sociology, politics and philosophy, and many of these are reaching sharply opposite conclusions. Given this situation, delimitation of the field of analysis becomes a necessary condition for the concept to achieve a modicum of precision.[10]

---

8   Kenichi Ohmae, *O Fim do Estado Nação*, Rio de Janeiro: Campus, 1996.
9   Michael Porter, *A Vantagem Competitiva das Nações*, Rio de Janeiro: Campus, 1993.
10 Michael Featherstone (ed.), *Global Culture*, London: Sage, 1990; Renato Ortiz, *Mundialização e Cultura*, São Paulo: Brasiliense, 1996; Paul Doremus *et al.*, *The Myth of the Global Corporation*, Princeton: Princeton University Press,

By examining recent shifts in the international structure of control over the means of production across the world the inherent contradictions in the ongoing regionalisation process, which have far reaching implications for the countries of the periphery, begin to become obvious. In a recent work Christian Palloix points out that neither classical economics, which initiated the notion of globalisation, nor neoclassical economics, anchored on the premise of the market as the provider of perfect equilibrium, offers a basis for understanding how the global coordination of market forces can be achieved. More specifically he says:

> in the nineties, the ideology and practices of globalisation represent, on the one hand, the weakening of the totality of the nation-state, speeding up of the processes of fragmentation and atomisation of the national jurisdiction and, therefore, the decline of national societies, and, on the other hand, the absence of a new global totality for filling the vacuum left by the former. It is this absence which explains the assumption of the hegemonic role of the nation gendarme by the United States of America.[11]

An advanced and innovative book for its time (first published in 1974), *The Global Reach,* dealing basically with the emergence and consolidation of big multinational corporations, foretold some of our current concerns:

> The men who manage global enterprises are the first ones in history to get the organisation, the technology, the resources and the ideology to make plausible an attempt to manage the world as a single and integrated unit.[12]

The authors of *The Global Reach* quoted Aurelio Peeci, at that time a director of FIAT Automobile and an organiser of the Rome Club, who had declared that global corporations were the 'most powerful agent at the time for promoting the internationalisation of human society.' Barnet and Müller pointed out one of the dominant trends in the

---

1998; Paul Hirst and Graham Thompson, *Globalisation in Question*, Cambridge: Polity Press, 1998.

11   Christian Palloix, 'Mundialização – Internacionalização – Globalização: Um conceito Impossivel', *Revista ANPEC*, No. 2, 51–62, Brasilia: Anpec, 1998: 61.

12   Richard Barnet and Ronald Müller, *Poder Global. A Força Incontrolável das Multinacionais*, Rio de Janeiro: Record, 1974: 13.

Mercosur and the New Global Order 63

seventies, namely, the transfer of big enterprises to third world countries.[13] They highlighted another important feature of globalisation, namely, the difficulty of market regulation as a result of the presence and sheer volume of the business carried out by MNCs. In some cases decisions made by MNCs, have a greater impact than decisions taken by governments;

> Those decisions influence where people will live, what kind of jobs they will have, what they eat, drink and wear, what kind of knowledge universities and schools need to encourage and what kind of society they will leave for their children [...] The most revolutionary aspect of global enterprises is not their size, but their global vision. Managers of global enterprises are trying to practice a human organisation theory that will alter deeply the national-state system around which human society has been established for more than 400 years.[14]

George Ball,[15] former US Secretary of State and president of Lehman Brothers, categorically affirmed:

> How can a government define with confidence an economic plan, if a management committee 8,000 km away can, changing its purchase power and production, affect deeply the economic life of the country?[16]

It is important to distinguish between the principal characteristics of globalisation and the global enterprise that flow from this process:

- Changes in the technological pattern, in product and processes, supported by computer, information and satellite systems;
- A new paradigm of industrial production – flexible automation, the new basis of competitiveness – with emphasis on information, know-how and high tech systems;
- The establishment of a Technological Innovation Systems with immense power for proliferation;

---

13   Ibid: 14.
14   Ibid: 15.
15   George Ball, 'Cosmocorp: The Importance of Being Stateless', *The Columbia Journal of World Business*, November 1967.
16   Ibid: 21.

- The establishment of pluri-national Trade Blocs: the European Union, NAFTA, Mercosur and Asean, among others;
- The concentration of capital: huge conglomerates growing in the tertiary sector, notably services;
- The reorganisation of labour markets with greater selectivity of workers;
- An increase in unemployment.

Also significant and prescient was the understanding of Barnet and Müller concerning the 'financial pre-eminence of wealth', a phenomenon that gave rise to the displacement of North American banks, from the mid seventies onwards, consolidating a market of euro-money independent of central banks and that guaranteed the movement of great corporations abroad: 'The 298 largest global companies of the USA, studied by the Dept. of Trade, obtain 40% of their total profits abroad.'[17]

There are many testimonies from managers of large corporations which, even in that early period, directly criticised regulation by nation-states. Thus Jaques Maisonrouge of IBM stated that the main problem at the time resided 'in the conflict between the search for the global optimisation of resources and the autonomy of the nation-state'. In 1967, some years before the oil crises, the conglomerate Business International proclaimed to its clients that:

> the nation-state is becoming obsolete. Tomorrow, at any rate, it will be dead, and the same thing is going to happen to those enterprises which will stay essentially national.[18]

These powerful global conglomerates, acting in all the major markets, have much greater profits than the sum total of the economies of many developed countries, and their presence in so many countries turns them into important political agents. It is known that the ten biggest industrial American enterprises now enjoy profits which are higher than Mercosur's GDP.

---

17   Ibid: 17.
18   Ibid: 19.

Mercosur and the New Global Order 65

Labour cost disparities was no doubt one of the first reasons behind the relocation of multinational companies in the sixties and seventies, when the average monthly salary of a North American worker was US$1,220 while in Korea and Taiwan it did not exceed US$68 and US$45 respectively.

Also relevant is the so-called North-American labour union obsolescence, a fact that would harm most trades unions around the world later on. During this period of the consolidation of the global market, a battle occurred between organised labour – the AFL-CIO – and global enterprise in the United States. The conflict came about not only because US companies were employing workers who performed all sort of dangerous jobs under very unsafe conditions, but also because they were attacking labour's traditional weapon of collective bargaining to such an extent that union members began to claim that the relocation of US enterprise abroad was transmuting the US 'into a nation of hamburger huts'.[19] In fact, at the beginning of the seventies, the biggest global US firms such as Ford, Chrysler, Kodak and Procter & Gamble, had more than one-third of their workforce outside the US.

The strengthening of big economic enterprises and the internationalisation of financial capital, aided by a vertiginous process of technological innovation based on microelectronics[20] and new methods of production and management by the end of seventies[21] gave birth to a new phase of capital concentration in the rich countries by the eighties. This was a consequence of the debt crises in developing countries and the increase in intercapitalist competition by the Triad countries.[22] By the nineties, the outline and crystallisation of this process became clearer. It was characterised by a new stage of internationalisation no longer circumscribed by the economy, but with many interfaces and connections with the politics, culture and society of whole countries and regions. This trend towards the amplification

---

19 Ibid: 302.
20 Christopher Freeman, *The Economics of Industrial Innovation*, London: Francis Pinter, 1982.
21 Manuel Castells and Jeffrey Henderson (eds.), *Global Restructuring and Territorial Development*, London: Sage Publications, 1987.
22 Giovanni Arrighi, *O Longo Seculo XX. Dinheiro, Poder e as Origens de Nosso Tempo*, Rio de Janeiro: Contraponto/UNESP, 1996.

of the geographical mobility of capital demands a greater understanding, capable of explaining the rise of emergent economies, the rise of new trends and the consequences of global changes.

At the same time, this new reality, revealed tensions which first manifested themselves in the high deficit of current accounts in the balance of payments, but also in the reduction of taxes on saving accounts in the US, which today represents one third of the total revenue from the same tax in OECD countries and less than a quarter of Japan's.[23]

The United States, from being the biggest global capital creditor and supplier, became the biggest debtor, with an external debt of over a trillion dollars.[24] This structural imbalance, emanating from the global economy's leader, profoundly affects the largest economies of Latin America, namely, Argentina, Brazil and Mexico.

The second focus of tension is in the disconnection of the Eastern European economies, which will continue to absorb external savings from developed countries without, in the short term, any possibility of paying them back. These countries represent a future frontier to the capitalist economy, above all in Europe and Asia, because they enjoy an advantageous position – in skilled labour or geographic proximity – in competitiveness in comparison to Latin American countries.

The third focus of tension is the computer revolution and technological upgrading, whose primary characteristics have, on the one hand, been impacting on industrial processes, thereby increasing unemployment and, on the other, operating as the core of the Third Industrial Revolution, generating new materials. The results are a great deal of export substitution of raw materials that used to come from third world countries, thus reducing the latter's comparative advantages, and thereby bringing about a decline in the price of commodities.

If one depicts in figures the present global market, the marginal position occupied by Latin America economies becomes clear: a share

---

23   Celso Furtado, *A Construção Interrompida*, São Paulo: Paz e Terra, 1992.
24   Lester Thurow, *Cabeça a Cabeça. A Batalha Econômica Entre Japão, Europa e Estados Unidos*, Rio de Janeiro: Rocca, 1993.

of 10% of global exports in the sixties, a fall to 5.3% in 1975 and only 3% in 1990.[25]

The total amount of Foreign Direct Investment to the region also fell considerably, dropping from 15.3% of the total in 1975 to 9.15% in 1985, which means that despite globalisation and an increase in world trade this process is much more related to the OECD countries, with the definite marginalisation of the Latin America countries.

By the beginning of the nineties the stock of Foreign Direct Investment existing in Singapore, Indonesia and Hong Kong, reached US$87.4bn, far more than the US$67.4bn represented by the joint FDI stock of Mexico and Brazil.[26] This is even more evident when the evolution of FDI is examined.

	Developing Countries					
	1976–80	1981–85	1986–90	1990	1991	1992
Asia	2.1	4.9	13.3	18.6	24.0	28.0
Latin America	4.1	5.0	6.3	7.3	12.0	13.0

Source: Reinaldo Gonçalves, 1994: 43; Bank for International Settlements, 63rd Report, Basileia, June 14, 1993: 90.

Table 1. Foreign direct investment in US$ billions.

It is in this context that the possibilities of Latin America's insertion into the global marketplace as well as the attempt to consolidate a regional trade bloc as a strategy to narrow the technological gap with the centre in order to relaunch economic development can be assessed. Such evaluation sheds new light on the Mercosur experience.[27]

The technological changes and management shifts that took place in the core countries in the last decade coincided with a period of stagnation and crisis in the Brazilian economy, which deepened the country's technological backwardness, including its most dynamic sectors, which are largely in the hands of big multinationals corporations. These multinationals control the hardcore of recent technological advances, i.e. they create and disseminate innovation. Furthermore,

25   CEPAL and UNESCO: 1992.
26   Reinaldo Gonçalves, Ô Abre Alas: A Nova Inserção do Brasil na Economia Mundial, Rio de Janeiro: Relume-Dumará, 1994: 53.
27   Paulo Roberto Almeida, O Mercosul no Contexto Regional e Internacional, São Paulo: Aduaneiras, 1993.

the transnationalisation of the Brazilian economy has had a significant impact on its domestic politics.

In this connection, it is necessary to ask some fundamental questions – many of them as yet unanswered – methodologically indispensable for the construction of a whole analytical field and the discussion of closely related themes. No doubt a better understanding will help shed light on the core issues such as the debate concerning multilateralism versus regionalism; the European Union versus NAFTA; the role of nation-states; the confrontation between welfare and neo-liberal models; the evolution of North–South relationships; the issue of globalisation; and, the search for historic and concrete models by which the international production system is articulated in national production subsystems.

It is relevant here to remember Castells' methodological warning that global restructuring manifests itself differently in different contexts and, therefore, one must look for the manifestation of some specific tendencies – local and regional – which appear as general tendencies.

> It would be absurd to pretend that a specific spatial form will derive automatically from the characteristics of the model of capitalist development implicit in the restructuring process. Specific spatial forms and processes will result from the interaction between the historically concrete restructuring policies and the attributes of each society, including its territorial basis.[28]

Would it be a mistake to think about the revival of regionalism in a world of ongoing capital interchange and financial globalisation? With the end of the Cold War, will NAFTA or the Initiative for the Americas, constitute a real attempt to consolidate a regional Free Trade Area for the United States, when it is well known that since the eighties and nineties Latin America increasingly means less to the North American economy?[29]

28   Castells and Henderson, 1987: 2.
29   Robert Pastor, 'NAFTA as the center of an integration process: The non-trade issues', in Nora Lusting, Barry P. Bosworth and Robert Z. Lawrence (eds), *North American Free Trade: Assessing the Impact*, Washington: The Brooking Institution, 1992; J. S. Tulchin, 'The Enterprise for the Americas Initiative', in Roy Green (ed.), *United States Trade Relations*, Boulder: Prager, 1993; Lia

The data in Table 2 show that although in recent years the region was not a commercial priority for the US, it does play a preponderant role in Latin America.

Some analysts assert that, in the medium term, NAFTA will encompass the entire continent, from Alaska to Tierra del Fuego. However, the basic concept of NAFTA is that of a free market, while Mercosur, inspired by the European Community, seeks a much deeper integration, not just a commercial one. Stimulated by the success of Mercosur, Brazil rejected a proposal to create ALCSA (South American Association of Free Trade) in 1994, and judging by its foreign policy, it has demonstrated itself ready to provide strategic leadership in the subcontinent, thus occupying the vacuum left by the US, at present much more closely engaged in trade relations with Asia and the European Union.

	United States		Latin America	
	Imports from Latin America	Exports to Latin America	Imports from US	Exports to US
1980	15%	18%	43%	42%
1990	10%	14%	57%	52%

Source: GATT (1989–90), International Trade; J. Tulchin, 'United States and Latin America'. *Política Externa*, 2(2), 1993: 102–32.

Table 2. US–Latin America trade.

If NAFTA has faced many difficulties and impasses, among them the Mexican crisis,[30] Mercosur for its part, year after year, amplifies its objectives. It does so by, for example, establishing preliminary agreements with Chile and Bolivia, evolving into full sub-regional integration with a spill over into the countries of the Andean Community. Despite the many controversies with Argentina since 1993,

---

Valls Pereira, 'Considerações preliminaries sobre a Iniciativa para as Americas', in João Paulo Reis Velloso (org.), *O Brasil e o Plano Bush*, São Paulo: Nobel, 1991.

30 The Mexican crisis initiated an entire sequence of macroeconomic turbulence, reaching as far as Thailand and its currency, the *baht*, and encompassing all East Asian countries.

resulting from a fall in the Brazilian exchange rate, Mercosur continues to go forward.[31]

Institutionally consolidated and in operation since 1 January 1995, Mercosur has been deepening its predisposition to intensify commerce between the member countries, business associations and such like. However, the external vulnerability of the two main Mercosur partners cannot be ignored. The main sources of this weakness are:

- an overvalued exchange rate which hinders exports and provokes deficits on their trade balances; in 1997 this deficit reached US$8.5 billion;
- a policy of high interest rates aimed at attracting external investments, resulting in high levels of unemployment and the increase of both the current account deficit and the public debt.[32]

Because economic growth, both in Argentina and Brazil, does not have a sustainable basis in the medium term, any increase in US interest rates or any speculative crisis damages Mercosur. Thus, 1999 proved a difficult year for the integration process in the Southern Cone, above all, due to the depreciation of the Brazilian real. Furthermore, the Multilateral Agreement on Investment[33] casts a rather large shadow over the possibilities of success for this integration process. Although the measures contemplated in the MAI were postponed because of world speculation crises and the proximity of the Millennium Round Table in Seattle, it represents a strong reminder of

---

31 Héctor Alimonda, 'NAFTABLUES', *Novos Estudos*, No. 39, Julho 1994: 222–37; Jorge Castañeda, *Utopia Unarmed*, New York: Vintage Books, 1995; L. S. Belluzzo, 'A crise do México e as forces do mercado', *Folha de São Paulo*, Janeiro 8, 1995.

32 The current account deficit of Brazil reached US$52.4 billion in 1977, almost 6% of GDP; while the public debt rose to US$306 billion, or 34% of a GDP of US$900 billion (Álvaro Zini, 'Rumo ao impasse fiscal', 1o. de Março, *Caderno Dinheiro, Folha de São Paulo*, 1998).

33 An idea conceived by the G-7 group, submitted to the OECD countries in 1998, to be submitted in turn to countries on the periphery and approved by referendum at a later date.

the dominant conceptions and penchant for free trade and globalisation. The agreement would represent the strongest measure to date toward economic deregulation in that it grants legal rights to multinational capital to sue national governments in a court of their choice. According to Tavares,[34] this project would lead to a 'completeness of foreign investors' rights; the subjective prevalence of foreign investors' criteria and the abdication of state sovereignty.' This is, without the slightest doubt, a question of utmost relevance and it is well known that the World Trade Organisation is already working on a 'zero tariff' scenario for 2025.

Judging by the recent diplomatic imbroglio between Brazil and North America over the *Area de Libre Comercio de las Americas* – Free Trade Area of the Americas – Mercosur, notwithstanding its many weaknesses, has already produced results.

In considering Brazil's trade relationship in the context of economic blocs, it can be seen that exports from Brazil to Mercosur grew almost seven times between 1989 and 1996, leaping from US$1,320bn to US$9,043bn. In this period, the value of trade of Brazil with Mercosur rose from US$2,885bn to US$18,668bn. The European Union, Brazil's main trading partner, buys 26.9% of Brazilian exports, while NAFTA purchases only 22%. Furthermore, Mercosur absorbs 15.3% of Brazilian exports which are made up of products with high value added. Even if Brazil is acknowledged as a global trader, the South American sub-regional market is already quite significant, since Brazilian exports to Mercosur are twice the amount of exports to Japan. In terms of imports, Brazil buys almost the same amount in dollars from the USA as from the European Union, roughly 26% of its total imports from each. Next is Mercosur accounting for 15% of Brazil's total imports in 1996.[35]

---

34 Maria da Conçeição Tavares, 'Acordos de investimentos, privatização e cidadania', *Folha de São Paulo*, Lições Contemporâneas, Caderno Dinheiro, Marzo 1, 1998.
35 Banco Central, September–December 1996.

Conclusion

The purpose of this contribution is not to put forward a blueprint for Mercosur's integration process and it therefore deliberately avoids a description of its historical evolution because it has already been accomplished elsewhere. This, however, does not rule out the need to look at the phenomenology of the actual events and processes leading to Mercosur's development.

From a methodological point of view, Mercosur already configures a whole 'programme of research' in the sense understood by Lakatos[36] or an 'analytical field', in Bourdieu's sense,[37] since it configures a 'history', a temporal trajectory with well known agents, different interests at play, and contrasting theoretical approaches. A fruitful examination of Mercosur therefore needs, first of all, studies to expand links, concepts and theses referring to the global economic process and its relationship with regionalisation. Any such examination should outline and discuss the main approaches to economic integration, comparative and competitive advantages, and the formulation and contextualisation of existing economic trade blocs.

A second axis of research would be the study of socio-economic and political changes wrought on Latin America in the period between the ascending post-war cycle until the end of the seventies and its descending phase in the early eighties – also known as the lost decade – and, in a more detailed way, the implementation of deflationary monetarist policies in the nineties in order to lay bare the issue of the sovereignty of the nation-state vs neo-liberal policies of deregulation. From our vantage point, such an approach would help better evaluate what was gained in the previous period, as well as the current prospects for the consolidation of regional integration. In this connection, it is worth pointing out the Mexican 'detachment' from Latin America by virtue of its inclusion in NAFTA. The dependency

---

36 Imre Lakatos, 'Criticism and the methodology of scientific research programmes', *Proceedings of the Aristotelian Society*, 69, 1968: 149–68.
37 Pierre Bourdieu, *A Economía das Trocas Simbólicas*, São Paulo: Perspectiva, 1992.

of this country on its trade with the US – surpassing 70% in value terms – turns Mexico into an additional star on the North American flag, but without the advantages of being a member of the Union.

A third line of inquiry would be the study of the consolidation of Mercosur emphasising industrial aspects as well as labour-related and science and technology issues. For this purpose, it would be fruitful to follow the deliberations of Technical Groups[38] – SGTs 4, 7 and 10 – relative to financial matters and macroeconomic coordination, as well as to examine the behaviour of private enterprise in Mercosur in order to determine the extent to which regional integration has contributed to bringing about and improving reciprocity, including industrial reconversion, at least between Brazil and Argentina.

The fourth axis, the energy question, is fundamental for regional integration and an outline of a single energy matrix has been emerging for South America, with the prospect of consolidating this around the gas reserves of Argentina, Bolivia, Peru and Venezuela.

A fifth axis is culture and civil society. The four partners in Mercosur have stayed very isolated from each other, with little interaction of any kind among them, a legacy of the colonial past under which interaction with Europe predominated. The democratic deficit is another problem; deeply rooted in authoritarian traditions, South American élites still stand firmly apart from the majority of the people. Extreme inequalities in consumption and income distribution demonstrate that, for example, in Brazil the bottom 10% of the population enjoy only 1% of national income, whereas the top 10% has 46.7%.[39] The poor, generally speaking undereducated, lacking in political experience and easily deceived by populist and/or corrupt politicians, scarcely know what is going on in the higher spheres of politics or in foreign affairs and this includes Mercosur.

---

38 In the institutional framework of Mercosur the Mercosur Council (CM) and the Mercosur Group (GM) were created to deal with intra-government decisions. The CM has, additionally, its own subordinate structures with advisory functions on technical matters, the SGTs of which there are ten: Trade; Customs; Technical norms; Fiscal and monetary policy related to commerce; Land and Maritime Transport; Industrial and technology policy; Agricultural policy; Energy; Macroeconomic policy; and Work and Social security.

39 World Development Indicators 2001. Washington: The World Bank.

Last but not least, a systematic examination of globalisation would be of value, looking as much to Bretton Wood's organisations, as to the unfolding power of financial capital and multinationals, globalisation's big players and which decide the rhythm of developments and dictate the possibilities that nation states have.

Studies and research in these directions are necessary in order to define a broad field of enquiry capable of intellectually enriching and replacing the thesis of overcoming Latin America's under- and late development which finds in Raul Prebisch its first and most consistent advocate.

A research programme based on Lakatos' conception will need both a whole new approach,[40] but also an understanding of the meso and micro aspects of regional questions. In this context, Brazil, given not only its continental dimensions but also its level of industrial development, would unavoidably be one of the central foci of analysis.

In conclusion, in order to gain the most accurate knowledge of Mercosur, even confining its analytical field into areas such as the economy, politics, geography, socio-cultural and environmental issues, it is necessary to adopt a holistic approach, as well as identifying and understanding the complex interaction between the global, regional, national and local dimensions.

It is clear that a consistent approach to the understanding of Mercosur cannot be dissociated from the analysis of 'big politics', namely, agents and social groups more directly involved in the process of regional integration. Nor should it be seen as a finished matter, but as *work in progress*; it is essential to establish the context with the greatest degree of accuracy, which to certain extent points to the diplomatic conflicts surrounding the Free Trade Area of the Americas. Under this agreement, thirty four American countries – with the exception of Cuba – have decided to abolish all common taxes and trade tariffs after 2005. Such prospect is the biggest challenge Mercosur faces in the immediate future.

---

40 Fernando Gewandsznadjer, 'Ciência natural: os pressupostos filosóficos', in F. Gewandsznadjer and A. J. Mazzotti, *O Método nas Ciências Naturais e Sociais*, São Paulo: Pioneira, 1999: 10–64.

Marcelo de Almeida Medeiros

Multi Level Governance and the Problem of Balance within Mercosur

Introduction

Since the second half of the eighties, the international political economy has been characterised by a worldwide movement towards regional integration. The momentous step the European Union has taken in the direction of a single market is likely to have operated as a kind of catalyst, inducing other countries to rethink their ways of conceiving the state. The state's relationships with both society and international actors places it in a conflictual position in which it is confronted with the problem of the internal requirements of work and welfare on the one hand and the demands of efficiency and productivity, on the other.

If regional integration emerges as a genuine means of achieving the conciliation of endogenous and exogenous claims, it also introduces a number of new issues that have to be faced. Economic circumstances, characterised by rapid technological development, the globalisation of trade and finance, and the information explosion, call for a regional political and administrative system which commands enough sovereignty to be able to take rapid decisions. This system should also command sufficient legitimacy from the constituent unities – national states, regions, federated states – thus giving it stable equilibrium, and could also possess adequate democratic principles to guarantee society's participation. It should, however, be pointed out that sovereignty, subsidiarity and democracy are all very tricky concepts, and are not necessarily understood by everybody in the same way.

The multitude of political cultures that distinguish a group of countries aiming to become integrated may reveal how difficult it is to find a pattern that is capable of combining every miscellaneous idiosyncrasy.[1] At the same time, sub-units of national states, particularly those belonging to federal systems, attempt to improve their bargaining power, setting up additional levels of negotiation. The internal struggle that takes place between federal and federated powers – in part as a result of the regional integration process – impinges directly on national political systems and, by feedback action, the regional integration process itself.

In Latin America regional integration is a long-standing and mature tendency. Since Bolivar's famous *Jamaica Letter* of 1815, which suggested three Spanish American federations, the continent has aspired to forming a single entity that could work as a strong united front against foreign interests, one in which the diversity of each individual society could be respected. Unfortunately, national demands were more powerful and the Spanish Empire broke up into the micro states of Central America and the medium-sized states of South America. Brazil was an exception to this, which due to a fairly smooth 'family' political transition to independence – compared to Spanish America – it preserved the central political power structures founded by Lisbon.

Despite several positive attitudes during the 19th and the first half of the 20th centuries towards regional cooperation, Latin American countries only started to think systematically about their economic integration after the Second World War. From 1948 the United Nations Economic Commission for Latin America onwards advocated a model of economic growth anchored on the import-substitution model and regional integration. The Latin American Free Trade Association (LAFTA, 1960), the Andean Pact (1969) and the Latin American Integration Association (LAIA, 1980), are examples of this. The failure of ECLA's policies for the bulk of Latin American economies, and the shift of political and economic assumptions, especially, after the debacle of the Soviet Union, brought liberal theories to the fore of the institutional debate within a state and regional framework.

Likewise, the indefiniteness of the GATT Uruguay Round and the evolution of administrated trade have pushed states into adopting an aggressive posture towards regional integration in order to ensure markets for their goods and capital. The North American Free Trade

1   Sidney Verba and Lucien Pye, *Political Culture and Political Development*, Princeton: Princeton University Press, 1965: 512–60.

Agreement, and the Asia-Pacific Economic Cooperation forum, can be pointed to as examples of this. The attempt to renew the regional integration process, supported by an association of market economy and 'minilateralism', can be fittingly represented in Latin America by the Common Market of the South: Mercosur.

Actually, Mercosur came into being as a response to the metamorphosis of the world political economy and as a means of reformulating state institutional structures. Mercosur took shape at a moment when military regimes, which had ruled for decades, were coming to an end, and society began to demand democratic reforms. Certain actors that had long been marginalised manifested their intention of returning to the political arena and were actively participating in its changes.

This article examines multilevel governance issues and the problem of balance within Mercosur. It begins with the analysis of the genesis of Argentine and Brazilian federalisms, essential to the comprehension of certain contemporary attitudes towards integration. It then approaches the relationship between the restoration of democracy and governance, taking into consideration its institutional aspect, as well as social practice. Next, the issue of domestic transformations on federal questions is placed in a broader context, in which international trends and integration in the Southern Cone are examined. Further, the confrontation between nation states vs sub-federal units is looked at in order to explain the rise of a complex power network in which the roles of the actors implicated in the integration process are not easily defined. Finally, before making some tentative conclusions, Mercosur's institutional structures are explored in order to offer a number of concrete landmarks, which are substantive for the understanding of its functioning and the relationships between its member states.

The genesis of Argentinian and Brazilian federalisms

The development of Mercosur's integration process has encouraged certain tendencies in the direction of the creation of an enlarged and more complex sub-regional network system. In reality, if in the international arena the economic rationale has called forth the elaboration of single commercial areas, in the domestic sphere the increasing progress of democracy has necessitated participation at local levels as a factor in the political legitimacy of citizenship. These contrasting trends have engendered a double confrontation, between economic and political forces on the one hand, and between society and state on the other. Despite the quasi consensus on the necessity of promoting the regional integration of Mercosur's member states, internal actors sometimes differ on how to accomplish this.

As a result of both their federal structures and their overwhelming economic power within Mercosur, Argentina and Brazil are important cases for the analysis of governance issues.[2] The concomitance between Argentine and Brazilian internal political reforms and the phenomenon of the Common Market of the South indicate that they have been part of a vast state modernisation project, which has been seeking to combine political pluralism and economically sustainable development. Its driving forces intend to construct this on the basis of an optimum conception of governance. However, the elaboration of this conception requires a reevaluation of their national federal systems, which are at present inserted into a larger international network relatively affected by the logic of sub-regional integration, procedures, and institutions.

Federalism, both in Argentina and in Brazil, as in most federal states, has been inspired by the North American Confederation Articles and the Philadelphia Constitution. Hamiltonian principles of centralism, as well as Jeffersonian ideas of self-government have swayed, in successive periods, the evolution of federalism in the Southern Cone.[3] Nevertheless, Argentina's and Brazil's common federal roots have also faced their own political idiosyncrasies,

---

2   Contrary to the European Union, where one can identify the 'big four' alongside medium and small countries, Mercosur membership breaks down into a continental country, Brazil, responsible for about 70% of both its GDP and population; a vast country, Argentina, which with Brazil represents 97% of its GDP and 95.5% of its population; and two much smaller countries, Paraguay and Uruguay.

3   James Madison, Alexander Hamilton and John Jay, *Os Artigos Federalistas (1787–1788)*, Rio de Janeiro: Editora Nova Fronteira, 1987.

resulting from the different way they were colonised and their dissimilar processes of independence.

As with most Latin American countries, except Portuguese-speaking Brazil, the Argentine federation was born out of the fall of the Spanish colonial empire. Indeed, the break up of the Spanish empire followed its fairly decentralised administration, based on *Virreinatos*, *Capitanias-Generales* and *Audiencias*, which gave birth to the new South American states at the beginning of the 19th century.[4] Both the succession problems of the Spanish crown and the Napoleonic invasion of the Iberian Peninsula led to Jose Bonaparte becoming the new King of Spain. This event dramatically threw the legitimacy of the metropolitan authority over its overseas Spanish dominions into question.

In the River Plate basin, Buenos Aires made efforts to succeed metropolitan royal authority legitimately within the territory of the La Plata Viceroyalty, but the remaining *Provincias* rejected its centralist dynamic.[5] Subsequently, the signing of the Pilar Treaty in 1820 outlined a type of federal project which, unfortunately, would later be altered by the unitary tendency of the *Provincias Unidas del Río de la Plata* as a result of the war with Brazil. Later, the 1831 Federal Pact set up a *de facto* confederation that functioned under Rosas' pragmatism, and is laid out in *La Carta de la Hacienda Figueroa*.[6] Finally, the 1853 Federal Constitution – established under Urquiza's auspices – and its subsequent modifications – under Mitre's patronage – which was introduced in order to incorporate Buenos Aires into the Federation, represents the outcome of half a century of constitutional

---

4   Guy Martiniere, *Les Amériques latines: une histoire économique*, Grenoble: Presses Universitaires de Grenoble, 1978.
5   At the outset there were only three *Intendencias*: Buenos Aires, Córdoba de Tucumán and Salta de Tucumán. Due to the lack of legitimacy of Buenos Aires' central power, communal autonomy increased, and some municipalities became the epicentres of the 14 new Provincias. (José Carlos Chiaramonte, 'El federalismo argentino en la primera mitad del siglo XIX', in Marcelo Carmagnani (coordinador), *Federalismos Latinoamericanos: México / Brasil / Argentina*, México: El Colegio de México / Fondo de Cultura Económica, 1993).
6   As a matter of fact, Rosas governed according to centralist principles (Ernesto Quesada, *La época de Rosas, su verdadero caráter histórico*, Buenos Aires: N. Moen, 1898).

and political efforts underlined by the dichotomy between the economic and demographic power of that *Provincia* and the military might of the others. However, the interests underlying this dichotomy would survive throughout the 20th century, both during military periods as well as in the Peronist era, in accordance with the natural tendency to favour Buenos Aires centralism.

Unlike Spanish colonial strategies, which were basically founded on the strong, decentralised power of the Viceroys and Captain-generals, Portuguese strategies were instead focused firmly on the King himself, even when General-governments and the *Capitanias Hereditarias* were responsible for local administration.[7] The repercussions of the Napoleonic wars in Brazil come out of the fact that the Portuguese royal family moved from Lisbon to Rio de Janeiro. The King's presence in Brazil was, without doubt, an important factor contributing to the centralisation and unity of the country. Brazil had its institutional status modified, moving from the position of mere colony to that of becoming a part of the United Kingdom of Portugal, Brazil, and Algarve.

Following Napoleon's fall, Portugal's *Cortes* attempted to restore the primitive colonial system in Brazil. As this regression seemed unacceptable to the Brazilian administration, independence was achieved. However, since independence was proclaimed by the King's son, Don Pedro I, there was no issue regarding the legitimacy of his power and centrifugal tendencies were, at least temporarily, fairly weak. Constituted as an Empire from 1882 until 1889, Brazil enjoyed a centralised and unitary system, even if it also experienced, during the *Regência* decade, a sort of rudimentary tentative model of decentralisation.[8] The social evolution linked to the abolition of slavery, positivist ideas, and the increasing organisation of military power after the Paraguay war gave rise to the advent of republicanism in 1889, and the improvement of the federal regime.

7   The *Capitanias Hereditarias* were the first administrative division of Brazilian territory. They are the seeds of the future states of the Brazilian federation.
8   As in 1831 Brazilian Emperor Pedro I abdicated and since his son was only five years old the country's executive power was held by politicians until 1840. The *Regência* was a very tumultuous period, marked by several separatist movements (Joao Pandia Calogeras, *Formaçao Histórica do Brasil*, Rio de Janeiro: Biblioteca do Exército Editora, 1957).

In fact, Brazilian federalism was created as a result of the transformation of the hitherto *Provincias*, belonging to a central and unitary state, into autonomous, though not sovereign, units. Each unit, now called a state, became a space for local politics with its own constitution, executive, legislative and judicial powers, even if it was linked to central power through the federal constitution. Therefore, unlike Argentina where the federal process took place via the independent units' voluntary cohesion, the birth of Brazilian federalism is characterised by the separation of the central administrative body and its concentrated power. As Camargo points out

> Brazil is the only country with a federal tradition in which the term 'federation', even today, is identified with decentralisation, rather than defining the organisation of the union, as is the case in the United States and elsewhere.[9]

Prior to 1930 the Brazilian federal system was characterised by a genuinely decentralised regime in which the governors, with the support of local oligarchies, constituted the real locus of power. There was minor political and economic integration among the bulk of states in the federation, and federal policy was likely to roughly represent the interests of a few powerful states.[10] Subsequently, and until the 1988 Magna Carta, the Brazilian federal system tended towards centralisation, even though the 1946 Constitution assigned room for manoeuvre to the federated states.

The federal evolution of both Argentina and Brazil has been marked by a pendulum-like movement, sometimes swinging towards decentralisation, sometimes in the direction of centralisation. Golbery do Couto e Silva used the cardiac metaphor of 'systole' and 'diastole' to describe these trends within the Brazilian political system.[11] As a matter

---

9   Aspásia Camargo, *La Federación sometida. Nacionalismo desarrollista e inestabilidad democrática*, in Marcelo Carmagnani (coordinador), op. cit.: 1993.
10 São Paulo and Minas Gerais were then, the two states which most influenced federal policy. This hegemony has been described as 'coffee and milk politics', because the former was a strong coffee producer and the latter an impressive milk producer.
11 Golbery do Couto e Silva, *Conjuntura Política Nacional: O Poder Executivo e Geopolítica do Brasil*, Rio de Janeiro: Livraria José Olympio Editora, 1981.

of fact, during past decades, both countries have sought to resolve their respective dilemmas of governance through the adaptation of their federal procedures to the new social and state realities coming out of the metamorphosis of the interests of domestic and foreign powers.

The restoration of democracy and governance

The restoration of democracy in Argentina and Brazil can be interpreted as the most significant recent domestic change. The heritage of centralised and bureaucratic administration, transferred by the military to civilian control, appeared inadequate as a response to new actors' demands and the pattern of modern efficiency which was founded mainly on the information revolution. The 1994 reform of the Argentine Constitution and the new Brazilian Constitution of 1988 – and its subsequent amendments – introduced modifications that seek to improve the conception of governance. In fact, this conception is based on the idea that, on the one hand, the state – at all levels – should limit its actions to the regulation of the economy, and play the role of a mere redistributive actor, while on the other hand, political decisions should be taken as near as possible to the citizens, in which case, the federal state should shift some of its power to lower levels of management. In essence, the liberal postulates and practices of regulatory subsidiarity.[12]

In Argentina, therefore, in spite of its traditional liberalism, the federal state has intensified its withdrawal from the productive sphere by privatising several enterprises and, in addition, the part played by *Provincias* and *Municipios* in the political process has been increasing. Articles 123 and 124 of the constitution, for instance, are a concrete demonstration of this phenomenon. The former asserts that every *Provincia* should be guaranteed municipal autonomy with regard to institutional, political, administrative, economic, and finan-

12 For an historical and EU contemporary view of the notion of subsidiarity, Jean Charpentier, 'Quelle Subsidiarité', *Pouvoirs*, No. 69, Paris: Avril 1994.

cial matters. The latter, that each *Provincia* can create regions of economic and social development and enter into international accords, so long as they are not incompatible with federal foreign policy and are communicated to congress. It also states that natural resources located within the territory of each *Provincia* belong to it.[13]

However, unquestionably more aware of developmental issues, Brazil included fewer liberal economic clauses in its 1988 Constitution, in which it pays attention, above all, to the affirmation of democratic beliefs. Nonetheless, stemming from those principles and in order to encourage the more effective participation of its citizens, the constitutional text moves in the direction of political and economic decentralisation. In addition, the new Magna Carta confers greater room for manoeuvre to the federated states and municipalities than they previously enjoyed. For instance, with the abrogation of the constitutional amendments No. 1/69/art.13 and No. 1/69/art.200 the federated states' power of self-organisation has been increased. The *Municípios* were first considered as federal entities by Art. 1, while Art. 30 assigned them particular political and economic competence.[14] Furthermore, articles 157, 158, 159, and 160 alter the former federal–provincial tax-raising powers, which largely favoured central power, granting the federated states and municipalities extensive economic autonomy.

Nevertheless, beyond the institutional aspects, often severely static, liberal and democratic precepts have taken a dynamic turn, permeating the social sphere. Both in the private and public realms, the actors concerned have sought to put organic regulation into practice in order to experience both the positive and negative consequences of economic liberalism and political pluralism. But, patently, the alteration of the principles of governance cannot be implemented by law alone, and the inertia of the oligarchy that still prevails throughout certain regions and in some social sectors in both Brazil

13 *Constitución de la Nación Argentina*, Buenos Aires: Depalma, 1995.
14 Neither the Brazilian nor the Argentinian constitutions were clear about the federal nature of the *Municípios*. This fact provoked a polemic doctrinal debate among politicians and legal experts (Manoel Goncalves Ferreira Filho, *Curso de Direito Constitucional*, São Paulo: Editora Saraiva, 1990; and Germán Bidart Campos, 'El federalismo argentino desde 1930 hasta la actualidad', in Marcelo Carmagnani (coordinador), op. cit.

and Argentina operates as a colossal obstacle for state transformation. Hence, time is necessary in order to permit the organising of new customs, and for actors to assume their new responsibilities, allowing for a smooth encounter between tradition and modernity, which constitutes a very substantial factor in the balance of governance.

International trends and integration in the Southern Cone

However, the Argentine and Brazilian domestic metamorphoses may be projected onto a broader world context. In fact, the international scenario has been characterised by the phenomenon of globalisation, which has been facilitated and encouraged by the development of informatics. Almost all areas of human life have been affected by this dynamic and, as a result, the horizon of comparison has been broadened. If, formerly, the parameters of effectiveness could be either local or sub-regional, nowadays they tend to be international.

Moreover, the world order has changed dramatically since the end of the Cold War. It basically has turned from a vertical, bipolar structure, based on nuclear deterrence and the predominance of political contingencies over economic ones, towards a horizontal[15] and multipolar structure, characterised by the hypertrophy of economic values and by the concept of 'world time' that praises 'market democracy'.[16] To offset this concept of 'world time' – an idea closely allied to developmentalist theory – Laïdi has proposed the idea of 'local time'. He points out the necessity of nationally internalising foreign

---

15 At the moment, we might say that relations are still 'diagonal', i.e. they are in an intermediate position between hierarchic (vertical), and non-hierarchic (horizontal) ones.

16 'The fall of the Berlin Wall showed us a marked international reality: that of "world time" – *temps mondial*. "Market democracy" – *démocratie de marché* – is from now on the matrix of the world, the legitimate concern of the international system' (Zaki Laidi (Dir.), *L'ordre mondial relâché – sens et puissance après la guerre froide*, Paris: Presses de la Fondation Nationale de Sciences Politiques, 2ème édition, 1993).

configurations, suggesting that the specificities of each society must be considered – an attitude closely related to cultural theory. The result is very likely to be that the choice is neither the passive acceptance of a given model nor its rejection, but the optimal combination between universal and particular values.[17]

In this context, one way in which the implementation of 'market democracy' has been taking place worldwide is in processes of regional integration. The European Union has attempted, in parallel to its economic development, to construct a 'political meaning' capable of responding both to democratic principles and world expectations. In fact, it has shown that this is a paradigm that could fit fairly well into the new international structure, composed essentially of three dynamics: of states, of economic and financial integration and of cultural interpenetration among societies.[18]

Argentina and Brazil's economic political reforms, aimed at the improvement of governance, have been influenced both by the notion of 'market democracy' and by the example of the European Union. Mercosur has demonstrated, on the one hand, the determination of its members to create a less traumatic way ahead for their international insertion and, on the other, their resolve to associate their democracies in order to forge an area in which sub-regional allegiances can allow for a more stable system of governance.

Nation states vs sub-federal units

In an atmosphere characterised by what Gilpin calls 'the rapprochement of liberal and nationalist theories', empirical relations between federal states and an overarching level of governance – Mercosur – are especially marked by two principal phenomena: firstly, even if liberalism has become almost commonplace, national intervention has progressively achieved great importance as a means of delineating

17 Ibid.
18 Zaki Laidi, 'Après les guerres, la mêlée généralisée', *Le Monde Diplomatique*, Janvier 1996.

multiple and various domestic actions, assigning to them the necessary coherence which is normally required for international transactions; secondly, the propensity of nation states to progress in the direction of regional integration has been compensated by the inclination of their sub-federal units to move towards a more direct participation in it.

These incongruities can be observed within the arena of Mercosur in the cases of Argentina and Brazil. In fact, ever since the inception of the Common Market of the South, both federal executive powers have acted as the most powerful actors. The political will of Raúl Alfonsín and José Sarney, and their respective successors, has been the cornerstone of Mercosur's achievement. However, as time goes on, the initial public and federal 'monopoly' of negotiation is starting to decline little by little, to the detriment of private and public sub-federal (*Provincias*, federated states and municipalities) actors.

On the one hand, businessmen, workers and consumers have progressively begun to consider their actions as impacting not only on their domestic national domain, but also on the substantially larger one, represented by Mercosur. Commercial statistics, the number of joint ventures, growth in the strength of dialogue with trade unions, and the increase of tourist and cultural exchange between Argentina and Brazil reveal a tangible participation of the private sector in the integration process.[19] Likewise, social manifestations are mutually felt by the populations of the two countries, and, gradually, these manifestations start to take on great importance in political discourse. An interactive mimetic process between Argentina and Brazil is beginning to emerge, accelerating the rapprochement between the two societies. Furthermore, from an institutional perspective, the constitution of the Economic and Social Consultative Forum by the 1994 Ouro

---

19 Currently, Argentine exports to Brazil represent about 30% of its total, whereas around 10% of Brazilian exports go to Argentina. With regard to the growth in trade union dialogue, one can point out the coordination task developed by the Coordenaçao de Centrais Sindicais do Cone Sul in recent years (Antonio Pecci, 'Priorizar novas açoes: trabalho deve ser uma preocupaçao dos governos', *Gazeta Mercantil Latino-Americana*, 6 January, 1997).

Preto Protocol confirms the trend of private actors to participate in the integration process in Mercosur.[20]

On the other hand, public sub-federal units (*Provincias*, federated states and municipalities) have also initiated attempts to participate more directly in the integration process. Since 1986, on the basis that the provincial area was not large enough to resolve certain economic problems, nine *Provincias* of the *Norte Grande Argentino* signed a declaration aiming at the closest integration between them. Their objective was to reinforce their position within the federal system, through both the creation of a stronger political and economic role for themselves and economic rapprochement with Brazil.[21]

On the Brazilian side, the South-eastern and the Southern regions, representing the most dynamic economic area, began to consider the River Plate border as a potential trading zone, and not as in bygone days, a region of military conflict.[22] In the wake of this tendency, some states in those regions created special secretariats of 'foreign affairs' demonstrating not only the economic importance of the new dynamic of integration, but its political significance; that is, the way in which it might be conducted within the federal system.[23] As Vicente Bogo, Vice-governor of Rio Grande do Sul stressed, there are several obstacles to Mercosur's integration process all firmly linked to the federal government making it 'necessary to shift the relations between states and Union' in order to facilitate certain proce-

---

20 The Forum is composed of trade unions, employers and consumer rights bodies. It forms part of Mercosur's institutional structure.

21 The nine Provincias are: Catamarca, Corrientes, Chaco, Formosa, Jujuy, Misiones, Salta, Santiago del Estero and Tucumán (Marie-France Prevot-Schapira, 'Argentine: fédéralismes et territoires', *Cahiers des Amériques Latines*, No. 14, 1992).

22 The South-eastern region is formed by: Espírito Santo, Minas Gerais, Rio de Janeiro and Sao Paulo. The Southern region is composed of: Paraná, Rio Grande do Sul and Santa Catarina.

23 The creation of the *Secretaria Extraordinária para Integraçao ao Mercosul* by the Santa Catarina state Governor Paulo Afonso Vieira is one example of this. It is true that sometimes the label varies from 'foreign affairs' to 'Mercosur integration', but the general idea is that these bodies seek to be more effective in Mercosur's negotiations (Andrea Leonora, 'Governo catarinense cria secretaria de integraçao', *Gazeta Mercantil / Por Conta Própria*, 21 June 1995.

dures. He suggests that 'it may be interesting, for instance, to transfer some frontier controls from the Union to the states'.[24]

The creation of the Crecenea-Codesul Governors summit[25] is the direct result, on the one hand, of the determination of the private sector and the Argentine *Provincias*, and of the Brazilian states, on the other, to enlarge their capacity for influence in Mercosur. Actually, this summit goes far beyond mere administrative speculation since it constitutes a political act in which Argentine *Provincias* and Brazilian federated states proclaim the importance of their role in the Mercosur integration process.

Whereas the federal authorities are likely to be particularly involved in the broad institutional lines of this process, the sub-national units are supposed to be concerned with its local implementation thus becoming significant actors in the integration dynamic. Closest to the citizen's everyday reality, the *Provincias* and federated states emerge as a more adequate level to respond to the economic and social demands of national actors with regard to Mercosur issues. As Angel Rozas, governor of the *Provincia* of El Chaco, asserts:

> Economic integration is important and it should be sustained, but it should also be expanded in the direction of the cultural, educational, environmental, transport and health spheres.

Fundamentally, those issues are addressed according to *Provincia* and state competencies.[26] On the other hand, for Antônio Britto, until recently Governor of the state of Rio Grande do Sul,

> there is the federal space and an enormous space for the Provincias and states. We must fit into it with solidarity and respecting the juridical and diplomatic [federal] legislation, but [...] recognising that the integration process takes place at the level of Provincias and states.[27]

---

24 Ubirajara Alves, 'Sul: autonomia na integraçao', *Gazeta Mercantil*, 23 October 1995.
25 Crecenea: Comissao Regional de Comércio Exterior do Nordeste Argentino; Codesul: Conselho de Desenvolvimento e Integraçao Sul. See fig. 1, p. 24.
26 Roberto Baraldi, 'Uma oportunidade histórica na fronteira', *Gazeta Mercantil Latino-Americana*, 24 June 1996.
27 Ibid.

In truth, *Provincias* and states have attempted to treat Mercosur as a means of aggrandizement, or at least of guaranteeing their own power of influence within the federation. Nevertheless, what they have postulated responds to both the necessity of economic efficiency and political democracy – which has characterised the present consensus in favour of 'market democracy' – conferring legitimacy on their demands. Thus, an added level of government above the nation state has worked as an actual factor for federal decentralisation, since it has induced parallel actions to central ones taking place in provinces and states. However, it seems that these actions are more compatible than antagonistic and the integration experience is likely to act as an external catalyst in the definition of the optimum domestic pattern of governance.

Along the lines of the rationale of decentralisation, one can also point out that the Mercosur integration process has provoked a deeper decentralisation movement that operates beyond the provincial and state level. As a matter of fact, in 1995, several mayors from Argentina, Brazil, Paraguay, and Uruguay founded a network of various Mercosur cities, aimed at the advancement of their cooperation. This 'league', known as *Mercocidades* (*Mercociudades* in Spanish), has established a set of nine specific commissions which have sought to develop projects of cooperation concerned with local issues. They have endeavoured to promote the insertion of the municipal level into the development of Mercosur trading strategies, favouring a micro-localisation of the industrial, commercial and service sectors. As Hermes Binner, mayor of Rosário, stressed:

> it is imperative in this context [Mercosur] to stimulate the functioning of the Mercocidades proposing that they discuss the trade accords signed between nation states.[28]

The cities are seen as the basic cells in globalisation, i.e. a locus through which economic and political strategies can be better implemented than at the provincial/state and federal levels. In contrast to the summit of Crecenea-Codesul Governors, the *Mercocidades*

---

28   Hermes Binner, 'A missao dos municípios', *Gazeta Mercantil Latino-Americana*, 2 September 1996.

have reached not only certain cities of the Southern and South-eastern regions, but also some cities of the other regions.[29]

Therefore, even though the *de jure* dialogue of the Mercosur integration process remains in federal hands, one can discern that a *de facto* procedure of consultation has been achieved between federal sub-units. It is yet to be ascertained whether this phenomenon has weakened the strength of central governments giving more leeway to those sub-units, or whether the federated units have only played the role that federal constitutions assigned to them.

However, it is hard to deny that Mercosur has incited Argentine and Brazilian élites to rethink the patterns of federalism and governance currently being debated. It has worked as a catalyst in awakening that familiar debate, introducing a new exogenous and significant component. Thus, an additional ambit of relationships characterised by a spider's web-like structure has been emerging; one in which nation states, *Provincias* and states, and municipalities, start to fix the limits of their political and economic competences.

Inasmuch as Mercosur has only been in existence a few years, these limits remain somewhat blurred. The static effects of institutional acts exert an influence of considerable inertia that frequently makes the entrance of these various levels of governance into bureaucratic administrations difficult, and it also obstructs their interaction with social actors. On the other hand, the dynamic effects, which are marked by the informal connections between actors, have operated as the concrete mainspring for the functioning of the Common Market of the South. As Rubens Antônio Barbosa, Brazilian Ambassador to the United Kingdom and former Sub-Secretary of State on Integration Affairs, has stressed, 'form must follow function and not the reverse.'[30] Accordingly, Mercosur's normative process has been limited to certain intergovernmental structures, which have operated in conformity with unanimity procedures. In this context, the 'official' place of social

---

29 Recife and Salvador, capitals of the north-eastern states of Pernambuco and Bahia are an example of this.
30 Rubens Antônio Barbosa, 'O Mercosul e suas instituiçoes', *Boletim de Integraçao Latino-Americana*, No. 14, Brasília: Brazilian Foreign Office, Julho–Setembro 1994.

Multi-Level Governance within Mercosur 91

actors is very modest, and the federal sub-units are not referred to. The Argentine and Brazilian federal governments keep the entire power of Mercosur's negotiating authority and maintain total control over their federal sub-units, even though they usually take local demands into consideration.[31]

Thus, before proceeding to draw some tentative conclusions concerning multilevel governance within Mercosur, a review of the Common Market of the South's institutional structure is essential to comprehend the relationships among all the actors involved in the integration process.

Mercosur's institutional structures

Following the signing of the Ouro Preto Protocol in December 1994, Mercosur's organs are:

- the Common Market Council (CMC)
- the Common Market Group (CMG)
- the Mercosur Trade Commission (MTC)
- the Joint Parliamentary Commission (JPC)
- the Economic-Social Consultative Forum (ESCF)
- the Mercosur Administrative Secretary (MAS)

---

31   In Brazil, the Foreign Affairs Minister, Luiz Felipe Lampréia, talked about 'federal diplomacy' in which his Ministry would seek to promote 'a permanent dialogue and information exchange between the federal Executive and the regions, states and municipalities.' Nevertheless, this does not mean that the federal sub-units can intervene directly in Mercosur institutional dynamics, but that they simply influence their federal states. It is true, for instance, that the north-east region has attempted to participate more actively in Mercosur, and that it has been the federal government that has encouraged and supported this local initiative. However, this region (as well as the others) has no official channel allowing it to affect Mercosur's decisions immediately (Luiz Felipe Lampreia, 'Speech given to the Commission of Foreign Relations of the Chamber of Deputies on 5 April 1995', *Diário da Manha*, 16 and 17 April, 1995).

The Common Market Council is the leading body of Mercosur, which is responsible for the political conduct of the integration process, and is formed by both the Economic and Foreign Ministers of the member states. It operates by unanimous decisions, which are binding on all member states, and its presidency rotates every six months in alphabetic order.

The Common Market Group is the executive body of Mercosur. It is responsible for proposing decision-making projects to the Common Market Council, and it also issues unanimous resolutions on subjects delegated to it by the CMC, which are binding on all member states. It is composed of four delegates representing the Foreign Ministry, the Ministry of the Economics and the Central Bank from each member state, and is made up of ten working groups.

The Mercosur Trade Commission is in charge of assisting the Common Market Group on questions related to trade policy. Its main task is to look after trade policy within Mercosur, and between it and third countries. The MTC also operates by unanimous directives, which are binding on all member-states, and considers any complaints arising out of trade conflicts in accordance with the Brasília Protocol.[32] It is composed of ten technical committees.

The Joint Parliamentary Commission is the representative body of member states' parliaments within Mercosur where national parliaments from each member state appoint the same number of deputies and senators. Its principal function is to accelerate national parliamentary procedures in order to adopt decisions, resolutions and directives at the domestic level. Its role is exclusively consultative, and it operates through recommendations to the Common Market Council.

The Economic Social Consultative Forum is, as its name suggests, the body representing economic and social sectors in Mercosur and it is formed by the same number of representatives from each member state as in the case of the JPC. The ESCF seeks to encourage

---

32   There is no Court of Justice within Mercosur. All disputes are resolved by *ad hoc* tribunals, formed especially for the occasion, which work in accordance with the Brasília Protocol ('Especial: Dois anos do Tratado de Assunçao', *Boletim de Integraçao Latino-Americana*, Brasília: Brazilian Foreign Office, March 1993.

more participation from ordinary people in Mercosur. Its function is purely consultative and it can formulate recommendations to the Common Market Group.

The Administrative Secretariat is an operational support body, whose main function is to publish Mercosur's *Official Journal*. It also organises the logistic aspects of all Mercosur's meetings and conferences and informs member states about the measures they need to adopt to incorporate norms issued by Mercosur bodies into their judicial systems.

Mercosur operates on two basic principles: intergovernmental procedures and unanimous decisions. It seeks to combine internal political democracy with external economic efficiency, and member states hesitate to disturb their principles of sovereignty. At present, Mercosur is subjected to both endogenous factors and exogenous forces and faces the challenge of finding its own way of overcoming this double constraint and avoiding 'Chamberlain's syndrome'.[33]

Tentative conclusions

It is probably too early to talk about an additional level of governance over and above that represented by federal states in Mercosur countries. As a matter of fact, the absence of any supranational procedures keeps nation states as the sole locus of sovereignty. Besides, there is no institutional body set up by the Treaty of Asunción that ensures the participation of *Provincias*, states and municipalities in Mercosur discussions. This situation is a far cry from, for instance, the operative participation of German Länder in

---

33 This expression was used by Jean-Louis Quermonne to describe the inertia which characterised the behaviour of the British Prime Minister, Neville Chamberlain, prior to the energising Winston Churchill instilled to British resistance to the threat from Nazi Germany (Jean-Louis Quermonne, 'La démocratisation du processus de décision communautaire depuis le Traité de Maastricht', paper presented at the *XVI World Congress of the International Political Science Association*, Berlin, 21–25 August, 1994. (Published in Portuguese in the journal *Política Hoje*, No. 3, Jan–June 1995.)

the European Union. Nonetheless, federal sub-unit officials, with the support of the private sector and social forces, have sought to develop their influence on Mercosur, through the creation of *de facto* sub-regional links among themselves. The summit of Crecenea-Codesul Governors and the Mercocidades are efforts in this direction.

The combination of these two trends, namely, formal negotiations based on federal principles and the fragility of Mercosur institutions on the one hand, and the informal constitution of sub-federal networks and the determination of federal sub-units to assert their own competencies on the other, has led to the emergence of a *Mercosurian* para-public space in which the three traditional levels of governance can meet. Therefore, this has given rise to new types of loyalties that will probably alter the prevailing system of governance. Beyond national allegiances, strongly sub-regional ones are emerging among certain actors that have attempted to take as much as they can from the integration process. Thus the economic and political stakes have become transnational and correspondingly far more complex. The interaction between Argentine and Brazilian national executives at all levels, as well as the rapprochement of their private and social actors, prefigures a new phase in the conception of their respective governances.

Indeed, these governances have historically evolved in different ways. In Argentina the process has been marked by an increase of central authority from Buenos Aires, founded on the quasi-perpetual coincidence of political and economic power. This phenomenon has generated a centrifugal dynamics among certain *Provincias*, which are aiming at setting up alternative economic and political ties. Actually, the roots of the Argentine federal process lie in sovereign states that gave birth to a confederation. Even though this ultimately matured into a federation, there has remained a residual sentiment of sovereignty among the *Provincias*.

In Brazil, the system of governance has been affected by the country's history of economic cycles – Brazilian wood, sugar, gold, coffee, etc. – but since the end of the 19th century the centre of political power no longer corresponds to the economic one (the São Paulo / Rio de Janeiro dichotomy). Since then, a sort of arrangement has emerged between these different centres of power with the most peripheral states enjoying more possibilities of establishing their own political and economic links. There is no monolithic *diktat* as the one operating from Buenos Aires. Furthermore, in contrast to Argentine federalism, the Brazilian model has its origins in the fragmentation of a unitary state. Consequently, Brazil's national sentiments are likely to be more tenacious than in Argentina making the issue of the sovereignty of the Brazilian federated states more abstract.

Following their pendulum-like movement, sometimes towards centralisation, sometimes in the direction of decentralisation, Argentine and Brazilian federalisms have been influenced by the development of Mercosur. If the future evolution of Mercosur depends on the minimum of coherence that each member state demands (which can be achieved easily by centralised governments), it is nonetheless true that Mercosur has been erected according to liberal economic postulates and principles of political pluralism, which, based on the logic of efficiency and subsidiarity, encourages decentralised systems of decision-making.

Therefore, the Common Market of the South has underscored some of the contradictions that have characterised the structure of the Argentine and Brazilian federal systems by entrenching these contradictions as well as expanding them to embrace a broad sub-regional level of interaction. These contradictions focus on three main pairs of confrontation:

- national state vs federal sub-units;
- state vs society;
- executive powers vs legislative powers.

In this web of mutual interaction the executive power of national states has operated as a spearhead for both the Mercosur integration process and the metamorphosis of national federal systems. Despite the active participation of social forces, federal sub-units and legislative powers in these developments – prompted by the return of the principles of economic liberalism and political pluralism – they have acted essentially as a stepping stone. Yet in contrast to previous integration processes in Latin America, Mercosur has displayed a greater capacity to promote their development. Nevertheless, there still remains an imbalance that operates to the detriment of social forces, federal sub-units, and legislative powers.

From an Argentine and Brazilian perspective, the problem of governance and balance within Mercosur is likely to be an issue on which specialists are faced with an array of new concepts, or rather, interpretations of old concepts, concerning issues such as federalism, sovereignty and democracy, among others. The understanding of the transformations undergone by these two federal systems has, at best, been contradictory. Thus for instance, French sociologist Alain Touraine considers that 'the federal state in Brazil is very weak',[34] North American economist Albert Fishlow asserts that 'what will support the [Brazilian reform] process will be the decentralisation of power, in opposition to what has happened for forty years.'[35]

Depending on the theoretical background, approaches can differ radically. Ultimately, however, only the evolution of the interaction of both domestic factors and international forces will settle the problem of the relationship between governance and the sub-regional integration process.

---

[34] Jorge Luiz de Souza, 'Amigos do presidente discutem neoliberalismo', *Gazeta Mercantil*, 12 November 1996.

[35] Maria Helena Tachinardi, 'Para Fishlow "Brasil está no caminho certo"', *Gazeta Mercantil*, 13 November 1996.

Tullo Vigevani
Karina Pasquariello Mariano
Marcelo Fernandes de Oliveira

Mercosur: Democracy and Political Actors

According to several authors there are a variety of motives for international cooperation as well as for regional integration. In a classic study, Aron[1] suggests that states build up relationships in different forms and level and among which, often determined by geographical location, there are temporary alliances and permanent coalitions.

From the late decades of the 19th century to the early years of the 20th, relationships between states often took the form of bilateral alliances. Until the end of the Cold War, roughly by 1990, the prevailing issues were those of power distribution and global or regional equilibrium. In South America, such issues have also been at stake, mainly concentrated around the La Plata Basin and, particularly, in the relations between Brazil and Argentina.

Aron also points out that

> states' behaviour towards others is not driven uniquely by power relations; but that decisions made by international actors are rather influenced by ideas and feelings,[2]

an issue intensely debated by contemporary constructivists.[3] Clearly then, the issue of the nature of political regimes and institutions, much dealt with at the end of the 20th century, was relevant to international relations in previous decades, particularly with regards to the various

---

1　Raymond Aron, *Paix et Guerre Entre les Nations*, Paris: Calmann-Lévy, 1962.
2　Ibid: 125.
3　Alexander Wendt, 'Collective identity, formation and the international state', *American Political Science Review*, 88(22), June, 1994; Emmanuel Adler, 'Seizing the middle ground: constructivism in world politics', *European Journal of International Relations*, 1997; Jeffrey T. Checkel, 'The constructivist turn in international relations theory', *World Politics*, No. 50, January, 1998.

forms of cooperation among states. The distinction made by Aron in 1962 between homogeneous and heterogeneous systems may enlighten us on this. According to him, a system is heterogeneous when the states involved are organised under different principles, whereas a homogeneous system assembles similarly organised states.

In the case of Mercosur, it may be said that one of the important factors that drove the integration process in the eighties, particularly between Argentina and Brazil, but also between Paraguay and Uruguay, as well as the free-trading associates Bolivia and Chile, was the perception of common values shared by their respective societies, especially the issue of democracy. Thus a starting point for the discussion on democracy and the involvement of political actors in Mercosur may be the recognition that for a successful integration process to occur some of the necessary conditions are present, though in themselves they are not sufficient.

From its inception the issue of democracy in Mercosur has been deemed vital for regional integration. Governments have always been concerned with ensuring the legitimacy of negotiations seeking to incorporate representatives of society in the process. In fact, concern with the democratic character of the countries taking part in Mercosur is becoming increasingly important in the process of regional integration itself. This is so, basically because the extent to which the effects of the integration process on society become tangible also brings about the mobilisation of the sectorial interests present therein. Thus, provided that the integration process does not suffer serious interruptions, and if, on the contrary, it intensifies – it is likely to generate new demands and the need for improving society's lobbying channels, including the creation of new mechanisms for influence, or intervention.

Ever since Mercosur's inception in 1991, there has been room for legislative participation by means of the Joint Parliamentary Commission. However, in the Brazilian case participating in this institutional forum has brought little influence to bear on the integration process itself and scant representation of political and social interests. This is also the case with the other member states. In the medium and long term, it is likely that such pressures and interests will be sufficiently organised so as to become determinant factors in shaping Mercosur. For the time being, and after almost ten years of its existence, the evolution of this regional bloc is still basically defined and controlled by government agencies in charge of its operation and, in the Brazilian case, the ministers of foreign affairs, economics, and planning.

The starting point of our analysis[4] is the belief that the integration process will be likely to give rise to issues beyond current trade matters, requiring the increased participation of political actors. Furthermore, results obtained so far tend to increasingly affect the everyday life of the populations involved, thus creating more propitious conditions for greater interest and mobilisation around the issue of regional integration. Such interest, in turn, may also lead to the incorporation of this issue on the negotiation agenda of political parties, even becoming both an issue of importance among voters and a vote winner to the point of polarising both politicians and voters as either pro or anti integration. Nevertheless, as will be seen later, the future direction, deepening, stagnation, or crisis of such a process cannot be determined in advance.

Within this framework, we aim to analyse the intersection between Mercosur's integration process and existing political interests, assessing the extent to which this very process is being incorporated into the interests of existing political parties. The issues of democracy and political actors are dealt with in their interrelations by examining four aspects: (a) the formal evolution of the issue of democracy in the constitution and development of Mercosur; (b) the structural reasons for the bloc of four countries to adhere to democracy; (c) the participation of Brazilian political parties and other agencies of representative democracy in the regional bloc, particularly in the Joint Parliamentary Commission, and examining its role and activity; and (d) a case study of the sugar industry, which exemplifies concrete forms of the mobilisation of political actors in their relations with society at large.

---

4   This text discusses some of the issues currently under analysis by CEDEC (Centro de Estudos de Cultura Contemporânea) in the scope of the project titled 'Mercosur: the emergency of a new society'.

Democracy in regional treaties

The understanding of many of Mercosur's recent problems is linked to an appraisal of how democracy is understood, and how so-called 'universal values' are shared among its various members. At the outset of the integration process between Brazil and Argentina in the mid eighties, during the administrations of Alfonsín and Sarney, policy-makers believed that the redemocratisation process taking place in both countries would be a lever that would make possible the necessary social consensus to strengthen their respective countries' capacity for international negotiations. Furthermore, the very alliance between them would be an important factor pointing towards the same aim. In other words, democracy and the rise of important forms of cooperation between the two countries concerned – for the first time in the region – would strengthen their protection in the face of the risks involved, and in the new phase the world economy was entering into at that time. This new phase was characterised by the United States' Trade Acts of 1984 and 1988, the GATT Uruguay Round since 1986, and the globalisation of production systems.

This was the time to seek to understand the changes operating at international level, to recognize the fall of ECLA's developmentalism that had prevailed through the fifties and sixties, and to accept that relatively protectionist economies would no longer be tolerated. On the other hand, the broadening of the economic space from national to regional might induce economic growth thus requiring increasing competitiveness in order to adapt to the new environment.

Democracy was an important theme for the integration process, even though it was not made explicit in the Treaty of Asunción. In fact, in the founding document of Mercosur, signed on 26 March 1991, by presidents Menem of Argentina, Collor de Mello of Brazil, Rodríguez of Paraguay, and Lacalle of Uruguay, the issues addressed were mostly economic. They are essentially related to the constitution of a common market – commodities, services, production factors, and common tariffs toward third countries – and the laying down of the grounds for the articulation of sectorial and macroeconomic policies. Though implicit, democracy was no doubt underlying the regional agreement and a clear indication of this being that Paraguay was only accepted into the negotiations after the end of the Stroessner era.

The historical reasons for such integration predate the 1991 treaty. A clear starting point was the agreement signed by the military regimes of Videla (Argentina) and Figueiredo (Brazil) in October 1979 as a result of tripartite negotiations regarding the waterpower potential of the Parana river, which led to the construction of the hydroelectric plants of Corpus (between Argentina and Paraguay) and Itaipu (between Brazil and Paraguay). Subsequent negotiations, since 1985 between Alfonsín and Sarney were aimed at strengthening their respective national economies. Achieving technical and economic progress within a context of democratic consolidation, alongside improving their competing capabilities in the world market, became the aim of these governments.[5]

Given this new disposition for cooperation in the Southern Cone, it is worth underlining the shift from a situation of non-cooperative competition, originating in the 19th century and prevailing throughout most of the 20th, to a situation where part of the national élites in both countries start to recognize the advantages deriving from regional integration policies. Within this perspective, the Iguazu Declaration was signed on 30 November 1985, emphasizing the consolidation of the democratic process, the combined efforts for the joint defence of both countries' interests in international fora, and the shared use of common resources. A full economic dimension of this new political relationship was reached on 29 July 1986, when the Argentine–Brazilian Integration Act created the Programme for Integration and Economic Cooperation (PICE), which led to the signing of 24 protocols.

Central to the understanding of the present difficulties involving Mercosur is the assessment of the two countries' basic motivations for the integration process: Brazilian policymakers, mostly at the Ministry for Foreign Affairs, were concerned with Brazil's international economic insertion, whereas their Argentine counterparts concentrated on modern-

5 Félix Peña, 'Pré-requisitos políticos e econômicos da integração', São Paulo [Paz e Terra; Programa de Política Internacional e Comparada/USP], *Política Externa*, 1(2), 1992.

ization and the possibility of reaching a market almost three times the size of their own.[6]

With such motivation, both countries signed the Treaty for Integration, Cooperation and Development (TICD), on 29 November 1988, establishing a ten-year period for setting up a common economic area with no tariffs or other barriers on commodities and services, as well as seeking the convergence of their macroeconomic policies. With the exception of the latter, these goals were reached within a much shorter time-span. The coordination of macroeconomic policies had certainly not been achieved by the end of the nineties, just one among the other factors contributing to the 1999–2000 crisis between them. Following the 1989 elections, the new presidents (Menem in Argentina and Collor de Mello in Brazil) openly supported free trade and economic liberalization and regional integration was seen as a means of implementing them. The two presidents signed the Buenos Aires Act in July 1990, setting 31 December 1994 as the deadline for establishing a common market between both countries, thus bringing forward by five years the constitution of the Custom Unions envisaged by the TICD for 1998.[7]

Uruguay, already linked to Argentina and Brazil by means of the Agreements for Economic Reciprocity within the Latin America Association for Integration, confirmed its adherence to a perspective of regional integration during this period. In August 1990 Paraguay was also invited to take part in the negotiations that would lead to the formalization of the regional bloc the following year.

Mercosur documents from the Treaty of Asunción onwards clearly show that economic themes prevail. The Treaty's 24 articles and 6 chapters deal only with economic, trade or administrative matters (likewise its 5 appendices). The Treaty's foreword deals with democracy only in its last paragraph, where it mentions the 'political will to lay the bases for ever closer links among their nations.' Besides, another

---

6   Dante Caputo and Jorge Sabato, *La integración de las democracias pobres: oportunidades y peligros*, Buenos Aires: mimeo, 1991.

7   Rubens Barbosa, *América Latina em Perspectiva: A Integração Regional da Retórica a Realidade*, São Paulo: Aduaneiras, 1991; Paulo Roberto Almeida, *O Mercosur: Fundamentos e Perspectivas*, São Paulo: LTr, 1998.

of the Treaty's considerations, namely, the 'evolution of world affairs, specially the consolidation of huge economic blocs and the importance of member countries' achieving an adequate insertion in the world economy' acquired political sense.[8] This was to become a matter of controversy between Argentina and Brazil at the end of the nineties.

Similarly, in all 12 chapters and 53 articles of the Ouro Preto Protocol, signed on 17 December 1994, – that formally instituted the incomplete 'Customs Union' thus bringing an end to the transition period for the establishment of the common market – also concentrate solely on organizational and economic matters.

This document established that the Common Market Council would be responsible for the political conduct of the integration process. However, the Council's responsibilities do not include those related to maintaining democracy or upholding democratic principles.

The Joint Parliamentary Commission, in operation since 1991 following the Treaty of Asunción, became a full part of Mercosur's institutional structure in 1995, after being assigned some new functions. Its role has not been broadened though: according to article 26 of the Ouro Preto Protocol, all it can do is refer recommendations to the Council through the Common Market Group. Nevertheless, as we shall see below, it is worth noting that the Commission has discussed its own possibilities of contributing to the integration process by, for example, accelerating internal processes, acting as a consultative agency for the Council, or cooperating in seeking legislation compatibility. At the formal level, however, it has not had any role in fostering democratic debate concerning the integration process nor has it had any supervisory control regarding the adherence to democratic principles by the four member countries.

The other agency created by the Ouro Preto Protocol was the Economic and Social Consultative Forum, which might have played a role in condensing social and democratic interests, and whose function is to give voice to representatives of economic and social interests. Besides its merely consultative character, restricted to making recommendations to the Council, its functions have not been defined with precision, which is compounded by operational difficulties.

8 Ibid.: 95.

In spite of the problems and controversies concerning defining the relationship between democracy and the integration process in Mercosur, there is no doubt that the regional bloc was useful in strengthening democratic principles by promoting and consolidating them. In order to examine this viewpoint it will be necessary to make reference to the universal debate on democracy and its meaning, so as to see how these principles may concretely influence the debates within Mercosur and its political evolution.

The motivations of democracy in the integration process

In order to examine the issue of democracy, or more precisely, the effectiveness of the informal democratic clause in Mercosur, doubts as to whether this regional bloc should be considered an integration process based on shared goals or solely on practical objectives should be clarified. This question will probably become increasingly relevant in the coming years. Will Mercosur, though surviving deep conjunctural crises, manage to consolidate itself on the basis of common interests within the societies that constitute it, or will it fall apart as a regionally integrated bloc, even though continuing as a mere free trade agreement?

So far, judging by the sovereign manifestations of the governments of its member states (on matters such as the United Nations Security Council, the proposal to integrate NATO, the FTAA negotiations, and currency devaluation), Mercosur cannot be considered a shared-goals association. This kind of integration process implies – employing an extreme metaphor – a common, though partial, *weltanschauung*. Conversely, a practical-objectives type of integration necessitates values indispensable for the relationships between member states, but which do not develop into a common aim. This indicates a situation in which member states are forced to join together, probably spurred on by concrete needs, but sharing no strong common perspective.[9]

9   Terry Nardin, *Lei, Moralidade e as Relações Entre os Estados*, Rio de Janeiro: Forense-Universitaria, 1987.

The post-Cold War era gives rise to a debate over whether existing integration processes are objective-led. This debate places issues such as democracy at the centre of international relations. According to Nardin, 'it is common practices, rather than shared goals, that offer conditions for international association'.[10] Thus the adhesion to democratic values would be one of the elements measured to assess the success or failure of regional integration. That is to say, the verification of the success or otherwise of the regional integration process, means corroborating that its establishment leads to the consolidation of common values. Alternatively, the process may barely constitute a practical association of convenience, however solid the association might be. In the latter case, there would be shared objectives, but not a strong common perspective.

Ever since Westphalia 1648, the international system has not shown common norms at the core of its basic conceptual structure – not, at least, until the end of the 20th century. Among others, one of the regional bloc's roles is to introduce mutually accepted common rules. These rules, even through the use of coercion, might be politically and legally accepted. In the analysis of the democracy issue within Mercosur, what matters is to understand the meaning of norms and the fact that, even if in most cases the rules are put forward by the strongest, they do not exclude the possibility of serving the weakest. Recent institutional crises in Paraguay in early 1996 and 1999, both linked to the role of the armed forces, particularly to General Oviedo, and Mercosur's reactions to them, seem to confirm the correctness of this assertion.

As is well known, Mercosur as a process of regional integration relies on the principle of intergovernability, the idea of supranationality having been rejected mainly by Argentina and Brazil. Bull supports the idea that through history the interstate system has permitted the harmonisation of norms, albeit haphazardly, leading *de facto* to the prevalence of common norms.[11] That is to say, despite intergovernability, democratic principles have in fact been reaffirmed within the

10 Ibid: 27.
11 Hedley Bull, *The Anarchical Society: A Study of Order in World Politics*, London: Macmillan, 1995.

regional bloc. This does not emerge spontaneously, but is directly linked to ongoing changes in the international system.

In April 1996, when General Oviedo threatened Paraguay's constitutional president, Wasmosy, coordination between the ambassadors from the US (Service), Brazil (Oliveira Dias), and Argentina (Auad), led rapidly to the failure of this attempt to break the country's constitutional rule. Threats to isolate Paraguay politically and economically, including the freezing of Paraguay's membership of Mercosur, brought about an agreement that basically secured the continuation of constitutional rule in that country.[12]

The trend towards the universal consolidation of democracy as a value is dependent on various factors. The matrix of this phenomenon is closely linked to the liberal-democratic values that have become hegemonic during the past fifty years. Side by side with, and complementing power relations, softpower has been gaining relevance with the double advantage of absorbing the idea of hegemony and of effectively serving peoples' interests.[13] Forces other than the state strengthen trends especially those linked to universal values. More actors play international roles and bring new interests onto the international scene. According to Bonanate,[14] if such interests resulted in international regimes they would thus be in a position to dictate the rules of the game. A radical interpretation of this would be that the behaviour of each individual nation state and each individual society would be ruled less by national developments and increasingly by universal values, whereby those values would be transferred to the spheres of both regional blocs and national states.

For influential sections of the Brazilian state the capacity of international regimes to impose their norms on individual states and societies is determined by the existence of a previous accord. Thus the

---

12   Karina L. P. Mariano and Marcelo F. Oliveira, *Mercosur: a emergencia de uma nova sociedade*, São Paulo: CEDEC, 1999 [Relatório final de pesquisa para o CNPq – 1ª Fase].

13   Joseph Nye Jr., *Bound to Lead: The Changing Nature of American Power*, New York: Basic Books, 1992.

14   Luigi Bonanate, 'Osservazioni sulla teoria dei regimi internazionali', in Luigi Bonanate, Anna Caffarena and Roberto Vellano, *Dopo l'Anarchia*, Milano: Franco Angeli, 1989.

acceptance of the infusion of democratic values into Mercosur by them stem from the fact that it results from the existence of a formal treaty. The same applies to national élites in Argentina, Paraguay, and Uruguay, and to a lesser degree, in Chile and Bolivia. These values might be in accordance with those prevailing in each of these countries, which might involve concrete action to support democratic regimes, even though they are backed by an international consensus with the explicit support of powerful countries.[15] Thus the sharing of some of these values by countries like Brazil indicates the positive potential for the establishment of increasingly stable rules, including regional policies, especially within Mercosur. The adherence to democratic values seems to be among the issues where there is agreement, thus favouring the stability of the integration process.

Inquiring into the reasons for Brazil's low profile and weak political prominence in matters related to softpower, Hurrel suggests that it could result in weakening the country's position in the international system, but it might also cause difficulties in the very process of regional integration itself, to the extent that other Mercosur member states seem to adhere more easily to the logic of the accord, thus weakening regional cohesion.[16] The fact is that for the Brazilian élites themselves – or for the majority of them – some hegemonic values (although not all) coincide with the interests of the country.

Within Mercosur, the issue of adherence to democracy apparently became a homogeneous question, given the existence in this regard of a high degree of understanding between governments and the most decisive sections of society. But the same cannot be said regarding other issues, because the views of the core countries are interpreted differently by each of the individual governments of the member states of Mercosur. This can be empirically verified. The relative homogeneity of the member states regarding the trial of Pinochet in Spain and his

15 Gélson Fonseca Jr., 'Anotações sobre as condições do sistme internacional no limiar do século XXI: a distribução dos polos de poder e a inserção internacional do Brasil', in Dupas and Vigevani (eds), *O Brasil e as Novas Dimensões da Segurança Internacional*, São Paulo: Alfa-Omega, FASESP, 1999.
16 Andrew Hurrell, 'Questions on Brazilian foreign policy', *Seminario no Centro de Estudos de Cultura Contemporânea*, São Paulo, 10 September 1999.

extradition by the United Kingdom may also be interpreted as concern for the democratic stability of Chile. There are also other interpretations, particularly those related to the value attached to national sovereignty.

In the current phase, another factor that must be taken into account when examining the issue of democracy in Mercosur is that besides states, non-state actors now enjoy growing importance. There is certainly an increasing amount of interest in Mercosur both from public opinion and from non-governmental organizations. Public opinion, organised movements and the media, all express powerful forces favouring not only democracy but also human rights, national rights, social rights and minority rights. The direction of such pressure is not fully disconnected from hegemonic interests. But, in most cases, these same pressures coincide with the objectives of important social groupings and classes.

Furthermore, at the regional level an apparently universal trend is also taking place excluding themes that had historically been functional to the logic of difference and competition – traditional in Argentina Brazil relations – making room for others that require cooperative forms. For instance, the very fact that Task Force 10 of the Common Market Group, devoted to labour and social issues, discusses legislation compatibility – so far with little result – strengthens the social actors involved, who, in turn, see in Mercosur a useful instrument for strengthening their bargaining position at a national level.[17] Such a perception is certainly not new: intergovernmental liberals had already analysed this in the early eighties showing that social actors in the European Economic Community saw in regional cooperation an advantageous tool to further their own interests.

Another issue to take into consideration when examining the basis for democratic motivations within Mercosur is linked to the debate on the so-called crisis of the state which, in addition to the effects of globalisation, fosters the role of non-governmental actors who, in turn, influence national, regional, and international agendas.

All processes of regional integration have had to deal with, and welcome, democratic aspirations of participation. Even though the

17 Tullo Vigevani, *Mercosur: Impactos para Trabalhadores e Sindicatos*, São Paulo: LTR, FAPESP, CEDEC, 1998.

European Union is the most developed model, democratic and participatory pressures have also been exerted within Mercosur and NAFTA, and are already visible in the negotiation processes of the FTAA and the proposed free-trade area between the European Union and Mercosur. In this connection, we understand democracy not as liberal political representation, but as participation. In the last ten years, civil society, pressure groups, public opinion – even though often intertwined with state interests – have become capable of influencing powerful states. In the case of Mercosur, a relatively new and less systematically studied economic bloc, it may be said that democracy encourages the integration process – a fact which is not obvious. Some studies show that, in general, the capacity of mobilisation of groups negatively affected by the integration process is greater than that of those who benefit from it. During crises, the fairly intensive mobilisation of social sectors in favour of deepening the integration process would be a manifestation of the fact that democracy weighs positively on the consolidation of the regional bloc.

The crisis experienced in 1999 showed that there is a broad social base for which Mercosur is a tangible reality and in whose view a setback to the integration process would be negative partly for the nation and their specific group interests. An example of this is that, during the 1999 presidential election campaign in Argentina, both candidates – Duhalde, *justicialista*, and De la Rúa, Radical-FREPASO – were led, probably by vote-winning motives, to declare themselves in favour of deepening Mercosur. To a certain degree this is the same position taken by the Brazilian government. In other words – and this seems an optimistic conclusion – a virtuous circle between the integration process and the consolidation of a democratic perspective would appear to be emerging, both in the Schumpeterian sense of respecting the rules of the game[18] as well as concerning the rise of democratic expectations, reminiscent of Dahl's analysis regarding the forms of integration of the broad mass of the people into democracy.[19]

18 Joseph Schumpeter, *Capitalism, Socialism and Democracy*, London: George Allen & Unwin, 1979.
19 Robert Dahl, *A Preface to Economic Democracy*, Berkeley: University of California Press, 1985.

Based on a certain notion of globalisation, the debate that is taking place would indicate that the concept of a cosmopolitan public sphere would partially apply to Mercosur.[20] This is so because the integration process stimulates the debate over what is known as 'an association of objectives' as against a practical-objectives association. The concept of a cosmopolitan public sphere, even if applied only at regional level, implies growing forms of homogeneity with regards to normative issues that would make up the collective will of the states in the regional bloc. The weakening or failure of democracy in one of the states of the bloc, for instance, would stimulate the debate about the formalisation of the democratic clause discussed by heads of state at their biannual meeting in December 1998, in Rio de Janeiro. Thus it follows that if one of the member states were to break democracy's rules of the game it would, in fact, be excluding itself form Mercosur.

Although nothing has been formally agreed in writing the issue surfaces in between the lines of presidential statements and is reaffirmed by them every six months. Within the framework of the cosmopolitan public sphere it must be highlighted that, as far as influential political and social actors, there is, at present, the impression that the democratic character of member states is determined by three convergent parameters: international hegemonic regimes, the four countries' recent democratic evolution, and the rise of a regional public sphere, which would lead to the exclusion of any undemocratic state. This perception favours the defence of democracy in the member states.

Once again, the 1996 and 1999 Paraguay experiences may be taken as examples. The three parameters showed to be effective during the unfolding of those crises. In terms of international relations, the relevant actors were the North American, Argentine, and Brazilian embassies, as well as European Union governments. In June 1996, Brazilian President Cardoso travelled to Asunción with the explicit intention of 'reaffirming both Brazil and Mercosur's interests in preserving democratic rule in Paraguay'.[21] In 1998, in the midst of the electoral campaign in Paraguay, on the occasion of the meeting of the World Economic Forum in Davos,

---

20 Daniele Archubugi, David Held and Martin Kohler (eds), *Re-imagining Political Community*, Cambridge: Polity Press, 1998.
21 Mariano and Oliveira, op. cit.: 267.

Presidents Menem and Cardoso issued a statement which made it clear that an interruption in Paraguay's democratic process would lead to the cessation of the country's benefits from Mercosur. In the crisis at the beginning of 1999, the intervention by the Mercosur countries, as well as the United States and the European Union, was again crucial in preventing a break in Paraguay's democracy.

In the search to understand the relevance of democracy in the integration process one final factor must be underlined: among the reasons for regional cooperation. There is the need, felt by each member state, to reduce the degree of uncertainty over each other's behaviour; thus leading over time to the creation of multiple structures within which mutually advantageous agreements may be negotiated. These structures, in turn, influence states' behaviour, which leads to expect other actors' actions to follow the rules, norms, and conventions previously established by all. Therefore, these structures represent an acknowledgment and acceptance of a given institutional framewrok, even in cases which stress intergovernability, exactly as in Mercosur. It is clear that the existence of a democratic regime in and of itself guarantees nothing with regards to the maintenance of the rules of the game. However, by complying with the constitution, laws and institutions, a more stable framework emerges.

In Mercosur, during moments of crisis (like the one in 1999–2000), some leading actors have pleaded for more developed institutional structures, such as a Permanent Arbitration Court,[22] revealing a trend for greater cohesion and the broadening of common structures. In fact, crises have been generated precisely by those unforeseen, or disagreed upon, actions, such as the Brazilian currency devaluation in January 1999, or the Argentine imposition of quotas on Brazilian imports such as shoes, textiles, and steel in June 1999. Such crises could be prevented by the creation of structures that might help avert, or at least manage the crises. Although these are measures of an administrative nature, the view underlying such proposals is that integration is of common interest. It must be stressed that transparency in the relations between states also strengthens integration.

22 Felipe Lampreia, 'A política exterior do Brasil', *Seminario no IEA/USP*, São Paulo: 4 October 1999.

According to Lafer,

> from the moment Argentine and Brazilian policy makers became aware that ambiguities of any nature did not serve their real interests, a change took place in the nature of their relations, so that all that previously appeared as a zero-sum game could now be seen as convergence and joint effort.[23]

Still, according to this author, Mercosur would be a means for the four countries to show the world that

> they have common interests and that to promote themselves as centres of a stable and peaceful sub-region does not threaten international peace and security; and as poles of a dynamic and open integration process, and as partners with regards to values [contribute] to build an international order based on democracy and human rights.[24]

From this perspective, democracy is not only intrinsic to the possibility of anticipating each other's next move, but also to the integration process itself and its unfolding, concerning both institutions and the compatibility of political and moral values.

Political participation in Mercosur

We have so far discussed the ways in which the idea of democracy has been incorporated into the process of establishing Mercosur, by trying to understand how this principle is viewed by the member states and how it is integrated into state relations within the bloc. In this section, we will examine the bloc's internal mechanisms of democratic control, seeking to understand the instruments used in the building of Mercosur and how the various actors pursue their own interests. For this purpose we have chosen to examine the position of Brazilian political parties and the role of the Joint Parliamentary Commission, since legislative processes are the basis of the democratic system.

23 Celso Lafer, 'Relações Brasil-Argentina: alcance e significado de uma parceria estratégica', *Contexto Internacional*, 19(2), 1997: 253.
24 Ibid: 260.

Building a legislative body is almost inevitable and has taken place in all known integration processes that aim to go beyond a mere free trade area. This is the case with the European Union, the Andean Pact, and so it is with Mercosur. There are two possible reasons for this: the need to create channels for the expression of society's demands, and the advocacy of democracy as a fundamental principle of the integration process itself. In the case of Mercosur, it may be argued that since the Iguazu Declaration (1985) through to the Treaty of Asunción (1991) and the Ouro Preto Protocol (1994), integration has been basically economic since the main actors have been top ranking government officials and business entrepreneurs – the latter deemed society's most dynamic agents. Simultaneously, given that a representative body expressing the views of the national legislatures, or even an elected body representing the whole of Mercosur's electorate – as with the European Parliament for the EU – would not be able to represent all interests, the Economic-Social Consulting Forum was set up.

From the outset parlamentarians in the four member countries have not mobilised to take part in the integration movement. This is possible because at the beginning it was unclear how cooperation would be carried out and, also because the domestic processes of redemocratisation in Brazil and Argentina gave rise to demands leading to the broad mobilisation of parties, parliamentarians and politicians at the purely national level. The intense concentration on domestic issues meant scant concern from society and its representatives on the institutional arrangements of the integration process. This gave Brazilian and Argentine negotiators relative autonomy to conduct the process of agreement according to their viewpoints. However, this type of development is not peculiar to Mercosur. According to Schmitter[25] and to functionalist theory in general, the adherence of parties and politicians to integration processes is linked to the degree to which the debate on integration yields benefits in terms of prestige and votes. Thus the actions of social and economic actors in general and politicians in particular, are conditioned by the impact of the

---

25 Philippe Schmitter, *How to Democratise the European Union: Citizenship, Representation, Decision-making in the Emerging Euro-polity*, Florença: Instituto Universitario Europeo, 1998, mimeo.

integration process. The present analysis rests on the idea that the higher the actors' sensitivity to Mercosur's decisions and its effects, the greater their mobilisation and desire to influence the process. Therefore, the extent to which Mercosur is incorporated into societies of the member states' everyday life, determines the importance it has on political parties' domestic agendas.

Brazilian political parties and regional integration

Brazilian political parties seem to follow what may be called a reactive logic that is, waiting for a policy impact to be felt and by treating regional integration as a matter of foreign policy, to be dealt with by the federal government and diplomats. So far, Mercosur has not been incorporated as a relevant issue into their political agendas and is only dealt with when congress discusses the approval of international agreements signed by the federal government. The lack of concern for the issue of integration is thus linked both to the broadness of the domestic agenda, and to the idea that foreign policy is not a matter for congress, except when it comes to ratification of treaties and such like.

Traditionally, Brazilian political parties assign priority to what is usually termed 'great national issues', namely, stabilisation, growth, the reduction of unemployment in the economic sphere, the reform of political and party systems, and the 'federal pact' in the political sphere and, education, health, and violence in the social sphere. Democracy and its consolidation underlie these debates. With such an approach, foreign policy is understandably neglected by congress, all the more so given that there is a federal body exclusively devoted to it, the Ministry of Foreign Affairs. This ministry, relying on its long tradition and experience in foreign policy, is more a think tank that designs strategies for the country's international rleations.

Though there is some logic in the parties' neglect of foreign affairs, in many cases foreign and home policies interact. According to Soares de Lima, in spite of a generalized belief in continuity and consensus, there have been significant changes in Brazil's international position brought about by alterations in the domestic political sphere.[26] Besides, Mercosur does not fit a clear demarcation between national and international responsibilities. On the one hand, it is a subject duly dealt with and coordinated by the Ministry of Foreign Affairs, on the other, its effects are closely linked to national issues. As integration deepens, Mercosur increasingly influences societies' everyday life, thus compelling social actor and their representatives to take clear stances. Brazil, being the largest country in the region, does feel the effects of Mercosur's decisions, although admittedly in a lesser fashion than the smaller member states.

In such a context, Brazil's political parties in general, having no established position as to the various aspects of the process of regional integration, are hardly prepared to face the novel challenges that it raises. Brazil's delegation to Mercosur's Joint Parliamentary Commission for the 50th national parliamentary term (1994–98) was made up of representatives from the biggest national parties (Table 1).

Party	Representative	Position	State of the federation, region
PMDB	José Fogaça	Senator	Rio Grande do Sul, South
PMDB	Casildo Maldaner	Senator	Paraná, South
PMDB	Paulo Ritzel	Deputy	Rio Grande do Sul, South
PMDB	Valdir Colatto	Deputy	Santa Catarina, South
PFL	Wilson Kleinubing	Senator	Santa Catarina, South
PFL	Romero Jucá	Senator	Roraima, North
PFL	Paulo Bornhausen	Deputy	Santa Catarina, South
PFL	Luciano Pizzato	Deputy	Paraná, South
PPB	Osmar Dias	Senator	Paraná, South
PPB	Espiridião Amin	Senator	Santa Catarina, South
PPB	Júlio Redecker	Deputy	Rio Grande do Sul, South
PPB	Dilceu Sperafico	Deputy	Paraná, South
PSDB	Lúdio Coelho	Senator	Mato Grosso do Sul, Center-West
PSDB	Franco Montoro	Deputy	São Paulo, South-East
PTB	Emília Fernandes	Senator	Rio Grande do Sul, South
PT	Miguel Rosseto	Deputy	Rio Grande do Sul, South

Source: Comissão Parlamentar Conjunta 1996, Encarte: 3.

Table 1. Brazilian representatives and their parties at the Mercosur Joint Parliamentary Commission, 1994–1998.

26 Maria Regina Soares de Lima, 'Ejes analíticos y conflictos de paradigmas en la política exterior brasileña', *Revista América Latina / Internacionales*, FLACSO, 1(2), 1994.

We have examined the programmes of all the parties with representatives in the Joint Parliamentary Commission, since they have the strongest say on the issue of integration. By reading through these parties' programmes, though, it may be claimed that none has incorporated the issue of Mercosur, except that occasionally, the regional integration is mentioned in a general way.

Party	Representative	Position	State of the federation, region
PMDB	José Fogaça	Senator	Rio Grande do Sul, South
PMDB	Casildo Maldaner	Senator	Santa Catarina, South
PMDB	Roberto Requião	Senator	Paraná, South
PMDB	Confúcio Moura	Deputy	Roraima, North
PMDB	Germano Rigotto	Deputy	Rio Grande do Sul, South
PFL	Jorge Bornhausen	Senator	Santa Catarina, South
PFL	Geraldo Althoff	Senator	Santa Catarina, South
PFL	Ney Lopes	Deputy	Rio Grande do Norte, North-East
PFL	Santos Filho	Deputy	Paraná, South
PSDB	Álvaro Dias	Senator	Paraná, South
PSDB	Pedro Piva	Senator	São Paulo, South-East
PSDB	Nelson Marchezan	Deputy	Rio Grande do Sul, South
PSDB	Feu Rosa	Deputy	Espírito Santo, South-East
PPB	Júlio Redecker	Deputy	Rio Grande do Sul, South
PTB	Emília Fernandes	Senator	Rio Grande do Sul, South
PT	Luiz Mainardi	Deputy	Rio Grande do Sul, South

Source: Câmara dos Deputados, 2000; Senado Federal, 2000.

Table 2. Brazilian representatives and respective parties at the Mercosur Joint Parliamentary Commission, 1999–2002.

The programme of the *Partido do Movimento Democrático Brasileiro* (PMDB), approved at the 1994 National Convention and ratified for publication at the 1996 Convention which contains the party's basic principles, states that

> it vigorously defends the national interest, understood as the Brazilian people's interest in preserving both territorial and national sovereignty, in strengthening cultural autonomy, productive and commercial capacity, as well as the defence of other national strategic goals.[27]

27 PMDB – Partido do Movimento Democrático Brasileiro, *Programa do PMDB*, www.pmdb.org.br/progrm2.htm [19 June 1998: 4].

For the PMDB, therefore, regional integration, hence Mercosur, is not linked to the issue of defending the national interest; the emphasis on the various aspects of Brazilian nationality (cultural, economic, etc.) is not followed by a concern for building a shared regional space via a process which seeks to provide better living conditions for all the peoples in the region.

With regards to international relations for the PMDB the nation state is predominant and exclusive and thus the party aims at formulating and carrying out a national project. Processes of regional cooperation must be taken into account only in so far as they are complementary to the national interest therefore the party's activity leads it to reaffirm differences and specific interests:

> The PMDB considers an active and strong Brazilian presence at the UN, GATT, IMF, World Bank and other international agencies, and at the Latin-American Parliament, Mercosur, Amazon Pact and other regional organizations and agencies, indispensable, seeking above all, negotiated solutions to bilateral or international issues. But the party will always be ready to oppose any obstacle that may hinder its national project.[28]

Thus, the party declares, a priory, the supremacy of the national interest over any obstacle that might be brought about by regional cooperation. Such an attitude narrows the country's capacity to negotiate and accommodate diverse interests. In other words, Mercosur is seen to provide a strategic way of consolidating the national project rather than a process of regional integration aimed at asserting the common interests of the member countries in the international arena. Theories on international cooperation suggest that the insertion of national interests in a regional perspective is a condition of the deepening of the integration process.

Part of the reason for such an attitude may be due to Mercosur's institutional structure, for all decision-making powers related to the integration process are held by the Executive. Thus, a party's autonomy from, or opposition to, the government might lead it to opposing the process of regional integration. On the other hand, the parties' activities at national level show that their own dynamics and

---

28 Ibid: 22.

links with society contribute to the formulation of their foreign policies. The fact that the PMDB operates only at national level, mostly on the bases of tactical considerations, obstructs its grasping of the importance of foreign relations, which are generally incorporated slowly by society except during periods of acute crisis.

The *Partido da Frente Liberal* (PFL) programme does not mention Mercosur or regional integration. The party's pragmatic stand reflects its views on foreign policy. This is a concise programme made up of ideological norms, principles and interpretations of the country's political, economic, social, and cultural reality formulated from a liberal perspective. These principles form the party's theoretical framework from which its parliamentarians draw the party's line with regards to the government and other domestic issues. Thus the PFL views on foreign policy, and particularly on Mercosur, are only manifest when the interests of party members or those of the economic and social élites that it represents are directly affected.

The *Partido da Social Democracia Brasileira* (PSDB) programme does not have a specific position on Mercosur. In fact, it barely sets out basic guidelines in connection with Brazil's foreign policy. Thus, according to the PSDB, it is up to the diplomatic service to be both vigilant regarding issues of regional integration in Latin America, and endeavour to achieve the country's long term objectives:

> Foreign policy has a strategic importance for the country's development. Brazil must continue fostering dialogue within the international arena, and relationships based on co-operation and non-confrontation. The traditional long-term goals of Brazilian foreign policy – sovereignty, self-determination, security, and territorial integrity – must be asserted through a more active diplomacy on issues such as Latin American integration, external debt, as well as in actions in favour of world peace.[29]

The stance of both the PSDB and that of the PFL differ from that of the remaining parties, in that they formed part of the ruling coalition under President Fernando Henrique Cardoso's two terms of office (1995–1998 and 1999–2002), a fact which, in the final analysis, makes

---

29 PSDB – Partido da Social Democracia, Programa do PSDB, www.psdb.org.br/programa.htm [19 September 1998: 11].

them co-responsible for the negotiations in Mercosur. Thus these parties' standpoint is linked to that of the Brazilian state. The omission of Mercosur in the PSDB programme is probably due to this not being deemed a central issue on the domestic agenda. For as long as Mercosur is not an important issue in social and political life domestically, and, especially if it has no potential to be a vote winner, its exclusion from the party programme does the party no harm. In other words, it seems that integration is not the subject of disputes concerning domestic political power.

The *Partido Progressista Brasileiro* (PPB) programme, Organizational and Administrative State Directives, establishes the party's stance concerning Brazilian foreign policy suggesting the country must sustain policies that

> maintain respect for other countries self-determination and the peaceful solution of conflicts; honour UN action and principles [...] as well as other documents which commits it to defending the country's participation in equal standing in all international bodies; avoid automatic alignment and foster frank dialogue with all members of the international community; promote increasing political and economic integration of Latin America aiming at strengthening regional agreements and the continental community; advocate further participation of developing countries in wealth benefits and a more equitable world political and economic power sharing; assure the protection of our country's natural resources as well as of the prices of our export commodities with a view to strengthening our currency and bringing in wealth.[30]

As can be seen, the PPB sketches broad, general lines for Brazilian foreign policy. Like the other parties' programmes, it supports regional integration in general, but without mentioning controversial issues.

The *Partido Trabalhista Brasileiro* (PTB, Brazilian Labour Party) programme, chapter 6, is devoted to international relations, and it reads:

> The PTB supports peoples' self-determination, non-intervention and non-interference in the internal affairs of other countries, as well as a peaceful solution to conflicts; the PTB recognizes a new world order and hopes that Brazil

30 PPB – Partido Progressista Brasileiro, *Manifesto Programa Estatuto de PPB*, 1996: 17.

benefits from it; the PTB supports all movements that foster world disarmament and the elimination of nuclear weapons; the PTB supports economic and cultural integration of developing countries and fosters the acceleration of Latin American integration, as well as the establishing of a Latin American common market; the PTB underlines the need for an orderly occupation of frontier areas, as well as the need for sufficient funds for improving their aerial control, roads and communications, in order to develop them and protect the territorial integrity of the nation.[31]

As with the other parties, the PTB's programme makes no specific reference to Mercosur, broadly alluding to regional integration processes and favouring a Latin American common market.

The *Partido dos Trabalhadores* (PT, Workers Party), expounds its position on foreign relations thus:

> As to relations between nations, the PT promotes a policy of international solidarity among oppressed peoples, and of mutual respect among nations, aiming at greater cooperation and world peace. The party clearly states its solidarity to national liberation movements and to all international movements that aim at providing [higher] living standards, justice, and peace for all humanity.[32]

In spite of the emphasis on cooperative international relations, there is no mention of Mercosur in its programme. However, it should be stressed that the PT has constantly discussed the subject, having carried out an internal debate concerning the impact of Mercosur on the working class, as well as supporting initiatives taken by several of its bodies. Incidentally, party members showing strong interest in the subject follow the same geographical distribution of the state of origin already seen in Tables 1 and 2. Internal debate resulted in further party documents such as the *Curitiba Letter*,[33] *Recommendations of the First PT National Seminar on Mercosur*, and *Notes on the Mercosur Integration Process*.[34] Furthermore, the PT has a strong presence in

---

31 PTB – Partido Trablahista Brasileiro, *Programa e Estatuto do PTB*, Brasilia, 1996: 12.
32 PT – *Programa do Partido dos Trabalhadores*, www.pt.org.br/prog-pt.htm [20 June 1998: 3].
33 PT – Partido dos Trabalhadores, 'Carta de Curitiba', Curitiba: *Primeiro Seminário Nacional do PT sobre o Mercosul*, 25 September 25, 1993.
34 PT – Partido dos Trabalhadores, *Notas sobre o Proceso de Integraçã do Mercosul*, São Paulo, 1995

the São Paulo Forum which assembles left and centre-left parties from all over Latin America, leading it to take part in activities alongside other parties from Mercosur member countries.

In view of the PT's nature, a party with intense internal debate, a contradiction has become manifest between what party bodies decide and its parliamentary practice. Whereas Mercosur is actively discussed internally, PT deputies show relative apathy with regards to the issue in the parliamentary terrain probably because any such discussion brings poor electoral returns.

Under Cardos, government and opposition political parties have in general shown little interest in Mercosur, treating it as a remote event. Opposition parties, though favouring regional integration in principle criticised some aspects of its current developments. The same occurred from time to time among non-opposition representatives, such was the case of deputy André Franco Montoro (PSDB, São Paulo), who criticised some aspects of the process, but wrote a favourable appraisal to ratify the Ouro Preto Protocol in 1995.

In any case, in the lifetime of the Joint Parliamentary Commission (nearly 10 years), it may be argued that the major difficulty has been to get political parties and their representatives interested and committed to Mercosur. They show a certain lack of knowledge about Mercosur negotiations and a detachment from its institutions is the prevalent attitude.

Weber's views may be useful in understanding the attitudes of Brazilian parties to Mercosur. For Weber[35] parties are either ideological, or 'compete among themselves by including in their programmes requirements from which they expect a higher impact'. In general, Weber goes on, parties combine both models since a political party is a group of individuals with the aim of seizing power within a given association. Consequently, if Mercosur's institutional structures were to provide political spaces from which power could be conquered to any party's benefit, parties would probably have much greater interest in it. Another reason for greater involvement would be the *weltanschaungspartei* – to use Weber's expression to signify a party's ideological

---

35   Max Weber, 'Parlamentarismo e governo numa Alemanha reconstruida', *Ensaios de Sociologa*, São Paulo: Abril Cultural, 1974: 26.

perspective through which party members endeavour to accomplish explicit political ideals. In such a case too, the role of the institutional structure, though linked to better-defined programme platforms, would be more important.

In our view, as long as the Mercosur decision making process remains concentrated on the Executive political parties will tend to have little interest in it, driving other social actors to seek different organisational forms to represent their interests in the integration process. This, no doubt, hinders the process of democratisation.

From the above we can draw two conclusions with regards to the issue of democracy in Mercosur. On the one hand, democratic values – following Schumpeter's rules[36] – tend to be reinforced within each member state and, as has been examined above, Mercosur practices simultaneously encourage their consolidation. On the other hand, the concentration of decision making on the executive weakens democratic control over the integration process itself and leads to a relative lack of commitment on the part of political parties, given the difficulties of using regional integration towards their objective of gaining political power.

Meanwhile, as their interests transcend national frontiers, certain economic and social pressure groups show an increasing desire to participate in regional politics. But when they find the Socio-Economic Consultative Forum inadequate to do so, they seek other means to forward their interests. At the end of the nineties this trend was resulting in serious problems for Mercosur and was hindering integration too. As we shall see in the last section of this article in connection with the sugar industry, economic and social groups do endeavour to advance their interests outside Mercosur's institutional mechanisms. It may be that such lobbying strategies are encouraged by virtue of the political parties' weak participation in the internal organs of Mercosur thus leading to the prevalence of private pressure.

---

36 Schumpeter, op. cit.: 1979.

The Joint Parliamentary Commission

The Iguazu Declaration, signed by Alfonsín and Sarney in November 1985, established the importance of the participation of all social sectors in the process of regional integration as the basis for the relations between the two countries. This item was nevertheless withdrawn from the June 1986 Argentina-Brazil Integration Act that created PICE, and mention was made only of entrepreneurs as active elements of the integration process. This prompted a debate on the democratic deficit of the integration process which led to the creation of the Joint Parliamentary Commission and, later, of Working Group 11 (renamed 10 as of 1995), in charge of labour and social issues. Thus far, there has been little room for society's participation in the integration process, with an emphasis on negotiations between states. The PICE document does not even mention ways in which business' leaders might participate nor the nature of their relationship to state agencies.

If, on the one hand, the governments of Argentina and Brazil saw Mercosur as an important strategic means to consolidate their respective domestic democratic processes, on the other, the preoccupation of high-rank officials and decision makers with ensuring closer relations between the two countries ended up becoming a factor in narrowing the scope for society's participation in Mercosur. As the integration process progressed and deepened, interest in participation grew slightly, particularly with regard to parliamentary involvement, which can be explained by society's growing fears about the effects of the integration process itself.[37]

However, while nationally organized groups and political parties focused attention on domestic affairs, thus neglecting discussion on regional cooperation, the very difficulties of participating have led to doubts about the democratic character of the process and to certain

---

37   This is a general rule of integration processes: political and social mobilisation comes about from the perception of its risks, rather than its advantages. Such generic interest appeared under various guises from different regions and social groups.

reluctance to take part in negotiations. A yawning gap can be perceived between their rhetoric on the concern for democracy and their actual practice since, contrary to expectations, the progress of economic integration would discourage the participation of society's organised groups, except for those with clearly defined sectorial interests. Therefore, a genuine concern with democracy combined with a situation of low participation created a favourable atmosphere for the emergence of a parliamentary body to oversee the integration process.

A Joint Parliamentary Commission was set up by the Treaty for Integration, Cooperation, and Development that had been signed by Argentina and Brazil in 1988. It was made up of twelve representatives appointed for two years by national parliaments of each country. Consultative in nature, its main function was to assess negotiation agreements prepared by government officials and make appropriate recommendations before sending them to their respective congresses for ratification. In this way the involvement of legislators in the integration process in a consultative capacity, a role inherited by Mercosur's Joint Parliamentary Commission created in 1991, was sanctioned. In and of itself, this does not fully exhaust the parliamentary experience of Mercosur, which, as discussed above, is largely shaped by (especially Brazilian) political parties, whose attitude toward Mercosur has influenced the way the Commission functions.

From the beginning, in 1991–92, the Commission has supported a broader type of integration, one that goes beyond trade agreements, but aimed also at improving the welfare of the populations involved. This integration model would represent an extension of the internal democratisation process into the realm of foreign relations, and would be an effective means of ensuring the transition of Mercosur from a practical-objectives association into a shared-goals association. However, while the Commission's rhetoric clearly supports broad and ambitious integration goals, its activities were limited both by the vague definition of its functions and the limitations set by the Treaty of Asunción. This does not, however, question its role within the integration process or its decision making powers but neither does I make the case to broadening them. This contrast between action and rhetoric is central to understanding the Commission's role in Mercosur.

According to Chapter VI of the Treaty of Asunción, the Commission must 'facilitate the progress of the establishment of a Common Market',[38] yet the Commission remains a consultative body and did not, at that time, belong to Mercosur's institutional structure. Its main activity remains processing the legislation related to agreements and treaties. The same vagueness is maintained in the Common Market Group's internal statute regulations, a body which according to Chapter II, assigns itself the role of 'establishing the necessary links with the Joint Parliamentary Commission',[39] without further explanation of how this should be done.

Throughout the 1991–1994 transition period, the Commission held several meetings which issued recommendations and resolutions, but with few concrete results. Its proposals addressing economic, trade, and infrastructure issues, barely reflected society's general concerns; in spite of the criticisms expressed by some Commission members when analysing their own role, most sought ways to support the role of the executive in carrying out the integration process.

According to Senator Dirceu Carneiro (PSDB, Santa Catarina), the Treaty of Asunción focused on trade, whereas Mercosur should have more ambitious goals. For him the Treaty should be thought of as a preliminary document to be complemented in subsequent years by the actions of the various parties involved, thus bringing broader issues into the debate on integration.[40]

Such contributions, though, have not been acted upon. Our research shows that no relevant Mercosur decision in the nineties is attributable to the participation of representatives from the legislature. That is, the Joint Parliamentary Commission has had no decisive influence on negotiations, nor has it proposed for debate any major issues aimed at developing and consolidating the integration process. Most of the time the Commission has been concerned with the economic aspects of the integration process, issuing recommendations that have been either vague or complementary to what was already being dealt with by other Mercosur bodies. Hence the Commission's

---

38 Almeida, op. cit.: 97.
39 Grupo Mercado Comum 1992.
40 Dirceu Carneiro, Interview, Brasilia, 12 April 1994

performance has not been significant for it has not introduced specific new themes into the negotiations.

It could have been otherwise, though. For Senator Montoro (PMDB, São Paulo), the Commission might have brought up issues that reflected social concerns within the scope of integration policies, thus creating channels for the expression of society's demands around issues such as the transparency of negotiations or proposals that expressed regional, sectorial and political interests. But the Commission's role remained weak, consisting merely of ratifying governments' decisions.

Nevertheless, the Joint Parliamentary Commission has always expressed concern about guaranteeing democracy and its institutions, as well as respect for human rights. This may be observed in several of most documents from its early period.[41]

Resolution No. 001, taken at the meeting of 13–15 May 1992, where the Commission condemns the continuous violation by Peru's government of the right to freedom of expression, democracy, and human rights, sends a note of solidarity to the Peruvian people through the Peruvian Congress, and reaffirms the validity of democracy as a means of uprooting poverty, social inequality, and corruption in Latin America.

Recommendation No. 004, 1992 states that the process that gave rise to Mercosur derives directly from democratisation in the rest of the continent, particularly in the Southern Cone; that according to the Treaty of Asunción, the integration process is closely linked to democracy; and, in the face of the frequent attacks against constitutional system in Latin America, judicial institutions must be strengthened. To this effect, the Commission recommends to Mercosur governments the signing of an Additional Protocol to the Treaty of Asunción, establishing as a condition of Mercosur membership the full functioning of democratic institutions and the adherence to human rights agreements in their respective territories.

On Resolution No. 001, 1993, the Commission decided: To urge the governments of the Mercosur member countries to unconditionally respect the democratic system and its institutions, fully aware that an

41 Commisão Parlamentar Conjunta, *Atas do Reuniones*, 1991 through to 1998.

interruption of the democratic order by any of the signatory countries of the Asunción Treaty would militate against the process of regional and continental integration; To support, by all means recognized in international law, all governments born from the people's will.

In another document in 1993, the Commission reaffirms its

> unshakeable belief that, in accordance with Recommendation No. 004, adopted in the city of Córdoba, Argentina, on 22 May, 1992, and Resolution No. 001, adopted in Brasília, on 5 March, 1993, a fully democratic system in member states is an imperative condition to the achievement of the goals set by the Asunción Treaty.

Recommendation 004 further reaffirms the Commission's commitment 'to be vigilant for the interests of the societies taking part in the integration process, thus exerting its prime function as representative body of the peoples concerned'. Hence it recommends member states: to have as the foundation principle of their relations with third countries, to support exclusively governments legitimated by the people's will; to be guided by the highest respect toward workers' rights, by assuring them a fair participation in the integration process as well as in all the benefits deriving from it; to adopt efficient and rapid measures, such as the setting up of a Common Compensation Fund to deal with industrial restructuring or adaptation of vulnerable sectors of the economy, as specified by Recommendation No. 001, 1993; to proceed as soon as possible to the elimination of non-tariff barriers for intraregional free trade, in line with Recommendation No. 002, 1993, approved by the Sub-Commission on Customs and Technical Norms; to adopt measures and procedures relative to Mercosur's policy for the transport sector concerning its professionalisation as well as controls at border customs, harmonisation of documents, insurance policies, zoological control, [...], as well as reducing economic and technical asymmetries relative to cargo and passenger transport [...] all in line with Recommendation No. 003, 1993, approved by the Sub-Commission on Transport [...].

In spite of innumerable resolutions and recommendations, the participation of the Joint Parliamentary Commission has not expanded. The emphasis on the importance of Mercosur's democratisation has not translated into effective implementation. Little attention has been paid to issues of interest to society at large, such as, for instance, labour and the environment. On these types of issues the Commission has made only vague references, not concrete proposals.

Answering a question they themselves had posed on why Mercosur has no parliament, Florêncio and Araújo suggest this is due to the fact that Mercosur's

> decision making bodies have no supranational character. All Mercosur-related decisions are made by national governments which are subjected to control by their own national parliaments. Since there is no common executive body, there is no need for a common parliament. Whilst the European Community Commission is not accountable to the member states national parliaments, if there were no European Parliament the Commission would be subject to no external control.[42]

This may be so but, bearing in mind what has previously been said on democracy being at the root of the integration process, it must be pointed out that the institutionalisation of political control over the integration process could be much improved.

It is true that the Ouro Preto Protocol (December 1994) incorporated the Commission into Mercosur's institutional structure. In the proceedings from the fourth meeting of the Ad Hoc Group on Institutional Aspects, held in Brasília on 28–29 September 1994, item C contains recommendations for Mercosur's Future Institutional Structure. It proposes that

> the Trade Commission and the Joint Parliamentary Commission be incorporated into the organic structure of Mercosur. It also raises the possibility of the creation of an Socio-Economic Consultative Forum.

These recommendations have indeed been incorporated into the 1995 Ouro Preto Protocol, which, in Chapter 1, article 1, stipulates that the Parliamentary Commission be an integral part of Mercosur's structure.

Yet the Commission has been assigned no further functions than those established by the Treaty of Asuncion. While the newly created Trade Commission has decisive responsibilities with effective power

---

42   Sérgio Florêncio and Ernesto Araújo, *Mercosur, proyecto, realidad y perspectivas*, Brasília: Vest-Com, 1997: 74.

concerning the integration process, the Parliamentary Commission, in spite of its activity during the preceding years, has remained a consultative agency, only able to make recommendations to the Council. Its subordination to the executive has provoked reactions within the Brazilian Congress. Criticism of the Commission assignments was voiced by Deputy Montoro, who drew attention to the risks of the new institutional arrangement:

> the future of integration will be determined solely by negotiation among national executives, the populations of the four countries having no direct participation in decisions concerning integration, since their representative bodies, as well as the Joint Parliamentary Commission and the Socio-Economic Consultative Forum, have merely consultative functions.[43]

Nevertheless, his report (destined for the Chamber of Deputies Commission on Foreign Relations) eventually recommended thorough approval of the Ouro Preto Protocol.

Further criticism came from opposition parties. Deputy Sandra Starling (PT, Minas Gerais) demanded that the JPC should function similarly to the European Parliament which, she recalled, exerts rigorous control over the Economic Commission, even being able to dismiss its members, approve budgets and so on. On her note of rejection of the Ouro Preto Protocol, she argues that such institutional choice

> overtly violates the constitutional principle of the separation of powers to the extent that it subordinates parliamentarians of the four countries to the requirements and directives issued by a body made up of the economics and foreign affairs ministers

Still according to her,

> the Joint Parliamentary Commission [...] can only make recommendations to the Common Market Council through the Common Market Group. Such recommendations may or may not be accepted by the Council, hence the

---

43 Ana Maria Stuart, 'Um balanço político da reunião do Mercosur', *Carta Internacional*, São Paulo: Núcleo de Pesquisa em Relaçõs Internacionais e Política Comparada, 1996.

Parliamentary Commission, unlike the European Parliament, will have no control over any of the Council or Group activities.[44]

Notwithstanding, the Parliamentary Commission's institutional position in Mercosur was approved by the national parliaments of the member states. And, as far as the control mechanisms of the process of regional integration, hardly anything had changed. The new situation, as of 1995, has not significantly mobilised Commission members to enhance their role within Mercosur's decisive structures. It may be concluded that generalised acquiescence has prevailed. The Joint Parliamentary Commission has incorporated into its internal statute regulations – of 3 August 1995[45] – the same assignments determined by the Ouro Preto Protocol in article 25: to make recommendations and contribute to the decisions made by the Common Market Group, the Trade Commission, and the Common Market Council.

The new phase, following the Ouro Preto Protocol, has not changed the Commission practices, its members began in 1995 with no clear goals. At their meeting in August of that year they issued Resolution No. 003 decided that the Commission Administrative Secretariat 'shall establish a work schedule and define the agenda to be dealt with by the sub-commissions in the coming six months.'[46] At the same meeting, the Commission's short-term goals were defined as:

> to capitalise on the Commission's role in Mercosur institutional structure, improve the follow-up of work developed by other Mercosur institutional organs and identify priority issues to be discussed.[47]

The analysis of these goals shows lack of continuity with the Commission's previous work (during the transition period) and, above all, lack of a strategic long term working plan that might allow for

---

44   Sandra Starling, '*Declaração de voto da Deputada Sandra Starling sobre o parecer de relator Deputado André Franco Montoro sobre o Protocolo Adicional ao Tratado de Asunção sobre a estrutura institucional do Mercosur*', Brasilia: Comissão das Relações Exteriores da Câmara dos Deputados, 1995.

45   Armando Garcia Jr., 'Conflito entre normas do Mercosur e direito interno', *Informativo Mercosur*, 2(6), 1997.

46   Comissão Parlamentar Conjunta 1995.

47   Ibid.

more effective action or the strengthening of the legislature within Mercosur's integration process.

Sector interest and political parties: the case of the sugar industry

We now turn to examine an example of political articulation that certain economic and social groups have put into action to forward their interests within Mercosur in compensation for the lack of adequate regional democratic and participatory structures. This is explored with reference to the issue of free trade in sugar within the regional bloc.

Free trade in (mainly Argentine and Brazilian) sugar has been a source of conflict within Mercosur. The adaptation of this sector to the operation of the Customs Union, that is, the operation of free trade and the application of a Common External Tariff (TEC), from being a purely technical issue has become a focus of political debate through which Brazilian and Argentine social and economic groups have endeavoured to forward their interests. Their intense lobbying in their respective parliaments brought about a confrontation between the two legislative houses, thus generating a diplomatic crisis.

This example may suggest that participation of political parties in Mercosur might grow if political representatives and parliaments were encouraged to actively intervene to defend their electoral interests. At the same time partnerships based on local and sectorial interests pose difficulties for the emergence of international alliances and coalitions between parties with common affinities in the four countries.

It must be borne in mind that an increase in political party participation within the regional bloc may be encouraged by incentives that favour integration as much as than by disincentives. The case of sugar is an example of the latter.

The genesis of the problem

At the meeting of Mercosur Presidents in Fortaleza, Brazil, in December 1996, the Common Market Council decided that compatibility regulations for the sugar industry should be defined by 31 May 1997. The ad hoc task force created at the time did not achieve the expected results by the deadline due to disputes between Brazil and Argentina on the issue. The ad hoc group notified the CMC of its failure unleashing a further dispute between Argentine and Brazilian negotiators that partly reflected the interests of the affected social and economic groups. Brazilian delegates proposed the adoption of a timetable, starting on 1 July 1997, 'for the gradual and automatic elimination of tariffs in the sugar sector',[48] arguing that it was not justifiable to be the only economic sector entirely excluded from the process of regional integration.

Argentine delegates, for their part, argued that the Brazilian proposal did not take into account the asymmetry of the sugar industry between the two countries, which required special mechanisms to make up for the existing imbalances. Argentina alleged that Brazil's policy on sugar-cane alcohol included government intervention by means of Proálcool – state agency in charge of enforcing a mandatory percentage of sugar-cane alcohol to be mixed with gasoline – and which ensures that government vehicles be fuelled with alcohol. To the Argentine side, Proálcool subsidies encouraged Brazilian sugar planters to produce more alcohol and less sugar, the former a by-product of the latter, thus reducing its cost, thus making Brazilian sugar prices lower than in the rest of Mercosur. Worse still, as sugar prices rose on the international market, Brazilian producers increased production, offering sugar within Mercosur and on the world market at more competitive prices thus displacing Argentine production. Domestically the situation in both countries took on political connotations leading to tension within Mercosur.

---

48 *Gazeta Mercantil*, 'Disputa pelo açúcar', 19 May 1997.

On the Argentine side

In May 1997, as a result of the impasse, the Argentine Congress approved a law subjecting the withdrawal of Mercosur import quotas on Brazilian sugar to the ending of Brazilian government subsidies to alcohol producers. Since the law opposed existing Mercosur agreements President Menem immediately and successfully vetoed it. According to the Brazilian government there had been no need to pressurise Argentina since both countries shared an interest in accelerating the integration process.[49]

The June 1997 meeting of the Common Market Group brought the negotiations no further forward, except for an Argentine promise to seek a solution to the deadlock. Argentine officials attending the meeting proposed that the issue be dealt with in 2001, by which time both countries were supposed to have achieved full deregulation of the sugar industry. This was a setback for the Brazilian negotiators as they had been expecting some progress at the negotiations on this unique sector within Mercosur whose tariffs had so far not been reduced.[50]

On 6 August 1997, the Argentine Chamber of Deputies rejected President Menem's veto proposing to enact the law preventing the reduction in quotas for as long as the asymmetry, supposedly generated by Proálcool, persisted.[51] The issue was handed over to the Senate which unanimously approved the law on 3 September 1997. This Sugar Law (No. 24,822) reads:

> The duties applied to imported commodities regardless of origin, [...] are to be applied and must not be reduced on these same commodities' imports from Mercosur member countries as long as the asymmetry brought about by the Brazilian sugar-alcohol system persists.[52]

The law obviously protects Argentine sugar producers, less competitive than their Brazilian counterparts, who, by way of the

---

49 *Gazeta Mercantil*, 'Argentina mantém proteção ao açucar', 27 May 1997.
50 Ibid.
51 Ibid.
52 *Gazeta Mercantil*, 'Senado argentino imobiliza Menem na negociação do açúcar', 8 September 1997.

subsidies were able to place their products on the international market at lower prices.

The overthrow of the presidential veto and the passing of the Sugar Law resulted from a broad national political coalition involving congressmen form various parties and sugar producers, mainly from the northern provinces of Tucumán, Salta, and Jujuy, who argued that the Argentine industry would not be able to compete with its Brazilian counterpart if the duties within Mercosur were reduced.

As the October 1997 legislative elections in Argentina came nearer, most congressmen were compelled to attend to the sugar producers' demands, as the latter threatened their reelection plans, should they find themselves unprotected in the face of Brazilian competition. The threat was real, for if sugar production were stopped, the ensuing unemployment would be blamed on the congressmen who had refused to support the Sugar Law, as well as on the Menem administration's policy on Mercosur. Congressmen would be associated with unemployment which would hinder their reelection plans. A purely domestic solution for this impasse meant a clash of interests between Argentina and Brazil within Mercosur. Whilst the Menem government feared the victory of the opposition Alliance of Radicals and FREPASO – which did come about – there was temporarily room for an alliance between *justicialistas* and sugar producers in order to be able to influence the negotiations of international agreements – otherwise an exclusive government preserve.

The conflict resulted from the enactment of the Sugar Law, causing great apprehension in and arousing criticism from the Brazilian government who, in Foreign Affairs Ministry note of 4 September 1997, urged the Argentine government to

> make prevail the international agreements and the commitment between the two countries, in accordance with the Mercosur spirit of understanding and cooperation.[53]

Pressure from the Brazilian ministry of Foreign Affairs led Argentina's government to adopt a defensive and controversial attitude: while explaining that the executive was not to blame, they

---

53 *Gazeta Mercantil*, 'Lampreia lamenta decisão', 5 September 1997.

asserted that congress had passed the law legitimately, but also recognized that the country's laws should not contradict international agreements, as these have constitutional validity. Nevertheless, top officials publicly stated that they were seeking the means and studying the alternatives for resolving the problem.

Argentina's internal situation at that time shows that the government had, in fact, no means of preventing the Sugar Law from being enacted as its own parliamentarians were being heavily pressurised by sugar producers, who were in a strong position due to the proximity of parliamentary elections. In order to avoid compromising the government, pro-Menem senators were absent from the session when the law was voted on. The Argentine government was trapped between binding international treaties and the need to reelect its own party representatives. The Sugar Law appeared as an electoral device for reelecting to congress a parliamentary representation strong enough to approve the reforms it was proposing, whilst at the same time, to Brazil and the other Mercosur countries, it had to appear as if it were not responsible for the law itself.

It is clear then that, in this case, Argentine political parties mobilized around defensive interests and not from the perspective of consolidating the cooperation process.

On the Brazilian side

Brazil's reaction came in the form of the already mentioned Foreign Affairs note of September 1997, warning the Argentine government and congress of the risk of a serious diplomatic clash between the two countries. In addition, in the Brazilian Congress, Deputy Paulo Bornhausen (PFL, Santa Catarina), then head of the Brazilian section at the Joint Parliamentary Commission, proposed a retaliatory law banning imports of Argentine wheat, arguing that

> it is well known that Argentine export wheat is heavily subsidised, which makes it impossible for Brazilian producers to compete with it in fair or at least reasonably acceptable conditions in the home market.[54]

54 *Gazeta Mercantil*, 'Câmara ameaça retaliação', 6 September 1997.

Bornhausen's attitude was primarily political: to remind Argentina that the wheat sector in Brazil had undergone a serious crisis due to Mercosur but, in contrast to their reaction, the Brazilian government had taken accommodating measures to avoid damaging the regional bloc. The proposed law also aimed at pressurising the Argentine congress: if it were enacted, Argentine wheat producers would certainly mobilize and put pressure on their congressmen who would then find themselves in a still more uncomfortable position, since wheat and export producers might withdraw their support in the coming elections. Moreover, a 'wheat case' would have still broader consequences given that Brazil absorbs almost half of Argentina's wheat exports. Any reduction, therefore, besides affecting a powerful sector would certainly affect Argentina's balance of payments. In other words, Brazil threatened mobilizing an Argentine economic sector to take action in Argentina in favour of its interests. In economic international relations, mobilising groups in other countries in one country's own interests has been a tactic increasingly employed.

Further reactions followed. On 8 September 1997, the President of the Brazilian Senate, Antônio Carlos Magalhães (PFL, Bahia), demanded a more forceful government reaction to the Argentine congress's decision on Brazilian sugar imports. In turn, the President of the Chamber of Deputies, Michel Temer (PMDB, São Paulo), offered his support to Bornhausen's proposal, but was careful to add, 'decisions like the Argentine Congress's represent a risk to Mercosur'.[55]

Magalhães's position, just like that of Argentine congressmen, reflects the interests of important economic and social groups from the Brazilian North-East, mainly of sugar producers, but also includes concern for the workers who depend on sugar production. Temer's position expresses concern about a major Mercosur crisis which affects the business sector as a whole. As for Bornhausen, though his southern state of origin (Santa Catarina) is not a wheat producer, he speaks on behalf of farmers from its two neighbouring states, namely, Rio Grande do Sul and Paraná, the country's major wheat producers.

---

55 *Gazeta Mercantil*, 'ACM cobra reação', 9 September 1997.

The logic of cooperation

In the case analysed, the interests of Mercosur countries were organised into the political manifestations described, aimed at having parliamentary impact. A coalition among different groups became strong enough to make the Argentine legislative ignore the international agreements signed with its Mercosur partners. In Brazil, in turn, initiated by the Foreign Ministry's policy, another coalition began to urge the Argentine government and parliament to find a solution that would not threaten Brazilian interests.

Pressure from both sides eventually led the Argentine government to move towards a solution. President Menem's advisors prepared a proposal to revoke the Sugar Law, while others examined the possibility of appealing to the Argentine Supreme Court regarding its legality since it contradicted agreements signed with Brazil in June 1997. Under these agreements both sides committed themselves to study the asymmetry between their countries' sugar sectors aiming to develop a common policy to fully integrate the sector into a Mercosur free-trading and common foreign tariffs policy. Argentine Economy Minister, Roque Fernández, made the rejection of his country's congress decision public, while requesting more time from the Brazilian government in order to find a better solution to the problem.[56]

The Argentine government's public standing against its own congress was aimed at preventing a possible Brazilian retaliation and playing for time for further negotiations. Playing for time was crucial, due to the political situation in Argentina: from July through October 1997, any error might mean losing votes in the sugar-producing provinces. The Brazilian government, although rejecting Menem's claim that he had been taken by surprise by the vote in congress, decided to postpone further measures. According to the Brazilian Minister for Foreign Affairs, Luiz Felipe Lampreia, 'the decision of congress cannot be fully dissociated from the federal government, who holds a majority in the house'.[57]

---

56 *Gazeta Mercantil*, 'Menem pode apelar à Corte Suprema', 7 September 1997.
57 *Gazeta Mercantil*, 'Em nota oficial, Itamarati manifiesta "seria preocupação"', September 5, 1997.

Throughout the latter months of 1997, means were sought to undo the two coalitions at the root of the diplomatic crisis between Argentina and Brazil – perceived more as a political, than a commercial crisis. According to Bornhausen, the crisis had been triggered by the Argentine congress in setting a grave precedent by trying to establish a deliberative forum parallel to Mercosur's institutional structure established by the Ouro Preto Protocol in 1994. For Bornhausen, were the same method to be used by parliamentarians in the other member countries, aside from harming the credibility of the custom union, it would eventually make regional integration unviable. The Argentine government partially accepted the criticism, reaffirming its will to settle the issue.[58]

The emphasis on the desire to cooperate originates partly from the perception that a sectorial crisis might threaten all the advantages brought about by the custom union. Furthermore, the holding in the same month (September 1997) of Mercosur's World Economic Forum, where both Argentina and Brazil sought to present the image of a mature, united and strong Mercosur, ready to attract investment, also helped to avert the crisis.[59]

From then on, the sugar issue has become a matter of negotiation between government officials, hence bringing it back to the institutional scope of Mercosur. The participation of political parties in the debate has decreased. Yet, in September 1997, representatives from the Congresses and Export Chambers of both countries gathered to examine the issue and assess its possible consequences. There was a consensus that, despite their wishes, the matter would take a long time to be resolved. Task forces were therefore established to study the differences between the sugar sectors of Argentina and Brazil and, later on, to implement a common policy designed to integrate this

---

58 *Gazeta Mercantil*, 'Menem reafirma posição contra proteção a açúcar', 8 September 1997.
59 At the time, a new round of FTAA negotiations tried to set a timetable for trade liberalization in the continent, which also encouraged Mercosur member countries to appear as a solid bloc.

sector into the free-trading and Common Foreign Tariff (TEC) mechanisms.[60]

Conclusion

Brazilian policy on regional integration has been a matter for its Foreign Affairs Ministry, body that has played a significant role in the process of integration in the Southern Cone. Our research suggests that neither within the Brazilian state, nor in society at large, there exists an alternative or an opposing perspective to prevent the current strategy to develop Mercosur from bearing fruit. It may be argued that a classical view on policy-making prevails: advancing one step at a time and consolidating every stage before advancing any further.

It is important to point out that Mercosur's decision making structure rests on intergovernmental negotiations, there being no supranational agencies as in the European case. Brazil has favoured this structure, largely supported by Argentina, because it is aimed at preventing the rise of a supranational structure autonomous from national states, which would thus develop its own logic and strategies.

Shared fairly evenly by foreign affairs policymakers, the Brazilian perspective on regional integration, at least for the time being, is that it must progress under an intergovernmental framework. A central element of the current Brazilian position is that, rather than redesigning negotiation mechanisms, Mercosur members must seek to improve existing ones. Thus the current structure must be maintained, as current coordination offices rely on administrative and political entities that have the necessary know-how and are able to identify the issues that relatively, or fully, meet the national interests.

Our analysis seems to suggest if the integration process deepens the existing forms for the representation of public and private interests

---

60 *Gazeta Mercantil*, 'Exportadores debatem crise do açúcar: reunião de brasileiros e argentinos avalia que solução para impasse ainda vai demorar', 17 September 1997.

of Mercosur member countries will become inadequate. The current structure will not be able to offer suitable channels for the representation of those interests, leading to hard to manage conflicts, mainly in ill-defined situations such as electoral campaigns, macro-economic crises, or tensions linked to sectorial interests. Economic, social, political, public and private groups, whose interests are threatened within Mercosur, will seek in one way or another to make up for their losses to the detriment of the integration process as a whole. The crisis surrounding the sugar industry confirms this.

The persisting difficulties in the articulation of interests concerning regional integration policies suggest the need for a better exchange of information and the improvement of existing decision making mechanisms in order to accommodate national differences. The integration process would be assisted if congressmen had the possibility of greater participation. This would in turn have a positive effect on the current indifference that most Brazilian political parties show toward Mercosur. This indifference might be reversed if they could enhance their role in the decision making process, including their role in the Joint Parliamentary Commission. Not an easy issue to deal with in view of the current imbalance among member countries, which hampers solutions that might address existing differences and met groups' demands.

Furthermore, measures must be taken to strengthen Mercosur agencies – task forces and the Socio-Economic Consultative Forum, for example – so that they may encourage private sector participation, thus transferring to these bodies, issues which, if dealt within national spaces, might otherwise hinder the integration process.

The fact that democracy as a value is shared by all the countries in the regional bloc but that it is formally applied only at national level without pervading Mercosur's institutional structures, may be one of the factors contributing to the negative perception there is of Mercosur. Thus there coexists a positive perception of the role of the democratic clause in the relations among Mercosur member states with a growing awareness of the in-built democratic deficit in this regional integration process.

Olivier Dabène

Does Mercosur Still Have a project?

The scepticism in the question, Does Mercosur still have a project?, does not have anything to do with the crisis that hit this process of integration after the Brazilian devaluation of January 1999. In fact, this crisis was less dramatic and damaging than initially expected. Nor does it have to do with the much more serious Argentine crisis of 2001–2002, which will not be easily overcome. It has to do with a more fundamental preoccupation concerning the 'engine' of Mercosur. If one admits that an integration scheme cannot be merely a process, but has to have a project,[1] i.e. a strategic objective, then it seems legitimate to raise some concerns about Mercosur's future.

This paper argues that the initial motivation for the revitalisation of the Argentine Brazilian dialogue in the mid eighties was to put forth a mechanism of democratic consolidation. This proved to be rapidly successful. At the time, the signature of the Treaty of Asuncion in 1991 as a first step toward the creation of a Common Market of the South (Mercosur), embodied an ambitious project, both in terms of the level of integration (common market) and the scope of integration (the south).

From a device for the consolidation of democracy Mercosur became a profound and enlarged integration process. Nevertheless, as a project it was no more than a way of sketching the horizon far in the distant future. No one can seriously consider that, at the beginning, Mercosur's objective consisted of building a common market with all the South American countries. Actually, during the first years of its existence Mercosur had to meet the challenge posed by President Bush's Enterprise for the Americas Initiative (1991) and subsequently

1   Admittedly, this postulate can be criticised in the light of the European experience. But in Latin America weak institutionalisation of integration schemes prevent them from being animated by a self sustained dynamic.

the setting up of the Free Trade Area of the Americas (FTAA, 1994). Meeting these challenges meant getting ready for hemispheric negotiations, and that implied both deepening (the Ouro Preto Protocol of 1995) and (by including Chile and Bolivia) enlarging the integration process. Indeed, for a while, this appeared to be Mercosur's objective. But after Mercosur, at the Santiago summit of the Americas (1998), and, up to a point, also at the Rio Europe/Latin America summit (1999), managed to gain respect it had once again to give serious thought to the type of strategic objective which would unify its four members.

Initially set up to support fragile democratic transitions Mercosur has now to contribute to a better quality democracy both by ensuring that democracy is to prevail in the member countries and in the nature of the apparatus of regional governance. But this contribution cannot confine itself to dealing with the decision making process only, as classical representative theory of democracy would have. It ought also to deal with the outcomes of political systems, as suggested by the redistributive theory of democracy, in order to assess how Mercosur can bring improvements to the welfare of the region's 200 million inhabitants.

Mercosur as a tool of democratic consolidation

Argentina (in 1983) and Brazil (in 1985) put an end to the era of military rule in these countries against a background of uncertainty. Both countries had every reason to look for ways of securing a successful transition to democracy.

Argentina had to cope with both the frustration and resentment of the army, which had surrendered political power after the humiliating episode of the Falklands war, and an acute economic crisis. The military opposed trials for human rights violations and attempted twice, in 1987 and 1988, to overthrow the democratic regime. Brazil's transition has been less shaky, but the economic situation was stabilised much later than in Argentina.

Does Mercosur Still Have a Project? 143

For both countries, regional integration appeared to be a good way of tying each other's hands, locking in the democratic reforms thus reducing the uncertainties inherent in any transition.

According to an observer:

> In 1984 we had a clear idea of the weakness of the institutional situation. So the consolidation of democracy was a theme very much discussed. And a fundamental idea that emerged was that of trying to build a so called democratic security network in Latin America. It was about trying to defend democracy, but not after breakdowns. The idea was to consolidate democracy so that there would be no more breakdowns. The decisive episode was Tancredo Neves' visit to Buenos Aires. There was a lunch at Olivos at the end of 1984. During the lunch, there were talks about consolidation of democracy, about the dangers that existed in both countries, and about what could be done. There had been ideas discussed before, but it was the first time an elected president and a president in exercise had a serious talk about it. After that episode ideas got more precise. In Argentina, as well as in Brazil, there were plans to create a mechanism, not yet of regional integration, but of democratic security.[2]

At the Iguazu meeting (30 November 1985), the first presidential summit to take place in a long time between Argentina and Brazil, the idea of launching a process of regional integration was presented both as a tool for consolidating democracy and as an instrument of economic development. The idea was that both objectives could feed off one another. Point 9 of the final declaration stipulates that both countries should make efforts to:

> find lasting solutions that allow the governments to take care of the main task that consists of providing welfare and development for their people, consolidating the democratic process in Latin America.

The last point of the declaration concludes that the presidents

> stress that the process of democratisation that is sweeping the whole continent will lead to closer relations and integration among the peoples of the region.[3]

---

2   Diego Achard, Manuel Flores Silva and Luis Eduardo González, *Las élites argentinas y brasileñas frente al Mercosur*, BID-INTAL, 1994.
3   Declaración de Iguazú, 30 November 1985.

Obviously there is some kind of circular logic in operation here: regional integration is supposed to facilitate economic development, which in turn helps consolidate democracy, and at the same time democracy facilitates the integration process that contributes to economic development.

We find this circular logic in many declarations. For instance, point 2 of the Argentine Uruguayan declaration of May 1987 states that

> this process of integration [...] is the basic condition of our possibilities of economic and social development, facilitated by the [ongoing process of] democratic institutionalisation, without which [regional] integration would fail as it has failed in many cases in the past.[4]

The same declaration also mentions the 'politics of democratic solidarity' and democracy is deemed a necessary condition for the integration process while the latter is expected to bring about the prosperity that in turn will help consolidate democracy.

Mercosur's circular logic

It is to be noted that the determination to lay down safety valves in order to consolidate democracy has not been altered despite politicians of different persuasion coming to office in the countries of the region. It is easy to understand the fears of the first post dictatorship democratically elected presidents. Sarney, Alfonsín and Sanguinetti looked for democratic solidarity to compensate for the internal weaknesses of their states. The integration process, during a phase of transition, can reduce uncertainty. But the situation was very different for Presidents Collor, Menem and Lacalle. Nevertheless they, together with Rodríguez, President of Paraguay, signed the Treaty of Asunción in 1991 and, in the following years, kept insisting on regional economic integration as a tool of democratic consolidation.

4   *Declaración conjunta Argentina-Uruguay*, Montevideo, 26 May 1987.

Does Mercosur Still Have a Project? 145

However, the treaty makes no reference to a project of democratic consolidation. This probably reflects the shared belief that by 1991 democracy was no longer under threat in the region.

Meeting	Extract from Declaration
CMC 2	'the full operation of democratic institutions is an indispensable condition for the existence and development of Mercosur.'
CMC 5	the Presidents 'reiterate their conviction that [regional] integration, so long as it contributes in a tangible way to the promotion of economic development and social justice, it strengthens and consolidates the democratic transitions in the four countries.'
CMC 6	the Presidents 'reiterate their conviction that [regional] integration contributes to the promotion of development and social justice and helps eliminate economic backwardness, thus consolidating the democratic transitions in the four countries.'
CMC 7	the Presidents 'reaffirm their [commitment to] consolidate democratic principles in Mercosur, which they deem essential for the final goal of integration [i.e. a common market].'
CMC 8	the Presidents 'once again manifest their full adhesion to democratic principles as a fundamental pillar on which the integration process rests.'

Table 1. Treaty of Asunción.

Nevertheless, thanks to Paraguay, the issue of democratic consolidation resurfaced in Mercosur. The will to use the integration process to defend democracy was put to the test when, on 22 April 1996, General Lino Oviedo tried to overthrow President Wasmosy in that country. Diplomatic pressure – from the United States, Argentina, Brazil, and the European Union – managed to stop what otherwise would have developed into the breakdown of democratic rule in Paraguay or the militarisation of the regime. Obviously, a breakdown of democracy in Paraguay would have discredited Mercosur. But such a breakdown would have violated only the spirit and not the Treaty of Asuncion itself. True, the Presidents of Argentina and Brazil made it clear that a successful military coup would have meant the expulsion of Paraguay from Mercosur, but had no legal basis on which to do so.

Mercosur had to close this loophole by adopting a democratic clause. This was done in two steps: first a declaration was adopted in June 1996, stipulating that democracy was an essential condition for co operation within the framework of the Treaty of Asuncion. This declaration of principle was then transformed into a protocol, adopted at the Ushuaia summit in July 1998.

ARTICLE 1
The full operation of democratic institutions in the member states signatories to this Protocol is an essential condition for the development of [Mercosur].
ARTICLE 2
In the event of a breakdown of the democratic order in any member state, this Protocol will be applied against that state as stipulated in the integration agreements among the states signatories to this Protocol.
ARTICLE 3
Any breakdown of the democratic order in one of the states signatories to the present Protocol will lead to the application of the procedures contained in the articles below.
ARTICLE 4
In the event of a breakdown of the democratic order in a state signatory to the present Protocol, the other member states will undertake appropriate consultations among themselves and with the affected state [aimed at reversing the situation].
ARTICLE 5
When the aforementioned consultations result in failure, within the terms of the existing integration agreement, the other states signatories to the present Protocol, will consider the nature and the scope of the steps to be taken in accordance to the gravity of the situation. Such steps will go from suspension of the right to participate in the bodies of [Mercosur] up to and including the suspension of the rights and obligations arising out of those very processes.
ARTICLE 6
The measures contemplated in Article 5 above, will be adopted through consensus by the member states signatories to the present Protocol within the framework of the existing integration agreements and communicated to the state in question, which will not participate in the relevant decision making process. These measures will be implemented from the moment that the [official] communication is made.
ARTICLE 7
The cessation of the measures referred to in Article 5 will take place [only] when the full restoration of the democratic order has been effected and verified […]/[…]

Table 2. Ushuaia Protocol on Democratic Compromise in Mercosur, Bolivia and Chile, Ushuaia, 24 July 1998 (extracts).

Thanks, in a way, to the situation in Paraguay, Mercosur implemented its method of democratic consolidation in 1998. Since that date, a breakdown of democracy in any member state can lead to its expulsion from Mercosur.

The Paraguayan crisis helped put back an issue that had disappeared from Mercosur's agenda and, as noted above, even from the Treaty of Asuncion. This means that Mercosur was successful in its

Does Mercosur Still Have a Project? 147

aim of consolidating democracy in the member states by means of unleashing a dynamic of integration even before the treaty was signed. Thus it comes as no great surprise to learn that the Treaty of Asuncion was not inspired by a grand political design, nor that Mercosur's first years of existence were characterised by an effort to complete negotiations on a free trade area and a customs union – until the Miami summit forced it to become more ambitious or risk being dissolved.

Mercosur and the FTAA challenge

Between 1994 and 1998, Mercosur's project consisted of defending Latin America's interests with regard to the United States' aim to build a Free Trade Area of the Americas as an extension of the North American Free Trade Agreement. We can consider Mercosur as being successful in pursuing this strategy.

The 1994 Miami summit agreed to conclude the negotiations for a Free Trade Area of the Americas as late as 2005. However, it took four years to agree the format of the negotiations that were opened at the second hemispheric summit held in Santiago, Chile in 1998. At the risk of oversimplifying, those four years can be characterised as a battle between Mercosur and NAFTA to set the format of the negotiations. At the centre of the debate there were four basic issues.

Who will negotiate?

At the Recife meeting of vice ministers of commerce (February 1997), it was decided that countries could negotiate individually or by blocs. The United States opposed the latter but the Latin American customs unions (Mercosur and the Caribbean Community) insisted on negotiating as blocs, and their position prevailed.

When will the negotiation start?

Until the Belo Horizonte meeting of ministers of trade (May 1997), the United States' position was to engage in simultaneous negotiations on all topics, while Mercosur was in favour of phased negotiations, leaving the tariffs issue for the end. In this instance, the North American position prevailed.

Rhythm and scope of negotiations

The United States sought to speed up negotiations on the issue of access to markets. The US wanted to take concrete measures for market access facilitation before the year 2000 by addressing the issues of tariffs, investments, norms, etc.

Mercosur proposed a three stage negotiation: trade facilitation until 1999, followed by norms and disciplines until 2003 and then tariffs until 2005. Mercosur did not wish to start by addressing the tariffs issue because it would necessarily involve drastic sacrifices. Mercosur's external tariff average is 13%, compared to 3% for the United States. Mercosur wanted to first negotiate the non tariff barriers to trade that penalise their exports to the United States.

How to negotiate?

Mercosur hoped for a single undertaking, while the United States wanted to sign partial agreements as they were reached. This was a fundamental issue for Latin America. There was fear that the United States would try to rapidly wrap up an agreement on tariffs and then slow down negotiations on non tariff barriers indefinitely. Mercosur was successful in imposing the single undertaking procedure.

All these issues were addressed during the three San José meetings (February and March 1998), but other problems emerged.

During the third Free Trade Area of the Americas preparatory committee meeting (of deputy ministers of trade), Mercosur proposed the creation of a special group to study the removal of obstacles to the

Does Mercosur Still Have a Project? 149

trading of agricultural products. The United States firmly opposed this idea.

During the fourth business forum, it was clearly evident that the Brazilians wanted to slow down the process of establishing the Free Trade Area of the Americas, while the North Americans wanted to speed it up. The Brazilian position received the support of the Latin American Industries Association (AILA).

In the end, the fourth meeting of trade ministers proved to be a success. The San José declaration constituted a milestone that allowed Latin American Presidents to officially open Free Trade Area of the Americas negotiations in Santiago, Chile, a month later.

Certain compromises concerning the format of negotiations were agreed upon. All decisions would be taken unanimously, as has been the case since the beginning, and the negotiation process would function with a rotating presidency and following a precise timetable. The presidency would change every 18 months at every ministers of trade meeting. Mercosur succeeded in being part of the presidency throughout, acting as either president or vice president, while NAFTA representatives were granted the presidency at the beginning (Canada) and at the end (co presidency between the United States and Brazil). As Mercosur had wanted, a total of nine groups were set up, including one focusing on agricultural issues. The United States imposed the themes of labour and environment, but only in as far as they would be objects of monitoring by special groups. Pressure groups concerning labour rights and the environment are powerful in the United States, but Mercosur opposed the inclusion of these issues. As a result of Mercosur's opposition, these groups were not granted even the status of consultative entities.

However, the United States managed to impose the idea of reaching partial agreements on trade facilitation. This position was defended by the American Chamber of Commerce, but opposed by Mercosur, in the name of the single undertaking methodology.

All in all, the 1994–1998 hemispheric negotiations previous to the opening of the 'real' Free Trade Area of the Americas negotiations, turned out to be fairly well balanced. Of course, the fact that the Clinton administration was not granted fast track authority to negotiate was crucial in this. Mercosur clearly managed to defend its positions, and was successful in securing relative control of the Free Trade Area of the Americas negotiations up until the end.

Period	Place of negotiation	
1 May, 1998 – 28 February, 2001	Miami	
1 March, 2001 – 28 February, 2003	Panama	
1 March, 2003 – 31 December, 2004	Mexico	
Period	Presidency	Vice presidency
May 1998 – October 1999	Canada	Argentina
November 1999 – April 2001	Argentina	Ecuador
May 2001 – October 2002	Ecuador	Chile
November 2002 – December 2004	Co presidency Brazil and United States	
Negotiating groups	Presidency and vice presidency for the first 18 months	
Market access	Colombia – Bolivia	
Investment	Costa Rica – Dominican Republic	
Services	Salvador – CARICOM	
Government procurement	United States – Honduras	
Dispute settlement	Chile – Uruguay / Paraguay	
Agriculture	Argentina – Salvador	
Intellectual property rights	Venezuela – Ecuador	
Subsidies, anti dumping and countervailing duties	Brazil – Chile	
Competition policy	Peru – Trinidad and Tobago	

Table 3. FTAA negotiation format.

However, the format of negotiations is one thing the central issue of the discipline of trade relations is another. Given that the North American Free Trade Agreement's economic discipline is more profound and stricter than that of the World Trade Organisation, the United States aims to negotiate on a so called 'World Trade Organisation +' (WTO+) basis. Latin America, experiencing difficulties in adjusting to World Trade Organisation discipline, opposes the idea of a 'WTO+' based negotiation process. Furthermore, the North American Free Trade Agreement treaty includes not only 'new issues' of trade (investment, services, intellectual property, and government procurements) but also 'brand new issues' like the environment and labour (supplementary agreements made in September 1993).

Most Latin American integration schemes have yet to address these 'new' and 'brand new' issues and Mercosur is no exception. For

Does Mercosur Still Have a Project? 151

Mercosur, a 'WTO+' based negotiation would involve fundamental sacrifices. Nevertheless, it could also mean anticipating an adaptation that would have to be made in the future in any case, as these issues might some day be addressed on a multilateral basis during World Trade Organisation rounds of talks.

In a way, it can be concluded that Mercosur contributed to a better international insertion of its member states in Free Trade Area of the Americas negotiations. This goal having been reached, the question of Mercosur's project is raised once again. As for democratic consolidation, Mercosur is the victim of its own success and needs to be innovative in order to continue on its path of success. Mercosur's new challenge, and new project, can only be a deepening of its political dimension.

The democratic deficit in Mercosur

At first sight, the European debate on the democratic deficit of the integration process does not seem relevant to Mercosur: due to its strictly intergovernmental dimension, decisions are taken by elected authorities. Nevertheless, if we think in terms of the classical participative and representative theory of democracy, it is interesting to examine the proliferation of working groups in Mercosur (for it is reminiscent of Europe's 'committee mania'), and assess the participation of civil society in the process.

The initial organic structure of Mercosur was extremely modest. The Treaty of Asunción created only a Common Market Council (CMC) and a Common Market Group (GMC). The Ouro Preto Protocol (17 December, 1994), which gave Mercosur its definitive institutions, added a Commission of Commerce (CCM), a Joint Parliamentary Commission (JPC), a Socio-Economic Consultative Forum (FCES) and an Administrative Secretariat (MAS). Since 1994, this organic structure has become increasingly complex. For instance, the superior body, the CMC, composed of foreign affairs ministers and ministers of the economy, relied upon a network of ministerial meetings to prepare its decisions. Between 1994 and 1998, other meetings were added to the initial list, and each of these created its own complex network of committees, working groups or technical commissions, of which there are currently dozens.

The GMC, the executive body of Mercosur, has gone through the same evolutionary process. The number of working sub groups in charge of assisting the GMC remains at eleven, but within each sub group, there has been a proliferation of commissions and committees. The same pattern can be observed regarding the ad hoc groups and the specialised meetings of the GMC.

Finally, the Commission of Commerce (CCM), which had ten technical committees in 1995, has added seven new ones, while committee number two, dedicated to tariff issues, gave rise to six sub committees and three ad hoc groups.

Growing institutional complexity characterises many integration processes, but it is particularly significant in the case of Mercosur due to its promoters' initial determination to avoid any type of bureaucratisation that would resemble the European or the Andean experiences. True, this bureaucratisation remains virtual as none of the working groups has an 'existence' of its own but it is noteworthy nonetheless.

Indeed, the decision making process, relying on the advice of unelected experts, has grown increasingly fragmented in Mercosur, Nevertheless, the description of an administrative structure does not say much about the democratic dimension of the decisions that are actually taken. One of the most important characteristics of the integration process in Mercosur is the extreme centralisation of power in the hands of the Presidents. This means that all important decisions are taken by the Presidents during their bi-annual meetings.[5]

Concerning the participation of civil society, a much debated issue, Mercosur possesses a Joint Parliamentary Commission (JPC) and a Socio-Economic Consultative Forum (FCES). These institutions try to incorporate political parties, business associations and trade unions within Mercosur, but they play only a very modest role. In

---

5   Or so it seems. More empirical research is needed in order to reach definite conclusions about the respective roles of experts and elected authorities in Mercosur's decision making process.

addition to these institutionalised means of participation, there has been a proliferation of regional organisations, such as the Industrial Council of Mercosur (CMI) and the Southern Cone Confederation of Unions (CCSCS), which are active in lobbying the different working groups of Mercosur. More important still, an integration process operating from below has emerged. Many activities now have their own regional organisation and many local authorities join in regional networks. Example of such networks are numerous, for instance, the Montevideo group (a powerful network of universities), the Crecenea-Cedesul group (north east Argentine provinces and southern Brazilian states), and the Mercociudades organisation (cities of Mercosur).

Whether institutionalised or spontaneous, the participation of civil society in Mercosur is definitely progressing. Should that lead us to conclude that democracy is underway in the integration process? In a way, the answer is positive. We are indeed witnessing the emergence of a public space for debate. However, progress remains modest, and it cannot be otherwise. As the integration process moves forward, there will always be sectors of society complaining that they did not participate in taking the decisions that affect their interests. This means that approaching the debate about the democratic deficit from the perspective of the classical participatory and representative theory of democracy, leads nowhere.

Thus it is necessary to supplement this perspective with another, inspired by a more representative theory of democracy,[6] one that is concerned with looking at the outcome of the political process, and focuses on 'who gets what'. In other words, the question revolves around assessing whether regional public policies contribute to the welfare of the member states and if they serve the general interest of the members of Mercosur. However, a major objection to this new perspective springs immediately to mind. To talk of a redistributive form of democracy within Mercosur seems irrelevant, given that Mercosur does not redistribute anything. There is no common budget and there are hardly any common policies. This constitutes a major difference with the European Union, one that is often stressed. But

---

6   See Giovanni Sartori, *Theory of Democracy Revisited*, 2 vols, Chatham: Chatham House, 1987.

although this is true, we find within Mercosur a will to create other modes for the collective regulation of common problems in the four member states. There is the intention to build regional governance in certain precise areas, which means that Mercosur has already gone beyond the negative integration stage (the elimination of obstacles to free trade) and is flirting with positive integration. Admittedly, most decisions in Mercosur concern the economic dimension of integration, but there are also many decisions to be made regarding population movements, police and justice, labour rights and cultural exchanges.

Furthermore, Mercosur has already fostered an impressive dynamic. Nobody can deny, for example, that this integration process has already contributed to making irreversible important market oriented reforms and has had a label effect for investors.

On all these points, one can try to evaluate the added value of the integration process in terms of collective welfare. But let us keep in mind that Mercosur's priority has always been to open up a broad market. Negative integration is clearly dominant within Mercosur, just as it is in other integration processes around the world.

We might argue, as many economists do, that free trade is for the common good, because increased trade generates improved welfare. In this sense, building up a large market would make Mercosur a redistributive democracy. This argument is not acceptable, though, for there can be no redistributive democracy where there is no political intention to redistribute or regulate. Although those who formulate an integration process always argue that their ultimate goal is to generate improved welfare for the population, the immediate consequences of any integration process lead, more often than not, to an aggravation of existing social problems.

There is another limitation to redistributive democracy in the integration process. We can not talk about redistributive democracy if those who benefit from a decision do not know who took it. In order to speak of redistributive democracy, citizens would have to believe that the outcome of the political process compensates for their lack of representation. In other words, people must be convinced that it does not matter that they did not designate the decision maker, so long as those decisions serve their interests.

Mercosur, by being strictly intergovernmental, member states are in charge of implementing decisions. We do not see in Mercosur the situation characteristic of the European Union where Europeans seem to hear about the Commission's decisions only when they are bad for them. Within the European Union, Brussels's publicised decisions are often the most controversial ones, and citizens could be forgiven for wondering who could have taken such decisions on their behalf, hence discovering the democratic deficit for themselves. In Mercosur, there is also a problem of transparency and, as elsewhere, a redistributive democracy will emerge at a regional level only when citizens get the chance to identify their decision makers. For the moment, citizens in the Mercosur region have the (correct) impression that the benefits generated by the regional integration process are, in geographical and social terms, unevenly distributed.

Not to lose the momentum of positive integration and to demonstrate the utility of a regional level of regulation and a problem-solving capacity seems to be Mercosur's major challenge for the future. Mercosur goal must be the consolidation of a redistributive type of democracy.

Peter Lambert

Paraguay in Mercosur: *¿para qué?*

Introduction

Amidst great international fanfare, the Treaty of Asuncion of March 1991 signalled the end of a process of regional negotiation and the launch of Mercosur, with the stated aim of the 'creation of a true common market in the region, and the coordination of macro-economic and sectorial policies of the member states in relation to foreign trade'.[1] At present, the imperfect customs union has harmonised over 90% of all trade between the member states, with exceptions in the Paraguayan case, due to expire in 2006.

For Paraguay, small, poor and landlocked, the potential economic opportunities of membership of Mercosur seemed attractive. With a population of 208 million and a combined GDP of US$1,102 billion, Mercosur is the world's fourth largest economic bloc. From within a regional trade bloc, Paraguay hoped for a higher international profile and bargaining power, increased regional and international trade and far greater Foreign Direct Investment (FDI) due to its natural resources, cheap labour and energy supply from the Itaipu hydroelectric dam. Moreover, close regional cooperation was presented as an integral component of the new democratic and modern Paraguay.

However, despite expectations, the 1990s was 'a dismal decade for Paraguay'.[2] Since 1995 economic growth has stagnated, averaging just 2.9% since 1991 and registering 0.4% and 0.5% in 1998 and 1999, while per capita income has fallen every year since 1995.[3] Moreover, with a fiscal deficit of $146 million in 1999 rising to $342 million in 2000, and a growing foreign debt, the government has been

1   Mercosur website: www.mercosur.com.
2   World Bank Country Brief 2000: 1.
3   Banco Central de Paraguay, Estadísticas, 2000.

forced to speed up its negotiations with the IMF, especially regarding privatisation.[4] This suggests not only disappointing results from regional integration, but also that the traditional model of economic growth, based on the triangulation of imported goods and the promotion of agricultural exports (with little value added), is now exhausted. While Mercosur has neither exacerbated nor improved this situation, it has clearly exposed the shortcomings of an outdated economic model.

This paper examines the model of economic development in Paraguay before and after joining Mercosur, above all in the areas of trade and FDI. It argues that Mercosur has not brought the expected economic benefits to Paraguay, in part due to the lack of necessary institutional and economic reforms, as well as the failure to implement a regional development strategy within Mercosur. The paper also analyses the limitations of Paraguay's membership of Mercosur and examines the case for withdrawal, suggesting that there is little hope at present of progress, unless major reforms, both domestic and regional, are implemented.

The entry of Paraguay into Mercosur

The traumatic events of the 1980s, including the debt crisis, the collapse of protectionist economic models, the rise of IMF-sponsored structural adjustment programmes and the transition from authoritarian to electoral regimes, led to increasing cooperation between the traditional economic rivals of Argentina and Brazil. Given their lack of competitiveness in an increasingly global market, regional cooperation was put forward as an alternative to regional competition. This led to the Programme of Integration and Economic Cooperation (1986) between the two countries, with the objective of gradually reducing bilateral trade imbalances and promoting bilateral trade. In 1988 they signed the Treaty of Integration, Cooperation and Development, with the more radical aim of creating a free trade area and common market within ten years based on harmonization of macro-economic, trade and tariff

---

4   Cámara de Comercio e Industria Paraguayo-Francesa, *Informe Anual*, 2000: 2.

policies. In 1990 the Buenos Aires Act reaffirmed commitment to a common market but cut the deadline by four years.

For Uruguay, integration was the result of a long-term strategy to consolidate traditional markets in Brazil and Argentina. Previous to 1991, it already had substantial bilateral trade agreements with both neighbours, dating from the 1960s and 1970s, which gave it some preferential tariff arrangements. These agreements were renegotiated with Argentina and Brazil in the 1980s, as Uruguay sought to be included in any regional development programme in order to maintain its favourable bilateral agreements and regional markets.

The case of Paraguay, however, was different. Under the dictatorship of Alfredo Stroessner (1954–89), Paraguay had pursued a policy of regional and international isolationism rather than integration, and while relations with Brazil were favoured, Paraguay did not benefit from significant bilateral trade agreements. Paraguay showed little interest in the initial talks preceding regional integration and was not even invited to the constituent meeting of Mercosur in 1990.

A further obstacle to regionally integrate was the structural differences between the economies of Paraguay, on the one hand, and Brazil, Argentina and Uruguay on the other. In the 1980s, the latter three had developed from highly protected and regulated economies, characterised by industrialisation, inward investment and an economically active state, through a painful process of adjustment to free market economies with an emphasis on investment in productive sectors. Paraguay on the other hand, had traditionally been the most open and macroeconomically balanced regional economy. Having undergone no significant industrialisation or modernisation process, it had carved out a comparative advantage through primary agricultural exports (principally cotton and soya) and in its role as a regional intermediary in triangular trade (exploiting regional tariff differentials to import goods for re-export).[5] Once the economic boom produced by

---

5   Triangular trade, mainly non-registered, grew considerably from the 1960s onwards, as Paraguay exploited tariff differentials between Argentina and Brazil. By the 1980s Paraguay had a growing industry in 'economic tourism', as Brazilians flocked across the border to purchase among other things, electronics, white goods, and computers at cheaper prices.

the construction of the Itaipu bi-national hydroelectric dam with Brazil receded after 1982, and the agricultural colonisation programme of the Eastern Border Region came to an end, the shortcomings of the economic model became evident as the economy began to stagnate.

The decision taken by Paraguay to perform a dramatic about-face and belatedly request membership of Mercosur was based on a number of issues. Despite having been (semi) democratically elected to power in May 1989, the government of Andrés Rodríguez and the Colorado Party which replaced the Stroessner dictatorship lacked democratic legitimacy; Rodríguez had been Stroessner's long term military ally and the Colorado Party had been a pillar of the dictatorship. They thus actively sought national and international recognition, legitimacy and support by seeking to promote Paraguay as a modernizing and democratic member of the international community.[6] After years of political isolationism, Mercosur provided a project which would immediately give Paraguay a higher degree of international standing than it had held before. Membership, therefore, rapidly became an integral part of the democratic discourse of the new government.

Secondly it was presumed that economic benefits, through increased trade and investment, would accompany integration. Given the extent of trade with Argentina and Brazil and the potential of access to previously closed or protected markets, it was felt that membership of Mercosur would allow Paraguay to develop institutional, infrastructural and productive capacity to compete more effectively on a regional and indeed international level. The alternative of isolation between two developing trade blocs, Mercosur and the Andean Pact, was felt to be unacceptable.

A number of points stand out regarding Paraguay's decision to join Mercosur. First, there was no debate or popular consultation. Indeed, no political party had endorsed it in the 1989 elections and elements of all parties opposed it. Second, there was no serious analysis of the costs and benefits of membership on a small, unpro-

---

6   General Rodríguez had been a supporter and senior military member of the Stroessner government, until his fall in 1989. Despite coming to power via elections in May 1989, Rodríguez was seen as lacking democratic credentials amongst national and international observers.

ductive and unreformed economy. With no long term development strategy in place, Paraguay could not condition membership to the introduction of regional policies to ensure preferential treatment or development funds to reduce the social and economic costs of membership. Third, Paraguay's entry to Mercosur was not only hasty, belated and ill-prepared but also a predominantly political decision. These characteristics would define Paraguay's future course within Mercosur.

Continuity within the development model

Under Stroessner the Paraguayan economic model had been based on a high degree of deregulation, its role within triangular trade, the export of agricultural goods (primarily cotton and soya) and high levels of imports. The resulting trade deficit had traditionally been covered by income generated by the construction of the Itaipu dam (until 1982), and short-term capital investment. For political, as well as economic motives, Stroessner also encouraged corruption, and as an extension, unregistered trade or contraband, as a mechanism of political control, or 'the price of peace'.[7] By 1991 when Paraguay joined Mercosur, it was emerging from a period of serious economic instability, suggesting the breakdown of the former model and the need for major reform.

However, both the administrations of Rodríguez (1989–93) and Wasmosy (1993–98) sought macroeconomic stability over economic regeneration. Rather than any transformation of the economic model, efforts were concentrated on stability and controlling inflation through a degree of liberalisation (such as deregulation of interest and exchange

---

7 See P. Lambert, 'Mechanisms of control: The Stroessner regime in Paraguay', in Will Fowler (ed.), *Authoritarianism in Latin America Since Independence*, London: Greenwood Press, 1996; and R. Andrew Nickson, 'Corruption and the transition', in Peter Lambert and R. Andrew Nickson (eds), *The Transition to Democracy in Paraguay*, London: Macmillan, 1997.

rates and a tax reform). The cost of such a policy was high interest rates, low purchasing power, and a lack of investment, especially in the agricultural and industrial sectors. Most significantly, there was no sustained effort to transform the economic model away from a dependency on primary agricultural exports and triangular trade.

The reasons for this were primarily political. Neither Rodríguez nor Wasmosy had any interest in radically altering the economic model since they themselves were supported by and formed part of the élite group of vested interests whose wealth was based on the economic model inherited from Stroessner. Indeed, one of the defining features of the transition to democracy in Paraguay has been that of continuity over reform, including the continuity of corruption, a politicised and inefficient state sector, and an outdated economic model. Factions within the ruling Colorado Party have sought to protect their economic interests rather than initiate reforms that might have repercussions that were politically or economically damaging to the interests of themselves or the Party.

Despite being the most open and stable regional economy with consistently the lowest rate of inflation, in the 1990s Paraguay recorded the lowest growth among Mercosur members.[8] GDP growth in Paraguay remained parallel to population growth, averaging around 3% and sustained by financial speculation. However, recessions in 1996 and 1998 led to economic stagnation, a situation exacerbated by two financial crises in 1995 and 1997, deterioration in cotton production and the gradual elimination of triangular trade as Argentina and Brazil lowered their tariffs, and border controls against contraband were tightened.

Agriculture represents 25.8% of the GDP, by far the most significant reliance in a region in which agriculture represents less than 10% of the GDP,[9] thus making Paraguay especially vulnerable to international price variations and natural disasters. Revenue from cotton production, the most significant sector in terms of family

---

8   Although inflation reached a high of 44% in 1990, since 1996 it has remained below 10% (BCP, *Estadísticas Económicas*, 2000).
9   In Argentina agriculture represents 6.4% of the GDP, in Brazil 8.6% and in Uruguay 9.1% (World Bank Date Profile 2000).

employment, has decreased by over 30% since 1990, due to pests, low international prices and the lack of appropriate technology to make it more competitive on the regional level. This is especially serious since cotton and soya exports still account for between 45% and 50% of total exports.[10] Rather than investing in agricultural production or diversification, the government has allowed an agricultural free market to prosper, which has led to the increased concentration of land, growing rural unemployment, inequality and poverty.[11]

Thus, no government since 1989 has ventured to implement significant reforms to transform or modernise the developmental model. This is in part due to the weakness and lack of representation of civil society in Paraguay, as well as to the power of vested private interests in the maintenance of the developmental status quo. As a result, successive administrations have been content to make slight adjustments to the limited, and some would say, exhausted, economic model inherited from the dictatorship. While this initially fostered macroeconomic stability, as the decade progressed it led to economic stagnation and decline.

	Paraguay	Brazil	Argentina	Uruguay
Population (millions)	5.4	168	34.8	3.3
GDP US$ billions	8.1	791.4	281.9	20.2
GNP p\c	$1,580	$4,420	$7,600	$5,900
Secondary school enrolment	59.3%	63.6%	71.9%	80.3%
Telephones per 1,000	55	120.5	203	250
Computers per 1,000	9.6	30.1	44.3	91.2
Paved roads (%)	9.4	9.2	29.5	87
Trade % of GDP	34.7	9.9	12.9	22.7
External debt US$ bn	2.9	220	150.5	7.5

Source: World Bank Country Date Profile 2000.

Table 1. Comparison of Paraguay and neighbours.

10   Banco Central del Paraguay (BCP), *Comercio Exterior*, 2000: 2.
11   See F. Masi, *Paraguay y el Mercosur: ¿Apertura sin Ganancias?*, Asuncion: Cadep, 1998; World Bank, *Paraguay: Poverty and the Social Sectors: a Poverty Assessment*, Washington: World Bank, 1994; Ramón Fogel, *Pobreza y Políticas Sociales en el Paraguay*, Asunción: El Lector, 1995.

Trade

Of the Mercosur partners, Paraguay has the most open economy as well as by far the highest reliance on trade as a percentage of its GDP. Since the lifting of most tariff barriers in 1995, intra-regional Mercosur trade has quadrupled, and trade with the rest of the world has also increased, although not at the same rate. Thus it would be logical to assume that Paraguay would have exploited the increased trade opportunities from within Mercosur and increased both intra-regional and overall trade.

Year	Imports	Exports	Balance
1990	1,193	959	–234
1991	1,275	737	–538
1992	1,237	657	–580
1993	1,478	725	–752
1994	2,140	817	–1,323
1995	2,782	919	–1,862
1996	2,851	1,043	–1,807
1997	3,099	1,143	–1,956
1998	2,471	1,014	–1,456
1999	1,725	741	–984
2000	2,038	852	–1,186

Source: BCP Informe sobre Comercio Exterior, 2001.

Table 2. Registered Trade Balance (in $millions).

Exports

As indicated by Table 2, over the past decade, while Paraguay has almost doubled its imports in real terms, mainly in consumer goods, thus underlining its historical tendency towards importation, exports have stagnated, despite a brief rise between 1996–98. Within these figures there are some interesting developments, including the growth of non-traditional exports (dairy products, fruit and vegetables and clothing) from 14.8% of the total in 1985 to 33% of the total in 1996.[12]

---

12   Masi, op. cit.: 15.

Paraguay in Mercosur: ¿Para qué?

Most importantly, the share of intra-regional exports to Mercosur increased dramatically from 35% of the total in 1991 to 63% in 2000,[13] with Brazil accounting for 62% of Paraguay's exports to Mercosur and 39% of total registered exports.[14] If unregistered exports were to be included, this figure would be far higher.

It should be noted that a central benefit of membership of Mercosur was to be access not only to regional markets but world markets, with a corresponding increase in trade. While trade to Mercosur rose by 41% between 1990 and 2000, trade to the rest of the world fell by roughly the same figure, 45.5%.[15] This indicates that rather than an increase in overall exports, Mercosur has led to a diversion to intra-regional trade. Likewise, a decrease in imports from the rest of the world has accompanied the increase in imports from Mercosur, again suggesting a diversion of trade. Paradoxically, the result has been a change from a commercial balance with Mercosur (although not in overall trade terms) of plus $US12 million in 1990 to a deficit of $583 million in 1999 and of $US536 million in 2000.[16]

Paraguay not only has the lowest increase in exports to Mercosur among member countries but is also the only member to register a decrease in exports to the rest of the world.[17] After a decade within Mercosur, Paraguay's export profile may have changed in terms of target markets, but the quantity of its exports has fallen, suggesting stagnation rather than growth.

The distortions of free trade within the region have contributed to the problem of decreasing exports. Brazil and Argentina have repeatedly erected legal obstacles to prevent the entry on an equal footing of certain Paraguayan non-traditional exports, ranging from fruit to tyres. A legacy of a culture of protectionism, informal protection has gone largely unpunished in the absence of a supranational arbitration body to resolve such issues.

---

13 Ibid: 14.
14 BCP, op. cit.: 4.
15 Ibid.
16 Ibid.
17 Masi, op.cit.: 120.

Unregistered trade

According to Banco Central de Paraguay (BCP) figures Paraguay has run a trade deficit since 1990, yet World Bank figures show that Paraguay has maintained a trade balance. The cause of the difference is not simply conflicting figures, but rather that the BCP records only show registered trade, while the World Bank includes unregistered trade, or contraband. Traditionally, Paraguay has carved out a competitive advantage as a regional intermediary for products from the rest of world, benefiting from the development of triangular trade in products from Brazil and South East Asia, due to high tariffs among its neighbours. Indeed, contraband has traditionally played a major role in offsetting trade imbalance.

Despite government measures since 1989 to reduce unregistered trade, it remained a main characteristic of the economy in the first half of the 1990s, representing approximately 45% of trade. However, since 1996, when Argentina and Brazil lowered tariffs on goods to 10%, combined with greater efforts to control contraband by the Brazilian authorities, unregistered trade has dropped to approximately 20% of the total.[18] A common tariff might have meant the lowering of tariffs for Argentina and Brazil, but for Paraguay it meant raising traditionally low tariffs (with obvious effects on imports), thus undermining its comparative advantage in triangular trade.

The fall in unregistered trade, which decreased by 29% in 2000, has serious implications for the Paraguayan economy.[19] This will become even more serious when full customs union comes into effect in 2006, spelling the end of triangular trade, and even of commercial balance. Although unregistered trade is not ideal in terms of loss of tax revenues, it has represented a form of comparative advantage that Paraguay developed over its neighbours, and upon which its economic balance became dependent. However, rather than seeking to radically restructure its economy or develop an alternative economic strategy in the light of such imminent trends, Paraguay has continued to operate as a (declining) regional trade intermediary to offset its commercial

18   BCP, op.cit.: 7.
19   Ibid: 2.

deficit.[20] Paradoxically, while the loss of triangular trade will inevitably have significant implications upon the Paraguayan economy, the image of Paraguay as a contraband haven remains.

Investment

A key attraction of Mercosur was a potential growth in FDI, attracted by Paraguay's natural resources, energy resources (principally Itaipu), low taxation levels, low inflation and a cheap and flexible workforce.[21] It was hoped that increases in investment would stimulate exports. Two laws covering promotion of investment (60/90), and exports (90/90), and the establishment of an Industrial Development Fund and a Peasant Development Fund were implemented under the Rodríguez administration to further encourage investment.

However, results were disappointing. Between 1990 and 1996 FDI grew by 2.5% while investment in other Mercosur members grew by over 10%, in part driven by privatisation.[22] There was, however, little evidence that this small increase was connected to Paraguayan membership of Mercosur. Between 1996 and 2000 FDI increased initially, only to fall drastically following the 1998 recession, resulting in recuperation of 1995 levels only in 2000. Significantly, FDI, which represents less than 2% of the GDP, has been concentrated in the non-traded construction and services sectors rather than the agricultural sector, thus having little important or lasting impact on the financing of export production or the expansion of productive capacity. To an

---

20   Although it does not represent an alternative economy strategy, the establishment of *maquilas* producing mainly electrical goods, clothes, chemicals and electrodomestics in the Central Region, is officially being put forward as such. While the benefits, apart from employment, remain uncertain, Paraguay is seeking to promote its image as a centre of cheap labour and low taxation within Mercosur.

21   Social and labour obligations in the Paraguayan Labour Code are significantly less demanding than the equivalents in Argentina, Brazil and Uruguay.

22   Dionisio Borda, 'Economía y estado en transición', in *Mercosur, Integración e Identidades*, Asunción: AEP, 1995.

even greater extent than its neighbours, FDI in Paraguay has been directed not towards extra-regional or even regional exports but towards the exploitation of domestic markets.

The disappointing levels and nature of investment have a number of possible causes. The most apparent is the weakness of Paraguay's infrastructure. Transport, communications, and coverage in terms of electricity, water and sanitation are the most underdeveloped in the region. Nor have they been improved significantly in the past decade, due to a decrease in public and private infrastructure development. Paraguay also has the worst regional indicators in terms of per capita income levels, education and healthcare, with only 11% of students finishing secondary education, and 47% having only primary education.[23] The result is that Paraguay lacks the basic levels of labour skills, communications and infrastructure to attract greater FDI. Meanwhile, domestic investment has been further discouraged by high interest rates which averaged 32.7% per year between 1990 and 1998 and rose to 35% in 2000.[24]

This has been exacerbated by a number of other features. Despite the dominance of the Colorado Party during the past decade, political instability has been constant, with the ruling party plagued by factionalism. The three bouts of political instability (1996, 1999 and 2000), have been almost permanently accompanied by fears of imminent military intervention. In the most serious of these cases, in March 1999 the Vice President Luís María Argaña was assassinated, leading to the flight of President Cubas Grau and the political strongman, Lino Oviedo, to Brazil. Since then, the government of González Macchi has been widely criticised for weakness, inefficiency and the inability to return stability to Paraguayan politics. In 2001 rumours of a possible coup and civil unrest continue to abound in Paraguay.

A further problem is that of the growth of institutionalised corruption which pervades Paraguayan society from the top echelons,

23 Dionisio Borda and Fernando Masi, 'Repercusiones del Mercosur sobre la economía paraguaya', in CADEP (ed.), *Estabilización y Ajuste de las Economías del Mercosur*, Asunción, Paraguay: CADEP, 1997: 112.
24 Figures from Masi, op. cit: 6, and Cámara de Comercio E Industria Paraguayo-Francesa, *Informe Anual*, Asunción: Cámara de Comercio E Industria Paraguayo-Francesa, 2000: 1.

Paraguay in Mercosur: ¿Para qué?

and is especially rife in the unreformed state sector. While this has its roots in the period of authoritarian rule under General Stroessner, it has grown since 1989 (Nickson 1997), reflecting the power of entrenched authoritarian enclaves in Paraguay's democracy. Ex-president Wasmosy is among many ex-officials currently facing accusations of corruption, while in 1998 Paraguay was rated as the most corrupt country in the world, bar Cameroon.[25] The reputation of Paraguay not only as underdeveloped and politically unstable, but also as a centre of corruption, goes far in explaining the low level of FDI.

The political advantages

The formation of Mercosur has had some positive political benefits on the regional level. The Protocol of Ushuaia signed in 1996, specifically demands that members adhere to internal democracy as a political system, and that a return to authoritarianism will not be tolerated. For nations which have emerged from particularly brutal military and authoritarian regimes in the past twenty years, forming part of a democratic bloc does offer a greater degree of protection of human rights, Rule of Law and democratic government, as well as a deterrent against support for a military coup, than if they were acting on an individual level. This has been seen as particularly relevant in the Paraguayan case, given the high level of political instability, the weakness of democratic government and the almost constant rumours of impending military coups. Indeed, in the three coup attempts in Paraguay of 1996, 1999 and 2000, the role of Mercosur partners in taking a strong stance in favour of democracy has been seen as decisive.

However, while the Mercosur partners stand united in support of democracy, hopes for an intra-regional hard-line policy against the threat of a resurgence of authoritarianism have been undermined. President Stroessner still has asylum and protection in Brazil despite

25 See Transparency International 1998 Corruption Perception Listings.

efforts by the Paraguayan authorities to deport him. The same is the case for ex-President Cubas Grau who fled to Brazil after his alleged involvement in the assassination of vice-president Argaña in 1999. Lino Oviedo, perhaps the greatest threat to democratic consolidation in Paraguay during the latter part of the 1990s, used his connections with the pervasive Mercosur mafias to gain asylum in Menem's Argentina for his alleged role in the same assassination. When Fernando de la Rúa won the presidential elections in 2000, sensing deportation, Oviedo 'escaped' house arrest and successfully sought asylum in Brazil, although extradition proceedings continue. This suggests that, despite the rhetoric regarding a democratic consensus, Mercosur is not pursuing a political role in favour of democracy to the extent that it could.

Given this, it is appropriate to ask what kind of democracy Mercosur, and especially Brazil, is defending through the Protocol of Ushuaia. Given the ambiguous stance towards anti-democratic elements in Paraguay by both Argentina and especially Brazil over the past decade, it would appear that it is a minimal model of democracy which enables Mercosur to present itself internationally as a democratic bloc. Provided elections take place, democratic institutions function and Paraguay is seen internationally to conform to the procedural criteria of democracy, Mercosur neighbours will be content. The details of Paraguay's limited democracy are simply not questioned.[26]

Paraguay in Mercosur: a dwarf among giants?

The underdevelopment and lack of organised infrastructure evident in economic policy is reflected in the government response to Mercosur. Paraguay was not only slow to join Mercosur, but was also slow to respond to the organisational necessities, once a member. Before 1994, there was little policy coordination between ministries, with the

26 See Peter Lambert, 'A Decade of Electoral Democracy: Continuity, Change and Crisis in Paraguay', *Bulletin of Latin American Research*, 19(3), 2000: 378–96.

Paraguay in Mercosur: ¿Para qué? 171

Ministry of Integration vying for prestige, funding and power with those of Foreign Relations, Trade and Industry, and Finance. This was exacerbated by a lack of continuity of personnel in key positions, as decisions based on political immediacy and preference took priority over ability, a situation exacerbated by under-funding in key areas, including training. Although this serious problem seemed to have been addressed by giving overall authority to the Ministry of Integration after 1994, the issue resurfaced when the Ministry was closed down altogether in 1999.

The result has been predictable. Paraguay has been ineffective in obtaining concessions in negotiations with well-trained and well-organised representatives from other member states, which have followed a detailed integration strategy. This is especially the case with the failure of Paraguayan demands for the lifting of illegal anti-competition measures implemented by Argentina and Brazil against Paraguayan products, the involvement of Brazil in environmental destruction (such as illegal logging by Brazilian companies in Paraguay) and the establishment of regional development funds, to compensate and develop the Paraguayan economy. The fundamental problem, however, remains the serious failure of the Paraguayan government to coordinate a national policy on regional integration. By 2001, a decade after the Treaty of Asunción, there was still no such policy.[27]

From its launch, Mercosur has never been a union among equals. Instead it is dominated and pushed forward by Brazil, which possibly has its own agenda in staking out a strong position as head of a democratic bloc in a possible Free Trade Association of the Americas against the US.[28] There are two major results of this. Firstly, the Paraguayan economy, historically linked to that of Brazil, has become even more structurally dependent on its neighbour. Economic growth in the early 1990s was linked to growth in Brazil, while recession was closely linked to the Brazilian economic crisis of 1998. Brazil accounts for 39% of the total of Paraguayan registered exports, but this figure

27 Interview with Juan Buffa, Vice-Minister for International Relations, Asunción, 8 January 2001.
28 See 'Pan-American Free Trade: Slow, but Ahead,' *The Economist*, 24 May 1997: 35.

increases to 70% of total exports if non-registered trade is included.[29] Any variations in economic growth in Brazil have immediate effects on Paraguay, especially in triangular trade which has a more elastic demand. This is not just limited to economic growth. The recent expansion of Brazilian cotton seriously damaged Paraguayan exports, while Brazil's aim of achieving self-sufficiency in this area will have significant effects on the Paraguayan economic model

Secondly, economic dependency is linked to political domination by Brazil. Having already secured extremely favourable prices for the purchase of electricity from Paraguay's share of Itaipu, Brazil has maintained a policy of giving little while insisting on concessions from Paraguay. For example, Brazilian pressure has forced Paraguay to implement measures to clean up the border city of Ciudad del Este, over which Brazil has concerns regarding security, drugs and contraband. Paraguay, however, retains only two serious bargaining tools: to refuse to sell Brazil electricity from its share of the Itaipu dam, or to withdraw from Mercosur, both of which, given the implications, would be measures of last resort. Thus, from a position of economic inferiority, Paraguay has been unable to obtain reciprocal concessions regarding further tariff exceptions, a crack-down on Brazilian logging in Paraguay, or agreements to control Brazilian migration to the Eastern Border Region.

The dominance of Brazil is a cause and consequence of a multilateral agreement in which bilateral agreements predominate and in which a supranational body to arbitrate on issues such as infringements of free trade, technical standards, and quality control is notable by its absence. Brazil can maintain tariffs to protect its sugar and automobile production, but Paraguay, despite being a sugar producer itself, cannot. This suggests a continuation of an individualistic outlook by countries within Mercosur as each member strives to put its own interests forward, even at the cost of fellow members. Both Argentina and Brazil continue to seek trade agreements with other countries, acting purely on a bilateral basis. As Paraguayan Minister of Trade and Industry, Guillermo Caballero Vargas stated

---

29   Fernando Masi, '¿A dónde va el Mercosur?', *Acción*, CEPAG, No. 203, 2000: 3.

Paraguay in Mercosur: ¿Para qué?

there is an unbearable hypocrisy: in international forums we defend the interests of the bloc to the end, but back home each country attempts to undermine the economy of its neighbour.[30]

Even more notably, despite growing economic inter-dependence there has been little progress in harmonisation and convergence of macroeconomic policy or common fiscal or monetary policies. The devaluation of the Brazilian real in January 1999, and its subsequent loss of over 40% of its value, had huge repercussions on the regional economy. In the case of Paraguay, exports to Brazil from triangular trade dropped dramatically, since by nature they have an elastic demand, aggravating the economic recession. However, Brazilian devaluation, an act which had serious ramifications throughout the region, was taken unilaterally by the Brazilian government, with no prior warning to fellow Mercosur members.

Should Paraguay remain in Mercosur?

Mercosur remains a 'virtual reality' for Paraguay, not just for the majority of the population who have not been informed or consulted, but also in terms of the promised benefits of membership.[31] Exports, rather than booming through increased access to world markets, have simply been concentrated within the region. FDI has been disappointing and it is questionable whether any increase registered has been due to membership of Mercosur. In both areas, Paraguay has been the member that has benefited least from regional integration.

There have also been some more worrying trends. Since 1991, Paraguay has concentrated its exports excessively into the regional

---

30   *El Mundo*, 19 August 1999: 4. The minister was referring to an initiative by Argentina to develop a free trade zone in Clorinda on the Paraguayan border in a direct challenge to the dominance of Paraguay in informal triangular trade. Plans were temporarily halted pending negotiations only when Paraguay threatened to pull out of Mercosur.

31   Interview with Dionisio Borda, CADEP, Asuncion, 4 January 2001.

market at the cost of more global relations, leading to a decline in trade with the rest of the world. This in turn has led to an increasing dependency not just on regional growth, but on the Brazilian economy in particular. Not only does Paraguay have little comparative advantage within Mercosur, especially given its inability to replicate the economies of scale available in Brazil, but its comparative advantage in triangular trade has been undermined by customs union, and is set to disappear in 2006.

The 1999 real crisis led to questions being raised within Paraguay, not just regarding its increasing dependency on Brazil, but also of its membership of Mercosur, the increased economic vulnerability it possibly produces and the lack of apparent benefits. Increasingly, concerns are being expressed which argue that the concentration on economic relations with Mercosur had been at the cost of increased relations with more lucrative economic partners, such as the US, Europe and Asia.[32] In effect, Paraguay should be looking to exploit its comparative advantage at a global level, rather than a regional one.

Paraguay remains a passive and junior member of Mercosur, with little bargaining power. Moreover, it has yet to see the promised benefits of membership. As a result, the only justification for continued membership of Mercosur in its present form is that it presents the lesser of two evils, or in the words of the vice minister of Foreign Relations 'we are in Mercosur because we have no choice.'[33] This does not suggest a long term commitment to membership of the bloc as it presently stands, and indicates that unless Mercosur actively seeks to address issues relating to regional development, the long term future of the bloc will remain uncertain.

---

[32] A recent study by Venezuelan consultant Laura Rojas, working with the IMF, argued precisely this point. See ABC, 5 March 2001.
[33] Interview with Juan Buffa, Vice Minister of Foreign Relations, Asunción 8 January 2001.

A strategy for a less painful Mercosur

National strategies

Paradoxically, Paraguay with previously the most open and balanced economy has benefited the least from regional integration among the members of Mercosur. Mercosur has clearly not been a springboard to economic growth, as the six straight years of negative per capita GDP growth reflect. However, it would be mistaken to view Paraguay simply as a victim among powerful neighbours. Much of its current position of weakness within Mercosur stems from national failings, most significantly the unreformed nature of its state and economy. As we have seen, the Paraguayan economic model based on the export of two primary materials, triangular trade and short-term speculation is clearly exhausted, and obsolete in a regional common market. If Paraguay is to survive within Mercosur as more than the junior member as a producer of increasingly uncompetitive raw materials and a supply of cheap labour, internal reforms must be undertaken.

Firstly, macroeconomic stability is important but it is no longer sufficient without investment in the productive sector. The current model of high interest rates and limited access to credit has allowed industrial and agricultural sectors to stagnate, with little investment in modernisation and technology. In the 1997 list of products to be exempted from a common tariff, finished goods for re-export were included, while manufactured goods were not. This reflects a greater government emphasis on a dying triangular trade over the productive sector, a policy that is clearly short-term and unsustainable.

Given the dangers of an increased reliance on regional markets and the fall of exports to world markets, Paraguay needs not only to increase its competitiveness on a regional level but also to diversify its markets on a global level. Intra-Mercosur trade might have quadrupled since its creation, but it has fallen since 1998 and amounts to only 20.7% of the total.[34] Paraguay needs to follow the example of its Mercosur partners and expand trade towards the European Union, the

---

34 'Another Blow to the Americas', *The Economist*, 3 March 2001: 67.

US and Asia. Since Paraguay's trade with the rest of the world has fallen since 1990, such a strategy needs positive government investment in export promotion bodies such as Proparaguay, and also encouragement of sectorial alliances within the private export sector.

The weakness of Paraguayan infrastructure has discouraged investment. Paraguay is simply not competitive on a regional basis given the weakness of its transport infrastructure (road, rail, river and air), its low level of telecommunications and more importantly its low coverage in electricity, water supply and drainage. Among these, the case of energy supply is the most worrying. Paraguay has not only allowed Brazil to negotiate low prices for electricity generated by Itaipu, but has failed to use the energy generated to either promote industrial development or even connect the country. Indeed, despite the proceeds and resources from one of the world's most powerful hydroelectric dams, the national electricity company, ANDE, is currently in deficit.

Despite promises, progress in infrastructure development has been slow. Clearly substantial investment needs to be made and orchestrated by government and where possible in collaboration with private funding. Such a major project would need improvements in government tax collection. Despite a tax reform in 1992, income stands at just 10% of the GDP, suggesting low taxation rates and high levels of evasion. Moreover, there is still no personal income tax in Paraguay. Tax reform, currently stagnating due to political wrangling, needs to be pushed through as a matter of urgency.

If Paraguay is to shed its image of corruption and inefficiency, thorough, transparent and effective state reform is necessary, to create a democratic and efficient state sector. The sector did increase by 33.5% in terms of personnel in the 1990s, but without a parallel increase in efficiency or professionalisation[35] it has become clear that it is yet to be affected by democratic change. Instead, it remains institutionally weak, characterised by poor planning and organisation, a lack of transparency and efficiency, low levels of training and frequent changes in personnel. Equally important, it remains a centre of *prebendarismo* and corruption, both fuelled by its close links to the ruling Colorado Party. Measures to

---

35   In 1989 there were 114,227 employees in the state sector. By 2000 this number had risen to 152,518 (CCIPF, 2000: 3).

introduce a substantial state reform programme have been slow and plagued by obstructionism by vested interests, chiefly from within the Colorado Party. Likewise, the judicial sector, despite reform in 1995, has shown little progress in efficiency and speed in dealing with cases, especially regarding corruption.

Finally, if Paraguay is to advance beyond offering itself as a pool of cheap, unskilled labour, educational reform is essential. Government spending on education has increased significantly since 1989, but without significant results in terms of enrolment and completion of further and higher education, since most investment has been spent on wages and increased personnel, rather than infrastructure. In higher education, the government has sought to resolve the traditionally limited number of university places in the two traditional universities in Asunción, by allowing a plethora of private, unregulated universities to establish themselves. As yet there has been no concerted reform of education at any level, suggesting that Paraguay still has far to go before it can encourage investment in industries reliant on skilled labour.

Regional Strategies

While many of the problems regarding Paraguay's position in Mercosur are due to internal insufficiencies, the continuation of Mercosur as a regional bloc is simply not viable unless it commits itself to reforms aimed to deepen rather than merely broaden the process of integration. The relaunch of Mercosur in April 2000 did make modest progress in agreements to harmonise economic statistics and to set common macroeconomic targets, but it failed to agree on common policy on eliminating either exceptions to the common tariff, or non tariff barriers (such as technical standards, health and safety and quality control). More significantly, it failed to create a Mercosur disputes-settlement body, to arbitrate in case of infringements of free trade. Brazil may argue that such bodies would imply a loss of its sovereignty, but they are fundamental to the future of Mercosur.

Most importantly, Mercosur needs to reconsider the issue of preferential treatment towards weaker economies within the trade bloc, on the grounds of comparative underdevelopment. This is essential in the case of Paraguay's productive sectors that will not be able to compete with rivals from the larger and more developed economies of the other members. In order to transform and modernise its economic model, to be able to create more equal competition and to share the benefits of Mercosur, Paraguay will need significant regional and social compensation. However, to date, efforts to create a regional development fund on the lines of the European model have been blocked, principally by Brazil. This is a key issue and one upon which its future development within Mercosur is dependent. Unless Mercosur reforms its present policy towards Paraguay from *'maltrato diferencial'* into *'tratamiento preferencial'*, the benefits of Mercosur to Paraguay will remain limited.

Conclusion

Membership of Mercosur has not led to a change in the model of economic development. Instead, Paraguay has maintained its role as an exporter of primary agricultural goods and an intermediary in triangular trade, an unsustainable model which is incompatible with forthcoming full customs union and which damages national development possibilities. Nor have the promises of increased trade opportunities, access to new markets, and greater international profile, materialised. Exports have been concentrated rather than increased, FDI has been disappointing and economic growth has stagnated. Paraguay has benefited least among the members of Mercosur, and the future remains uncertain, especially since in 2006 remaining tariffs will be harmonised, effecting not least Paraguay's triangular trade. In economic terms the present and future benefits remain unclear.

The above does not necessarily mean that the potential for benefits cannot be attained in the future. Mercosur does offer the potential to expand exports, increase investment and obtain greater economic development. In order to do this Paraguay needs to implement major reforms of its economic model, its infrastructure and its state, as part of a long term strategy of regional integration. Given the track record since 1989, this is unlikely to happen in the short term. Despite the transition to democracy, there has been a lack of fundamental political change in key areas such as state reform, political corruption, Colorado Party hegemony, and the nature of politics. While politics remains a means by which to control the state and its assets for personal and party political benefit, there is little incentive for governments to invest in forward-looking public policy initiatives and reforms for the national interest.

However, the success of domestic reform also depends on regional reform. Mercosur will continue to fail until it accepts the necessity of its role to combat corruption, encourage the growth of civil society and develop regional democracy. Equally importantly, if Mercosur is to succeed, it needs to urgently reconsider the establishment of supranational bodies to coordinate economic development, offer arbitration, and harmonise competitive advantage and establish a regional development fund to finance reform, aid development and reduce socio-economic disparities in Paraguay and within the region. Unless such a major change of policy takes place and such wide-ranging reforms are implemented, Paraguay will continue to *'figurar como florero'* and receive minimal benefits from membership. More importantly, not only Paraguayans, but others will increasingly ask the question of *'Mercosur: ¿para qué?'*

Suranjit Kumar Saha

Core-Periphery in the Americas: Understanding the Political Economy of Mercosur and FTAA

Introduction

The Rio Grande divides the American landmass into a rich northern part and a poor southern part. In 1999, the southern part, i.e. Latin America, accounted for 62.6% of the Western Hemisphere's population, but only 17.9% of its gross domestic product. The northern part, i.e. the US and Canada, accounted for 37.4% of its population but as much as 82.1% of its GDP.[1] The United States alone, with only one-third of the hemisphere's population, accounted for more than three-quarters of its GDP. The annual per capita income of the United States was US$30,600; that of Canada US$19,320. The average per capita income in Latin America was, on the other hand, only US$3,840, ranging from US$430 in Nicaragua to US$7,600 in Argentina. The United States and Canada are members of the Organisation of Economic Cooperation and Development (OECD) and of the G7 and are, therefore, at the very core of global capitalism, while Latin America is part of the periphery of that system. Any project for building a trading bloc that embraces the whole hemisphere has to take into account this fundamental asymmetry.

In 1988, the United States and Canada joined together to form a free trade area. Mexico also joined this bloc in 1993 and in January 1994 the North American Free Trade Area (NAFTA) was launched. Mexico, with a per capita income of only US$4,400 in 1999 or one-seventh that of the United States, joined the rich man's club as a poor relative. The dominant core countries thus unite into one trading bloc,

---

1   *Direction of Trade Statistics*, Washington, DC: International Monetary Fund, 2000.

drawing into its fold a part of the periphery as well, while the rest of the periphery remained fragmented.

Historically, the countries of Latin America and the Caribbean have been more open to Europe and to the United States than to each other. Until as late as the first half of the twentieth century, little effort was made to build complementarities and common interests amongst these economies. However, things began to change with the signing of the Treaty of Rome and the establishment of the European Common Market in 1957. There was a growing realisation in the intellectual circles of Latin America that the continent's economies needed to work together to gain some collective strength in dealing with the rest of the world. Among the relatively ineffectual efforts to build trading blocs within Latin America were the Latin American Association of Free Trade (Associación Latinoamericana de Libre Comercio – ALALC), followed by the Association of Latin American Integration (Associación Latinoamericana de Integración – ALADI) which operated from 1960 to 1980. In addition, there are the Caribbean Common Market (CARICOM), which currently has 14 members and the Andean Pact, launched in 1969, which includes Bolivia, Colombia, Ecuador, Peru and Venezuela. Mercosur is the only trading bloc south of Mexico's southern border which shows the potential to effectively negotiate with the dominant core countries of the United States and Canada on the basis of collective strength. The significant point about emerging free trade negotiations between the core and the periphery in the Americas is that the core is now firmly united in NAFTA, whereas the periphery is fragmented into several blocs, only one of which is showing some signs of effectiveness.

The vision of Latin America-wide economic integration now faces the rival vision of hemisphere-wide integration led by the United States, i.e. that of the Free Trade Area of the Americas (FTAA). Most Latin American intellectuals and politicians seem to agree that the continent needs to emerge as an economic power in its own right and make a clean break from its historic role as the backyard of North American economic and foreign policies. Smaller Latin American countries, however, seem to fear domination by the larger ones more than they do that of the United States. Cutting through this kaleidoscope of conflicting national rivalries, the long-term vision of a Latin

American economic entity free from domination by outside powers, lives on.

The concept of core (or centre) and periphery was first introduced in development economics by American scholars way back in the 1950s and 1960s as a means for understanding the problem of persistent regional disparities within and between nation states.[2] Their common conclusion was that poorer countries and poorer regions within countries are not likely to benefit from interacting with richer countries on the basis of unregulated market forces. Myrdal puts the idea across succinctly:

> That there is a tendency inherent in the free play of market forces to create regional inequalities and that this tendency becomes the more dominant the poorer the country is, are two of the most important laws of economic underdevelopment and development under *laissez faire*.[3]

The moral that Myrdal and other proponents of the spatial disequilibrium thesis derive from these 'laws' is that the states of the periphery have a duty not to leave their economic relationships with richer countries entirely in the hands of market forces, but to regulate those forces in ways that they may, on balance, function to their advantage and not entirely to the advantage of the richer countries.

The actual definition of the core-periphery concept in any given context is, of course, subject to an infinite regression of relative situations. In the Americas, the United States is without doubt the core country *par excellence* in view of its hegemonic power and dominance. In South America, however, Brazil seems to be a core country to most of the other nations of the continent. Smaller and economically weaker countries like Uruguay and Paraguay are likely to consider even the middle-sized Argentina a powerful and dominant core country.

---

2   Gunnar Myrdal, *Economic Theory and Under-Developed Regions*, London: Gerald Duckworth, 1957; Alberto O. Hirschman, *The Strategy of Economic Development*, New Haven: Yale University Press, 1958; J. Friedmann, *Regional Development Policy: The Case Study of Venezuela*, Cambridge, MA: MIT Press, 1966.

3   Myrdal, 1957: 85.

This paper seeks to argue that the key challenge in the Americas today is to manage two sets of core periphery relationships effectively.

- Between the United States on the one hand and the rest of the hemisphere on the other (Canada and Mexico will be more likely to be on the side of the United States in this equation than on the side of the 'rest'), and,
- Between the larger countries of South America on the one hand and the smaller ones on the other.

The two parts of this challenge are inextricably interrelated. If the FTAA is to work for the benefit of all the peoples of the Americas, it cannot just be built on the unquestioning acceptance of US hegemony by the rest of the hemisphere. South America needs to protect its economic independence and consolidate its social foundations of technology generation and capacity building, which alone are the real guarantees of its long-term economic strength and competitiveness.

At the same time, South American countries cannot acquire effective negotiating strength in their talks with the United States unless they are able to reconcile and harmonise rivalries and contradictions of interests amongst themselves.

Mercosur vs FTAA: in search of economic integration without hegemony

On 26 March 2001, the Common Market of the Southern Cone (Mercosur) celebrated its 10th anniversary in a low-key ceremony at Montevideo which none of the presidents of its four member countries attended. Less than a month later, on 20 April, the third Summit for the Americas took place in Quebec City inaugurated by a grand ceremony in which thirty four heads of states and governments, representing the entire landmass of the Western Hemisphere, participated. Cuba was not invited to this summit, as had been the case in the earlier two summits.

During the ten years of its existence, Mercosur has certainly achieved success in terms of boosting trade among its four member states. The total volume of intra-Mercosur exports had increased fivefold since its establishment – from US$4 billion in 1990 to US$20.1 billion in 1998. More recently, this volume has, however, declined to US$15.5 billion in 1999, rising again to US$18.5 billion in 2000. Intra-Mercosur trade, however, continues to account for a relatively small part of the bloc's exports. In 1999, the total volume of its exports stood at US$74.3 billion, of which only 20.7% was intra-trade.[4] In 1990, only 9% of their exports and 15% of their imports formed part of intra-trade. In 1998, 25% of their exports and 21% of their imports was intra-trade. The proportion of total exports going to industrialised countries has fallen substantially during the same period, from 61% to 45%. The proportion of imports from industrialised countries during the period has, however, remained about the same: 57% in 1990 and 56% in 1998. For Uruguay and Paraguay, however, their Mercosur partners are now far more important trading partners than the industrialised countries. Brazil and Argentina, on the other hand, are continuing to trade with industrialised countries to a much greater extent than they do with each other or with the other two Mercosur countries. Brazil sends only 17% of its exports to the other three Mercosur countries and draws only 15% of its imports from them. The corresponding figures for Argentina are 36% and 25% respectively. Between the two larger member countries, Mercosur appears to be of much greater importance as an export market to Argentina than to Brazil (see Tables 1 and 2).

The FTAA project, the idea of a free market extending across the whole of the Western Hemisphere, emerged from the Enterprise of the Americas Initiative, proposed by President George Bush Sr. in June 1990. It was given the shape of a concrete agenda for negotiations by his successor Bill Clinton in the first Summit for the Americas held in December 1994 in Miami. The Declaration of Principles agreed at that summit states:

> For the first time in history, the Americas are a community of democratic societies, united in pursuing prosperity through open markets, hemispheric integration, and sustainable development. We are determined to consolidate and

4 *The Economist*, 31 March 2001.

advance closer bonds of cooperation and to transform our aspirations into concrete realities.[5]

	Share of exports in 1990				Share of exports in 1998			
	Brazil	Argentina	Uruguay	Paraguay	Brazil	Argentina	Uruguay	Paraguay
Brazil		11.52	29.25	29.35		30.12	33.77	28.10
Argentina	2.05		4.74	5.17	13.19		18.53	25.60
Uruguay	0.94	1.19		1.13	1.72	3.19		1.21
Paraguay	1.21	2.13	0.35		2.44	2.32	3.03	
Mercosur	4.20	14.84	34.34	35.65	17.35	35.63	55.33	54.91
Industrialised countries	68.07	49.74	38.61	37.54	54.70	29.87	24.77	29.39

Source: IMF, 2000.

Table 1. Direction of exports of Mercosur member countries: 1990 and 1998.

	Share of imports in 1990				Share of imports in 1998			
	Brazil	Argentina	Uruguay	Paraguay	Brazil	Argentina	Uruguay	Paraguay
Brazil		17.61	23.01	16.95		22.57	20.82	34.80
Argentina	6.72		16.86	12.37	12.96		22.03	16.83
Uruguay	2.64	2.84		0.74	1.69	1.66		2.34
Paraguay	1.49	1.03	1.14		0.56	1.11	0.42	
Mercosur	10.85	21.48	41.00	30.06	15.22	25.34	43.28	53.97
Industrialised countries	55.49	58.90	34.93	43.82	58.63	54.42	36.16	32.49

Source: IMF, 2000.

Table 2. Sources of imports of Mercosur member countries: 1990 and 1998.

The third Summit for the Americas, which took place in Quebec City from 20 to 22 April 2001, adopted a declaration, which spelled out the following vision in its first paragraph:

> We, the democratically elected Heads of State and Government of the Americas, have met in Quebec City at our Third Summit, to renew our commitment to

5   AmericasCanada.org, 2001.

hemispheric integration and national and collective responsibility for improving the economic wellbeing and security of our people. We have adopted a Plan of Action to strengthen representative democracy, promote good governance and protect human rights and fundamental freedoms. We seek to create greater prosperity and expand economic opportunities while fostering social justice and the realisation of human potential.[6]

Despite the lofty ideals stated in the declaration, Latin American intellectuals, particularly the Brazilians, have long been suspicious of US enthusiasm for the FTAA. They are unsure whether the Monroe doctrine of 1823, which regarded the continent as the backyard of US interests, is really not still alive and well in the minds of contemporary US policy makers. The fundamental economic reality is that the US and Canada together comprise 82% of the total GDP of the FTAA, the four Mercosur countries another 10% and the remaining 8% is shared among the twenty-eight other countries of the hemisphere. Any arrangement for a common economic bloc that does not take into account this glaring disparity in the wealth and income distribution of its members, cannot be said to be built on solid ground.

The main attraction of the FTAA for Latin American countries is that it will be a mechanism for low or zero tariff entry of their exports into the lucrative US market. A Brazilian economist called such expectations 'a false glitter'.[7] He points out that average tariff rates are already considerably lower in the US (less than 3%) than in Brazil (14%). But it is not tariff barriers which have been consistently keeping Brazilian exports like steel products, orange juice, shoes and other leather goods and textiles out of the US market, but a whole plethora of non tariff barriers like anti dumping laws and a network of hidden subsidies given to the farming and other sectors. The US has an immense, complex and well-entrenched apparatus of laws, regulatory regimes and institutional arrangements to 'adjust' free trade to its own advantage, and Latin American negotiators have very little experience or expertise in steering focused discussion towards these crucial matters. Negotiations are more likely to focus on improving quotas for

---

6   AmericasCanada.org, 2001.
7   Mercadante, Alizo, 'ALCA: mais de mesmo', *Folha de São Paulo, Caderno de Dinheiro*, 15 April 2001: B-2.

products like orange juice, tobacco and sugar, the effect of which will be to encourage the continued concentration of Brazilian and other Latin American exports into primary products. This will perpetuate Latin America's technological dependence and will also tie the fate of its economies to stagnant and volatile commodity prices. Reduction of tariff barriers, another natural outcome of the FTAA negotiations, will also bring asymmetrical advantages to the US. Latin American countries will lose the capacity to protect strategic sectors of their economies which they need to consolidate in order to close the technology gap, while the US will continue to practice protectionism via non tariff barriers. The crucial issue is this:

> For us the major question relates to the incompatibility of the FTAA in terms of the way it is being proposed. It bears on our strategic interests, in other words, on the preservation of our capacity and autonomy to construct our own future, which refers to the economic, social, political and cultural necessities and preferences of our people. This is the centre of the problem. The rest is accessory.[8]

This is how Mercadante sees the challenge:

> Brazil needs to value its self-respect as people [...] (and) lead the resistance to the expansionist policy of the United States inaugurated in the 19th century with the Monroe doctrine of 1823, when it proclaimed itself the guardian of the American continent.[9]

Rubens Ricupero, the Secretary General of UNCTAD and Brazil's Inland Revenue Minister in the Itamar Franco government, argues that the current approach to FTAA negotiations is fundamentally slanted against Latin America and makes a strong case for 'balancing the game' *(equilibrando o jogo)*. He points out that Brazil has strong competitive advantages in the export of steel, shoes and other leather goods, orange juice, sugar, tobacco and other agricultural products. These are precisely the items to which the US is applying anti-dumping measures or unfairly favouring their own farmers by various kinds of subsidies, seeking to keep them out of the arena of negotiations. On the other hand, the US is looking to focus negotiations on intellectual property

---

8 Ibid: B-2.
9 Ibid: B-2.

Understanding the Political Economy of Mercosur and FTAA 189

rights, trade in services and government purchases, the areas in which Latin America does not currently enjoy competitive advantage and therefore needs protection. Ricupero characterises this US attitude as one of: 'what is mine is mine, what is yours, is negotiable'. The result is: 'exports entering the FTAA would be those in which we are weak and have no competitive strength; those in which we are competitive and the Americans have problems, would be kept excluded from it'. His case is this: 'We must find a way to stimulate everybody's commitment to look for a more inclusive world system which makes the present asymmetric game a little more even'.[10]

Nearly all sectors and branches of Brazil's economy and civil society have expressed worries regarding the creation of the FTAA, though not all of the same kind. In a recent survey of views from different segments of Brazilian industry, the Associação Brasileira de Agribusiness (ABAG) which represents large-scale mechanised farmers, welcomed the FTAA but demanded that the US discontinue subsidies to its farmers, pointing out that in December 1999, the US congress approved US$78.1 billion of financial assistance to the farming sector for the financial year 2000–1, making it impossible for Brazilian farmers to compete on a fair basis.[11] Associations representing various branches of the Brazilian farming sector said that they had no problem in competing with US farmers and mill owners, but that the US must bring down current high tariff levels against such key Brazilian products as orange juice, beef, pork, chicken, sugar, alcohol, timber, coffee and tobacco. Associations representing cloth-making, garment and knitwear branches of the textile industry also expressed confidence in their own competitive strength, pointing out that it was the US and not Brazil which feared free trade and open competition in these areas. The US must phase out the quota regimes in these products before the FTAA becomes a reality. Brazil's steel industry also considered itself more efficient and competitive than its US

---

10 Rubens Ricupero, 'Equilibrando o jogo', *Folha de São Paulo, Caderno Folha Dinheiro*, 15 April 2001: B-2.
11 The current figure for agricultural subsidies in the US is about $500 billion.

counterpart, but its major problem resided in the US anti-dumping laws which were being unfairly imposed on its products.[12]

Brazil and Argentina within Mercosur: conflicting fears of domination

Good bilateral economic and political relations between Brazil and Argentina are of course essential prerequisites for Mercosur to function effectively, or indeed survive. The two countries together comprise 96.2% of Mercosur's combined population and 97.2% of its GDP. At the same time, Brazil's population is four and half times larger than Argentina's; its GDP, three and a quarter times larger. It is therefore natural that an undercurrent of rivalry and the fear of domination in the minds of Argentine policy makers will always characterise all projects of collaboration between the two countries. Brazilian policy makers need to understand this and show sensitivity towards it. Effective management of this undercurrent will always need to be a core requirement for the good management of Mercosur.

A significant factor in Brazil Argentina bilateral relations is that Brazil is a great deal more important to Argentina as a trading partner than Argentina is to Brazil. Its volume of trade with Brazil is also much larger than that with the United States. In 2000, it exported US$6.8 billion worth of goods to Brazil, which was more than twice the value of its exports to the US (US$3 billion). Its imports from Brazil were valued at US$6.9 billion, while those from the US totalled US$5.1 billion. Brazil accounts for 25.7% of Argentina's exports and 27% of its imports; the corresponding figures for Argentina's trade with the United States are 11.3% and 20.2% respectively. For many years, Argentina has enjoyed a positive trade balance with Brazil, but

---

12   Luís Eduardo Galvão, 'Área de Livre Comércio das Américas: Ela vem aí, o Brasil está pronto', *Rumos*, 25(179), 2000: 26–33; recently the Bush administration raised protectionist barriers on the imports of steel to about 30%, Brazilian steel exports to the US been hard hit.

a negative one with the United States. For Brazil, however, the United States is a far more important trading partner than Argentina, and indeed the whole of Mercosur put together. In 2000, the US accounted for 23.5% of Brazil's exports and 23.2% of its exports imports, Mercosur, for only 13.7% and 14% respectively, much of it with Argentina. Mercosur is, therefore, much more important as a trading bloc to Argentina than to Brazil. The rest of the FTAA region, outside Mercosur and the United States, is almost as important to Brazil as its Mercosur partners with regard to its exports, but less so with regard to its imports. In relation to Argentina's international trade, the rest of the FTAA is indeed of marginal importance (see Table 3).

Destination of exports and source of imports	Brazil			
	Exports		Imports	
	US$ bn	%	US$ bn	%
Intra-Mercosur	7.7	13.7	7.8	14.0
US	13.2	23.5	12.9	23.2
Rest of FTAA	6.4	11.4	5.0	9.0
FTAA Total	27.3	48.7	25.7	46.1
World Total	56.1	100.0	55.7	100.0
Destination of exports and source of imports	Argentina			
	Exports		Imports	
	US$ bn	%	US$ bn	%
Intra-Mercosur	8.4	31.5	7.7	30.3
US	3.0	11.3	5.1	20.1
Rest of FTAA	1.2	4.5	0.3	1.2
FTAA Total	12.6	47.2	13.1	51.6
World Total	26.7	100.0	25.4	100.0

Source: IMF, 2001.

Table 3. Direction of Trade of Brazil and Argentina in 2000.

Devaluation of the Brazilian real and its effect on Brazil–Argentina relationships

When the Brazilian currency, the real, was floated on 15 January, 1999, its value dropped from 1.32 to the dollar on 13 January to 1.58 to the dollar a week later. This was not a precipitous fall by any means, but it fell further in subsequent months. The value decreased to a monthly average of 1.97 in October, rising slightly to a monthly average of 1.85

in December. The value of the real against the dollar touched an all time low of 2.80 in early October 2001, and then rose a little to 2.30 in January 2002. The Argentine peso remained pegged to the dollar at one-to-one parity throughout this period. Argentines have been complaining ever since January 1999 that the progressive devaluation of the real has been cutting into their competitiveness, not only within Mercosur, but also in the world market in general and that this was against the spirit of a common market. They have also been backing up their complaints by repeatedly invoking the possibility of dollarisation as a way out of their economic difficulties. The imposition of tariff duties by Argentina on imports of sugar, textile and iron and steel products from Brazil and by Brazil on imports of food and animal products from Argentina also emerged as serious disputes. To smooth out these growing frictions in the relationship between the two countries, Cardoso paid a state visit to Argentina on 7 June 1999, to hold the famous Quinta de Olivos summit with Menem. There, the two leaders announced their 'policy decision' to integrate macroeconomic policies, to set target dates for balancing public finances, and for harmonising rates of interest, inflation and budget deficits. Menem also used the opportunity to clarify the fact that his earlier references to dollarising Argentina was only one of several long term possibilities, and that evolving a common currency for all the Mercosur countries was another such possibility. The two leaders referred to this summit as a 'mini Maastricht'.[13]

As the Brazilian real continued to fall in relation to the US dollar, reaching an all time low of 2.80 in October 2001, it became increasingly difficult for Argentina to maintain its peso–dollar parity, a major underpinning of its monetary policy and, in Cavallo's view, also of its economic stability. On 26 October 2001, Cavallo publicly criticised Brazil for letting the real fall in value saying 'the model of trade relations with countries which are given to the luxury of doing what they wish with their currencies is now exhausted.'[14] Setting aside the normal diplomatic courtesies, Brazil's foreign minister, Celso Lafer,

---

13   Carlos Eduardo Lins da Silva, 'Mercosul pode ter seu "Maastricht"', *Folha de São Paulo, Caderno Folha Dinheiro*, 8 June 1999: 1–4.
14   Quoted in Clóvis Rossi, 'Brasil não aceita mais negociar con Cavallo', Folha de São Paulo, 29 October 2001b, A-9.

announced that his country would no longer negotiate with Argentina as long as Cavallo remained in office. De la Rúa had to step in, affirming that Mercosur was Argentina's priority state policy and distancing himself from the comments of his economy minister.

Argentina's slow descent into economic collapse

After taking power as president of Argentina on 10 December 1999, Fernando de la Rúa had to force through seven successive austerity plans, each tougher than the preceding one. Fears about imminent debt default by Argentina and doubts about the ability of de la Rúa to manage the country's economy effectively were on the increase from the time he assumed office. In October 2000, Mario Vicens, the country's treasury secretary made a dash to Washington, DC to meet IMF officials, fuelling speculation that he was seeking an additional loan on top of the US$7.2 billion standby credit already committed by the international agency. Government borrowing needs for 2001 was estimated at US$18 billion and this was at a time when international banks and investors were becoming increasingly reluctant to lend to Argentina. This raised fears that the treasury would increasingly depend on local banks for its borrowing requirements, starving the domestic economy of investment funds and consumer spending power – a recipe for the further deepening and prolonging of the recession.[15]

The last austerity package of the de la Rúa administration was launched by Domingo Cavallo, his new economy minister in April 2001, within a month of his taking up office. It aimed at achieving a zero deficit budget. This would have involved trimming total government spending by US$1.5 billion in 2001 and US$4.3billion in 2002, cutting down the salaries and pensions of central government employees by 13% over a three-month period (August–October 2001), cutting back the resource transfers to provincial governments and forcing the pension funds to exchange short term bonds for longer-term ones at a 'patriotic' interest rate. Local banks and pension funds duly complied, agreeing to swap some US$50 billion of their high-

---

15   *The Economist*, 11 November 2000.

yield bonds for longer term pieces of papers at only 7% interest, the maximum imposed by the central bank on peso loans.[16] This was to save the government US$4.5 billion in 2002.

To boost the economy out of prolonged recession, Cavallo introduced tax-breaks for industrialists and tariff cuts on imports of capital goods; with regard to machinery needed by domestic manufacturers, the tariff rate was set at zero in early April 2001. Brazil protested, claiming that this would hurt its exports of capital goods, particularly of IT and telecommunications equipment, and that losses would amount to US$620 million. Brazil's development minister, Alcides Tápias rushed to Buenos Aires for an urgent meeting with Cavallo to convey his country's concern. Cardoso cancelled his state visit to Argentina which had been planned for 16–17 April. Cavallo relented, partially by taking IT and telecommunications equipment out of the arena of the zero-tariff measure.[17]

To compensate for revenue loss, he introduced a 35% tariff on consumer goods and a new tax on financial transactions at 0.25%, thus making money expensive for non-manufacturing sectors. All of this was a direct challenge to the requirement of all Mercosur countries to adhere to a common external tariff regime. Brazil reluctantly agreed to this effective suspension of Mercosur's customs union status, but only as a temporary measure. Argentina insisted that the measures would apply until 31 December 2002.

These measures, and persistent rumours about the imminent devaluation of the peso, led to a rapid collapse of peoples' confidence in the national currency and the banking system, triggering a run on peso deposits and the flight of dollar deposits to foreign banks. Between 1 January and 30 November 2001, dollar deposits in Argentina's banks dropped from 51 billion to 48 billion; peso deposits fell more precipitously, from 32 billion to 21 billion. During the same period the central bank's net reserves dropped by US$1.7 billion.[18] The government

16   *The Economist*, 21 July 2001.
17   Clóvis Rossi, 'Cavallo recua e se derrete em elogios ao Brasil', *Folha de São Paulo, Caderno de Dinheiro*, B-2, 6 April 2001a; Ariel Palacios, 'Cavallo volta atrás na decisão de zerar tarifas', *O Estado de São Paulo*, 6 April 2001: B-1.
18   *The Economist*, 31 March 2001.

responded by issuing a new decree introducing stringent exchange and banking controls. Argentine tourists were prohibited from taking more than US$1,000 on foreign trips. Within the country, bank withdrawals of more than US$1,000 were also prohibited. It became illegal to pay wages in cash; all wages henceforth were to be paid by cheque. All future loans were to be denominated in dollars. Banks were obliged to allow their customers to change their existing peso deposits into dollars at par, free of charges. De la Rúa remained determined to keep the rigid one-to-one exchange rate peg between the dollar and the peso, despite the damage it had been doing to the country's competitiveness in the export markets.[19]

On 20 December 2001, de la Rúa resigned in the face of widespread rioting and looting in Buenos Aires and elsewhere, and had to be plucked from the presidential palace by an airforce helicopter. On 1 January 2002, Eduardo Duhalde, the leader of the opposition Peronist party and the candidate de la Rua had defeated in the presidential election of October 1999, was sworn in as the new president. In his inaugural address, Duhalde said this:

> Argentina is bust. It's bankrupt. Business is halted, the chain of payment is broken, there is no currency to get the economy moving and we don't have pesos to pay Christmas bonuses, wages or pensions.[20]

Duhalde was not far wrong. Despite the 'no-deficit' law, the de la Rúa administration had run up a budget deficit of US$9 billion by the time of its collapse. The economy had been in recession since early 1999. The annual growth rate of 4% in 1998 had turned into a negative growth of minus 3.2% in 1999 and –0.8% in 2000. The contraction of the economy continued all through 2001; the rate of contraction reached –4% in the last quarter. One estimate, by the Argentine economist Miguel Angel Broda, puts the annual rate of contraction of the economy in 2001 at 15%. The official rate of unemployment had risen from 13.1% at the beginning of 1998 to 18.3% by the middle of 2001. In the two years prior to December 2001, the number of absolute poor, those who did not earn enough to

19   *The Economist*, 8 December 2001.
20   Quoted in *The Economist*, 5 January 2002: 40.

pay for their basic food needs, had doubled to reach 5.5 million.[21] The extent of the decline is better appreciated in the context of the fact that Argentina is the richest country in Latin America.

Duhalde's room for manoeuvre was nearly non-existent. If he opted for debt default, he would antagonise powerful international financial agencies like the IMF and international bankers and creditors. If he chose to abandon the peso–dollar parity instead, he would hurt the middle class, e.g. the salaried professionals and businessmen. This group formed the main support base of the country's long-enduring political establishment, of which he was a leading member, because its loans were denominated in dollars. In the end, he decided to do both. He formally admitted that Argentina was in no position to continue with its debt repayments. On 6 January he devalued the peso by 29%, setting a new official exchange rate of 1.40 pesos to the dollar, but this was to apply only to export earnings, imports being regarded as essential along with most capital transactions. The rest of the economy and Argentine tourists had to buy dollars at the rate determined by the market, where pesos rapidly sank to 1.60 to the dollar, sinking as low as 2.05 at one stage. Several other safeguards were also put in place to cushion the impact of the devaluation on the population. Banks were required to convert all dollar loans of less than US$100,000 into pesos at par. A week later, the government decreed that loans greater than that amount could be repaid at the official rate of 1.40. This was still lower than the market price of the dollar and thus of assistance to big business borrowers. Tariffs charged by the privatised telephone, electricity and water companies, which were hitherto pegged to the dollar and indexed to the US inflation rate, were now switched to the devalued peso at par and unlinked from US prices. Duhalde's administration thus tried to pass on the bulk of the cost of devaluation to the banks, which are mainly foreign owned, and to the privatised public utilities, which are also substantially foreign owned. The volume of outstanding bank loans not covered by the requirement of one-to-one peso conversion is around US$37 billion, US$33 billion of which is the government debt. The banks will, of course, suffer huge losses if borrowers are allowed

21   *The Economist*, 5 January 2002: 41; 20 January 2002: 50.

to repay them in pesos at the official rate of 1.40 while the market value of the peso drops to more than two to the dollar. The government's offer to compensate banks for their losses by taxing oil revenues to the tune of US$700 million a year will cover only a fraction of their likely losses.

Argentina is currently negotiating a new loan of US$15–20 billion with the IMF, which will, at the very least, insist on the resumption of debt repayments, adequate compensation to banks for their losses and a new austerity package involving tighter squeezes on incomes and consumption as conditionalities. It will be interesting to see how Duhalde squares his populist inclinations with the harsh economic realities of neo-liberalism.

Two different visions of South American integration: the Brazilian and the Argentinean

Brazil's and Argentina's policy behaviour towards Mercosur, and by extension to the FTAA, is guided by the different visions they have of South American integration. Brazil is the nearest thing there is in the whole of the Western Hemisphere which can potentially aspire to constitute a political and economic rival to the United States, and both of them know this fact. The Brazilian position is neatly summarised by Lima thus:

> Without recourse to diplomatic rhetoric, it can be said that Brazil's attitude to the unfolding of the FTAA process since 1994 stemmed not so much from a reaction to NAFTA, but from the need for a defensive strategy of strengthening a South American bloc as a means to secure a better a position for itself in the sphere of international political and economic relations.[22]

---

22   Marcos Costa Lima, 'Mercosur at the crossroads: a common market for South America or for the Americas', in Saha and Parker (eds), *Globalisation and Sustainability of Development: A Perspective on a New Economic Order*, Cheltenham: Edward Elgar, 2002: 147; 165.

On 1 September 2000, Brazil convened a summit meeting of the 12 presidents of South America at Brasília. This was the first time in the history of the continent that all its presidents had sat around the same table without outside mediation to discuss the modalities of continent wide integration. This was a major coup for Brazilian diplomacy. The occasion signalled a milestone of success for Itamaraty's efforts to establish South America as a coherent geopolitical unit and free-trade zone, functioning as a counter-weight to the US-dominated NAFTA. This is how one British commentator saw the development:

> The Brasília summit, therefore, raises some intriguing questions. Foreign policy specialists are asking if the Western Hemisphere is beginning to evolve into two separate blocs, one in the north dominated by the US and the other in the South, guided by Brazil. More specifically, they are wondering whether closer South American unity presents a challenge to US influence in the region. There is also the question of whether greater Brazilian influence will affect the talks to create by 2005 a 'Free Trade Area of the Americas', stretching from Alaska to Tierra del Fuego.[23]

Brazil has indeed been trying to seize every opportunity to project itself as the champion of South American sovereign interests, at times against intrusive US intervention in the continent. It successfully opposed US calls for sanctions against Peru in 2000 because the latter did not like the electoral process which looked as though it would bring left-leaning Toledo to power. It has expressed support for Venezuela's new president, Hugo Chávez, at times when the US has been expressing irritation at his populist, and seemingly anti-business, measures at home and his trips to Iraq and Cuba. Its armed forces intervened in Paraguay to forestall a military coup there in May 2000. It helped to stabilise the situation after the short-lived military coup in Ecuador in January 2000.

For Brazil, Mercosur is, in the main, a geopolitical project, the core purpose of which is to prevent US domination in the hemisphere. Once the US is kept out of the formal membership of a South America-wide trading bloc and customs union, Brazil is the natural candidate to slot into the leadership position, giving a strong voice to

---

23 Geoff Dyer, 'Brazil's plan for a resurgent South America', *Financial Times*, 1 September 2000: 17.

Understanding the Political Economy of Mercosur and FTAA 199

the common interests of the continent. The strengthening and consolidation of Mercosur has to be the first essential step towards reaching the goal of a South American trading bloc. Brazil knows that it has to move towards this objective without fanfare and with extreme care and sensitivity. Heavy-handed moves towards asserting regional leadership are certain to stoke adverse nationalistic reactions in other South American countries and drive some of them into the embrace of the United States. It also wishes to secure better access for its exports into the US market and therefore cannot afford to be seen to be single-handedly orchestrating opposition to that country's economic interests in South America.

For Argentina, Mercosur is an economic, and not a geopolitical, project. It sees Mercosur primarily as a mechanism by which to gain easy access for its exports into the large Brazilian market. It also fears the weight of Brazilian manufacturing exports bearing down on the continued viability of its much weaker manufacturing industries. This fear was greatly exacerbated after the Brazilian currency crisis of 1998–99. Bernal-Meza expresses this fear thus:

> If we took into account the fact of increased trade interdependence among the member countries, the answer [to this problem] has to be in the affirmative. The downside of this picture, however, lies in the growing asymmetries within this interdependence, particularly with regard to the trading relations between Argentina and Brazil. This became clearly evident during the Brazilian exchange rate crisis in 1998–1999. Unilateral measures taken by Brazil at the time [...] triggered a serious economic regression in Argentina. The asymmetry of interdependence thus clearly generates costs that tend to fall on the smaller economies.[24]

Argentina recognises the advantage of South American countries jointly acquiring a strong negotiating position vis-à-vis the United States, but does not see the latter as a potential or actual rival. In fact, Guido di Tella, its foreign minister for much of the 1990s, once declared that his country wanted renewed 'carnal relations' with the United States after 50 years of estrangement. It wants low-tariff access of its farm products into the US market and does not wish Mercosur to

---

24 Raúl Bernal-Meza, 'Latin American integration: regionalism or globalisation?', in Saha and Parker (eds), *Globalisation and Sustainability of Development: A Perspective on a New Economic Order*, Cheltenham: Edward Elgar, 2002: 182.

impose high external tariffs on the imports of machinery and capital goods from the US. It is this desire to gain privileged access into the Brazilian as well as the US markets at the same time that would seem to explain the periodic contradictions in its foreign policy – expressions of a strong commitment to Mercosur, followed by determined efforts to open direct trade negotiations with the US, bypassing the institutions of Mercosur.

Argentina's new foreign minister, Carlos Ruckauf, appointed by Duhalde in January 2002, however, announced that 'in foreign affairs, I am polygamous.' This new commitment to polygamy was aimed at assuaging the concerns of Brazil. When Duhalde set up an international team of policy advisers to boost the country's credibility abroad, he appointed Arminio Fraga, the chief of Brazil's central bank, to the team. Duhalde also showed renewed enthusiasm for Mercosur, even talking about the need for a new common currency for the four member states. The US is apparently none too pleased about this new Argentine rapprochement with Brazil. An Argentinean journalist is said to have overheard a US State Department official saying to an Argentine journalist: 'who is going to put up the money for your economic plan? Brazil?'[25] While he needs the support of the US in raising a new loan from the IMF, it is also difficult for a Peronist president to be seen to be enthusiastic about the neo-liberal policies which the US and the IMF are seeking to impose on Argentina. He may well feel that a stronger Mercosur will give him that bit of extra space to manoeuvre in his negotiations with the IMF. This is a position which is very close to that of Brazil.

Effect on Uruguay: what happens to the periphery of the periphery

Knock-on effects on Uruguay of the economic difficulties faced by its two giant neighbours, particularly the floating of the Brazilian real in January 1999 and the slow-motion economic collapse of Argentina,

---

25 *The Economist*, 26 January 2002.

have indeed been harsh. Brazilian devaluation severely squeezed the competitiveness of its exports. Selling Uruguayan products in Brazil became more difficult because they were now substantially dearer in that market. Selling them in Argentina also became harder because that country's buying power for imported goods simply evaporated under the pressure of successive IMF-imposed austerity measures. Uruguay was forced to loosen its currency's 'crawling peg' in January 2002 for the second time in a 12-month period, letting its peso devalue under the pressure of market forces. As most public loans are in dollars, the falling peso led to a rapid increase in the level of indebtedness, from 28% of the GDP by the end of 1998 to 46% in January 2002. Most business and household loans are also denominated in dollars, which raised the costs of production of domestic industry and squeezed the consumption of the general population. These facts in turn led to the deepening of the recession and bigger budget deficits. Its tourist industry, an important foreign exchange earner, nearly collapsed as the flow of tourists to the country, the mainstay of the industry, dried up.

When Argentina introduced a zero tariff on capital goods imports in March 2001, unilaterally breaking Mercosur's common external tariff (Tarifa Externa Comum) rule, Uruguay's exasperated trade minister, Sergio Abreu, compared Mercosur to *Doña Flor e Seus Dois Maridos*, invoking the analogy of Jorge Amado's famous novel, in which a widowed cookery teacher remarried but the ghost of the deceased husband also returned, thus initiating a love triangle. 'We never know what we are going to be – a custom's union or a free trade zone', he said.[26]

Mercosur: a stepping stone to negotiating strength at FTAA

Mercosur members have also been deviating from the established practice of presenting a united front in trade talks with outsiders. In November 2000, Chile initiated bilateral free-trade talks with the United

26   Reported in *Folha de São Paulo*, 6 April 2001: B-4.

States shortly after announcing that it would be seeking full membership of Mercosur. This led to the signing of a trade agreement with the United States in December which firmly stated Chile's intention to join NAFTA as soon as possible. In March 2001, three Mercosur members initiated direct discussions with other countries, by-passing the negotiating mechanism of Mercosur. Uruguay's foreign minister hinted that his country would be seeking its own trade deal with the United States.[27] Both Brazil and Argentina held separate trade talks with Mexico and the Andean countries. Argentina also initiated direct trade talks with the US. Cavallo defended this decision thus: 'Argentina and Brazil have to use all the opportunities which improve the lives of their peoples, expand their markets and create new jobs.'[28] The significant fact was the timing of these developments. They had all taken place less than a month before the approaching third summit of the FTAA in April 2001. This could hardly have been a coincidence.

This divergence of positions taken by individual member states of Mercosur in their discussions with parties outside the organisation stems from their inability to reconcile the differences of their interests within the bloc. Bernal-Meza describes the problem thus:

> [...] the objectives and interests of the member states of Mercosur are themselves not all that homogenous. There are immense fluidities in the identification of national groupings of interests within Latin American countries that cut across the membership of all regional trading blocs in Latin America.[29]

Some of the key issues which have been causing simmering tensions in intra-Mercosur relations are the following:

- Sugar: The average tariff on intra-bloc imports of sugar is currently 22%. Brazil wanted to reduce it to zero by December 2001, but Argentina insists on achieving this in 10 years, Paraguay in 20. Uruguay and Argentina also want Brazil to phase out all incentives and subsidies in the sector.

---

27 Galvão, 2000: 26; *The Economist*, 31 March 2001: 67.
28 Quoted in Rossi, 2001a.
29 Bernal-Meza, 2002: 185.

- Automotive sector: Brazil and Argentina have been negotiating the thorny issue of establishing a common external tariff on imports of cars and automotive parts. The intention is to achieve this by the end of 2004. These tariffs are higher in Brazil than in Argentina. Argentina is insisting on fixing a minimum percentage of domestically produced parts which must be integrated in cars manufactured in the country before agreeing to raise its tariff levels to those of Brazil.
- Chicken: Argentina has been complaining for several years about the alleged dumping of chicken meat on its market by Brazil. In November 2000 it established a minimum price on all imports of chicken from Brazil as an anti-dumping measure. The dispute has remained unresolved.
- Custom duties: Brazil, Argentina and Uruguay want to abolish all custom duties charged at border posts and frontiers between member countries. This is necessary to avoid double taxation on intra-bloc trade. But for land-locked Paraguay, which has no ports, these duties are a major source of revenue, which it cannot afford to lose. Its three partners have shown no inclination so far to give it special dispensation.
- Anti-dumping measures: The four countries have not yet evolved a common definition of what constitutes dumping and unfair competition, nor a common methodology for detecting them.
- Dispute resolution: While the Brasilia Protocol had created a general framework for resolving disputes between member states involving trade matters, the specific and uniform rules and procedures necessary for the functioning of tribunals or arbitration panels have not yet been established.

Now that January 2005 has been agreed at the Quebec City summit as the deadline for concluding the FTAA talks, these intra-Mercosur issues need to be resolved quickly, and in any case, long before that deadline. Ideally, specific understandings of common interests should also be achieved between Mercosur, ALADI and Andean Pact countries as soon as possible, if South American interests are to be adequately protected in those talks. But this is unlikely to happen anytime soon. Mercosur, providing a strong common voice for the 215 million people of its four member countries at those talks, will still be a far better option than each of them fighting their own corner single-handedly.

Bibliography

Achard, D., Flores Silva, M. and González, L. E., 1994, *Las élites argentinas y brasileñas frente al Mercosur*, Buenos Aires: BID-INTAL.
Achugar, Hugo and Caetano, Gerardo, 1993, 'Mundo, Region y Aldea. Identidades, Políticas Culturales e Integración Regional', *Colóquio sobre Identidades, Políticas Culturales e Integración Regional*, Montevideo, Uruguay, 21–23 Julho.
Adler, Emanuel, 1997, 'Seizing the middle ground: constructivism in world politics', *European Journal of International Relations*, 3(3): 319–63.
Alimonda, Héctor, 1994, 'NAFTABLUES', *Novos Estudos*, No. 39, Julho: 222–37.
Almeida, Guy de, 1998, 'Mercosul nas Universidades', Promer Site mercobol@pucminas. br, Belo Horizonte: PUC Minas.
Almeida, Paulo Roberto, 1993, *O Mercosul no contexto Regional e Internacional*, São Paulo: Aduaneiras.
——, 1998, *O Mercosur: fundamentos e perspectivas*, São Paulo: LTr.
Andrews, Christina and Kouzmin, Alexander, 1999, 'Re-legitimating "voice" and "loyalty" within economic theories of democracy and accountability: Brazilian exemplars', *International Review of Administrative Sciences*, 65 (3): 395–409.
Análisis Político Special edition, 1999, 'Análisis de la agenda del siglo XXI', Revista Politeia, Colombia, Venezuela: Instituto de Estudios Políticos y Relaciones Internacionales and Universidad Nacional de Colombia.
Archibugi, Daniele, Held, David and Kohler, Martin (eds), 1998, *Re-imagining Political Community*, Cambridge: Polity Press.
Aron, Raymond, 1962, *Paix et guerre entre les nations*, Paris: Calmann-Lévy.
Arrighi, Giovanni, 1996, *O Longo Século XX*, São Paulo: UNESP.
Ball, George, 1967, 'Cosmocorp: The importance of being stateless', *The Columbia Journal of World Business*, November: 25–30.
Banco Central, 1996, *Mercosul, Informações Selecionadas*, Dez, No. 26.
Baraldi, Roberto, 1996, 'Uma oportunidade histórica na fronteira', *Gazeta Mercantil Latino-Americana*, 24 Junho.
Barbosa, Rubens A., 1991, *A América Latina em perspectiva: a integração regional da retórica à realidade*, São Paulo: Aduaneiras.
——, 1994, 'O Mercosul e suas instituiçoes', *Boletim de Integraçao Latino-Americana*, No. 14, Brazilian Foreign Office, Brasília.
Barnet, Richard and Muller, Ronald, 1974, *Poder Global. A Força Incontrolável das Multinacionais*, Rio de Janeiro: Record.
Bernal-Meza, Raúl, 2002, 'Latin American Integration: Regionalism or Globalisation?', in Suranjit Kumar Saha and David Parker (eds), *Globalisation and*

Sustainability of Development in Latin America: A Perspective on a New Economic Order, Cheltenham: Edward Elgar: 168–88.

Bidart Campos, Germán, 1993, *El Federalismo Argentino desde 1930 hasta la actualidad*, in Marcelo Carmagnani (coordinador), *Federalismos latinoamericanos: México, Brasil, Argentina*, México: El Colegio de México: Fideicomiso Historia de las Américas: Fondo de Cultura Económica.

Binner, Hermes, 1996, 'A missão dos municípios', *Gazeta Mercantil Latino-Americana*, 2 Setembro.

Boletim De Integraçao Latino-Americana, 1993, *Especial: Dois anos do Tratado de Assunçao*, Brazilian Foreign Office, Brasília, March.

Bonanate, Luigi, 1989, 'Osservazioni sulla teoria dei regimi internazionali', in Bonanate, Luigi, Caffarena, Anna and Vellano, Roberto, *Dopo l'anarchia*, Milano: Franco Angeli.

Borda, Dionisio, 1995, 'Economía y estado en transición' in *Mercosur, Integración e Identidades*, Asuncion, Paraguay: AEP.

——, 1998, *Los límites de la Transición. Economía y Estado en Paraguay en los años noventa*, Asunción, Paraguay: CIDSEP-Universidad Católica.

—— and Masi, Fernando, 1997, 'Repercusiones del Mercosur sobre la Economía Paraguaya', in Dionisio Borda and Fernando Masi (eds), *Estabilización y Ajuste de las Economías del Mercosur*, Asunción, Paraguay: CADEP: 105–53.

Boron, Atilio, 1999, 'State Decay and Democratic Decadence in Latin America', in Leo Panitch and Colin Leys (eds), *The Socialist Register*: 209–226.

Bourdieu, Pierre, 1992, *A Economia das Trocas Simbólicas*, São Paulo: Perspectiva.

Bresser Pereira, Luiz Carlos and Spink, Peter (eds), 1999, *Reforming the State: Managerial Public Administration in Latin America*, Boulder: Lynne Rienner.

Bull, Hedley, 1995, *The Anarchical Society: A Study of Order in World Politics*, London: Macmillan.

Cademartori, José, 1998, *Chile. El Modelo Neoliberal*, Chile: Ediciones Chile America CESOC.

Camargo, Aspásia, 1993, 'La Federación sometida. Nacionalismo desarrollista e inestabilidad democrática', in Marcelo Carmagnani (coordinador), *Federalismos latinoamericanos: México, Brasil, Argentina*, México: El Colegio de México, Fideicomiso Historia de las Américas, Fondo de Cultura Económica.

Caputo, Dante M. and Sabato, Jorge F., 1991, *La integración de las democracias pobres: oportunidades y peligros*, Buenos Aires (mimeo).

Castañeda, Jorge, 1994, *Utopia Unarmed*, New York: Vintage Books.

——, 1994, 'Crise mexicana, o começo do fim,' *Teoria e Debate*, 8(28): 45–7.

Castells, M. and Henderson, J. (eds), 1987, *Global Restructuring and Territorial Development*, London: Sage.

Cámara de Comercio e Industria Paraguayo-francesa, 2000, *Informe Annual*, Asunción, Paraguay.

CEPAL and UNESCO, 1992, *Educación y conocimiento: eje de transformation productiva com equidad*, Santiago de Chile: CEPAL.

Bibliography

Charpentier, Jean, 1994, 'Quelle Subsidiarité?, dans Europe, de la Communaité à l'Union,' *Pouvoirs*, No. 69, Avril: 49–62.
Chant, Sylvia, 2000, 'Population, migration, employment and gender', in R. N. Gwynne and C. Kay (eds), *Latin America Transformed. Globalization and Modernity*, London: Arnold.
Chiaramonte, José Carlos, 1993, 'El federalismo argentino en la primera mitad del siglo XIX', in Marcelo Carmagnani (coordinador), *Federalismos latinoamericanos: México, Brasil, Argentina*, México: El Colegio de México, Fideicomiso Historia de las Américas, Fondo de Cultura Económica.
Checkel, Jeffrey T., 1998, 'The constructivist turn in international relations theory', *World Politics*, No. 50, January.
Comissão Parlamentar Conjunta, 1991–1998, *Atas das Reuniões*, Brasilia.
Constable, Pamela and Valenzuela, Arturo, 1991, *A Nation of Enemies: Chile under Pinochet*, London: W.W. Norton.
Couto E Silva, Golbery do, 1981, *Conjuntura Política Nacional: O Poder Executivo & Geopolítica do Brasil*, Rio de Janeiro: Livraria José Olympio Editora.
Dahl, Robert A., 1985, *A Preface to Economic Democracy*, Berkeley: University of California Press.
Diniz, Eli, 1997, *Crise, reforma do Estado e governabilidade: Brasil, 1985–95*, Rio de Janeiro: Fundação Getulio Vargas, Editora.
Domínguez, Francisco, 2000, 'Latin America, Spain, the European Union and the United States', in Francisco Domínguez (ed.), *Identity and Discursive Practices: Spain and Latin America*, Oxford: Peter Lang.
Doremus, Paul, Keller, William W., Pauly, Louis W. and Reich, Simon, 1999, *The Myth of the Global Corporation*, Princeton: Princeton University Press.
Featherstone, Mike (ed.), 1990, *Global Culture*, London: Sage.
Figueiredo, Argelina and Limongi, Fernando, 1997, 'As medidas provisórias: delegação ou abdicação?' *Novos Estudos*, São Paulo, CEBRAP, No. 47: 127–54.
Florêncio, Sérgio and Araújo, Ernesto, 1997, *Mercosur, proyecto, realidad y perspectivas*, Brasília: Vest-Com.
Fogel, R., 1995, *Pobreza y Políticas Sociales en el Paraguay*, Asunción, Paraguay: El Lector.
Fonseca Jr., Gélson, 1999, 'Anotações sobre as condições do sistema internacional no limiar do século XXI: a distribuição dos pólos de poder e a inserção internacional do Brasil', in Gilberto Dupas, and Tullo Vigevani, *O Brasil e as novas dimensões da segurança internacional*, São Paulo: Alfa-Omega, FAPESP.
Freeman, Christopher, 1982, *The Economics of Industrial Innovation*, London: Francis Pinter.
Friedmann, J. P., 1966, *Regional Development Policy: the Case Study of Venezuela*, Cambridge: MIT Press.
Furtado, Celso, 1992, *A Construção Interrompida*, São Paulo: Paz e Terra.
Fukuyama, Francis, 1992, *The End of History and the Last Man*, Harmondsworth: Penguin.

Galvão, Luís Eduardo, 2000, 'Área de Livre Comércio das Ámericas: Ela vem aí, o Brasil está pronto', *Rumos*, 25(179): 26–33.

Garcia Jr., Armando Á., 1997, 'Conflito entre normas do Mercosur e direito interno', *Informativo Mercosur*, 2(6).

Gewandsznadjer, Fernando, 1999, 'Ciência Natural: os Pressupostos Filosóficos', in F. Gewandsznadjer and A. J. Mazzoti, *O Método nas Ciências Naturais e Sociais*, São Paulo: Pioneira: 10–64.

Gonçalves, Reinaldo, 1994, *Ô Abre Alas: a nova inserção do Brasil na Economia Mundial*, Rio de Janeiro: Relume-Dumará.

Gonçalves Ferreira Filho, Manoel, 1990, *Curso de Direito Constitucional*, Sao Paulo: Editora Saraiva.

Green, Duncan, 1995, *Silent Revolution*, London: Latin American Bureau.

Griffith-Jones, Stephanie and Sunkel, Osvaldo, 1986, *Debt and Development Crisis in Latin America. The End of an Illusion*, New York: Oxford University Press.

Grupo Mercado Comum, Regimento Interno, in Paulo Roberto Almeida (coordinador), 1992, *Mercosur: textos básicos*, Brasília: Fundação Alexandre de Gusmão; Instituto de Pesquisas de Relações Internacionais.

Gwynne, Robert N. and Kay, Cristobal (eds), 1999, *Latin America Transformed, Globalization and Modernity*, London: Arnold.

Habermas, Jurgen, 1990, *O Discurso Filosófico da Modernidade*, Lisboa: Publicações Don Quixote.

——, 1995, 'O Estado-Nação Europeu Frente aos Desafios da Globalização', *Novos Estudos*, No. 43: 87–101.

Hirschman, A. O., 1958, *The Strategy of Economic Development*, New Haven: Yale University Press.

Hirst, Paul and Thompson, Graham, 1998, *Globalisation in Question*, Cambridge: Polity Press.

Hurrell, Andrew, 1999, 'Questions on Brazilian foreign policy', *Seminário no Centro de Estudos de Cultura Contemporânea*, 10 September.

IMF, 2000 and 2002, *Direction of Trade Statistics*, Washington DC: International Monetary Fund.

IRELA Briefing, 1996, 'European Union–Latin American economic relations. Statistical profile', Madrid, Instituto de Relaciones Europeo-Latinoamericanas, 15 November.

Lafer, Celso, 1997, 'Relações Brasil-Argentina: alcance e significado de uma parceria estratégica', *Contexto Internacional*, 19(2).

Laidi, Zaki (Dir.), 1993, *L'ordre mondial relâché – sens et puissance après la guerre froide*, 2ème édn, Paris: Presses de la Fondation Nationale de Sciences Politiques.

——, 1996, 'Après les guerres, la mêlée généralisée', *Le Monde Diplomatique*, Janvier.

Lakatos, Imre, 1968, 'Criticism and the methodology of scientific research programmes', *Proceedings of the Aristotelian Society* 69: 149–186.

Bibliography

Lambert, Peter, 1996, 'Mechanisms of control: the Stroessner regime in Paraguay' in W. Fowler (ed.), *Authoritarianism in Latin America Since Independence*, London, Greenwood Press: 93–108.

——, 2000, 'A decade of electoral democracy: continuity, change and crisis in Paraguay', *Bulletin of Latin American Research*, 19: 379–96.

Lampreia, Luiz Felipe, 1999, 'A política exterior do Brasil', *Seminário no IEA/USP*, 4 October.

——, 1995, 'Discourse pronounced to the Commission of Foreign Relations of the Chamber of Deputies on April 5, 1995', *Diário da Manha*, 16 e 17 Abril.

Lander, Edgardo, 1995, *Neoliberalismo, sociedad civil y democracia*, Caracas: Universidad Central de Venezuela.

Larrain, Jorge, 1999, 'Modernity and identity: cultural change in Latin America', in Robert N. Gwynne and Cristobal Kay (eds), *Latin America Transformed, Globalization and Modernity*, London: Arnold.

Leonora, Andrea, 1995, 'Governo Catarinense cria secretaria de integraçao', *Gazeta Mercantil / Por Conta Própria*, 21 Junio.

Lima, Marcos Costa, 1994, 'A Caminho do 1º Mundo? – O México e o Tratado de Comércio da América do Norte', *Temáticas*, ano 2, No. 3: 139–146.

——, 1996, *MERCOSUL. Obstáculos e Vantagens da Integração*, Textos para Discussão, Recife: UFPE/CFCH.

——, 1999, *O Mercosul no Contexto da Nova Ordem Mundial*, Tese de Doutorado, Campinas: UNICAMP/IFCH.

——, 2002, 'Mercosur at the crossroads: a common market for South America or for the Americas', in Suranjit Kumar Saha and David Parker (eds), *Globalisation and Sustainability of Development in Latin America: A Perspective on a New Economic Order*, Cheltenham: Edward Elgar: 136–70.

Lima, Maria Regina Soares, 1994, 'Ejes analíticos y conflicto de paradigmas en la política exterior brasileña', *América Latina/Internacional*, 1(2).

Madison, James, Hamilton, Alexander and Jay, John, 1987, *Os Artigos Federalistas (1787–1788)*, Rio de Janeiro: Editora Nova Fronteira.

Mariano, Karina L. P. and Oliveira, Marcelo F., 1999, *Mercosur: a emergência de uma nova sociedade*, São Paulo: CEDEC, [Relatório final de pesquisa para o CNPq – 1ª Fase].

Martiniere, Guy, 1978, *Les Amériques latines: une histoire économique*, Grenoble: Presses Universitaires de Grenoble.

Masi, Fernando, 1998, *Paraguay y El Mercosur: ¿Apertura sin Ganancias?*, Asunción, Paraguay: Cadep.

——, 1999, 'El Paraguay ante la Crisis Brasileña' in *Carta Internacional*, No. 72, Sao Paulo: Núcleo de Pesquisa em Relações Internacionais da USP.

——, 2000, '¿Adónde va el Mercosur?', *Acción*, No. 203.

Mattoso, Jorge (org.) *et al.*, 1996, *Crise e Trabalho no Brasil*, Campinas: Scritta.

Mazzotti, A. J., 1999, *O Método nas Ciências Naturais e Sociais*, São Paulo: Pioneira.

Moulián, Tomás, 1998, *Chile Actual. Anatomía de un Mito*, Chile: Lom – Arcis.

Myrdal, G., 1957, *Economic Theory and Under-Developed Regions*, London: Gerald Duckworth.

NACLA, *Report on the Americas*, XXX (6), 1997, New York, May/June (Special issue: 'Latin America in the Age of the Billionaires').

Nações Unidas, 1959, *El mercado comum latinoamericano*, México: Publicación de las Naciones Unidas, No. de venta 59.

Nardin, Terry, 1987, *Lei, moralidade e as relações entre os Estados*, Rio de Janeiro: Forense-Universitária.

Nickson, R. A., 1997, 'Corruption and the transition', in P. Lambert and A. Nickson (eds), *The Transition to Democracy in Paraguay*, London: Macmillan: 24–44.

Nye Jr., Joseph S., 1992, *Bound to Lead: the Changing Nature of American Power*, New York: Basic Books.

O Estado de São Paulo, 1997, 'Ministro argentino condena taxação do açúcar', São Paulo, Diplomacia, 8 September: A6.

Ohmae, Kenichi, 1996, *O Fim do Estado Nação*, Rio de Janeiro: Campus.

Ortiz, Renato, 1996, *Mundialização e Cultura*, São Paulo: Brasiliense.

Palacios, Ariel, 2001, 'Cavallo volta atrás na decisão de zerar tarifas', *O Estado de São Paulo,* São Paulo, 6 April: B-1.

Palloix, Christian, 1997, 'Mundialização – Internacionalização – Globalização: Um conceito Impossível', *Revista ANPEC*, No. 2: 51–62.

Pandia Calogeras, Joao, 1957, *Formaçao Histórica do Brasil*, Rio de Janeiro: Biblioteca do Exército Editora.

Pastor, Robert, 1992, 'NAFTA as the center of an integration process: The non trade issues', in Nora Lusting, Barry P. Bosworth and Robert Z. Lawrence (eds), *North American Free Trade: Assessing the Impact*, Washington: The Brooking Institution.

Pecci, Antonio, 1997, 'Priorizar novas açoes: trabalho deve ser uma preocupaçao dos governos', *Gazeta Mercantil Latino-Americana*, Rio de Janeiro, 6 Janvier.

Peña, Félix, 1992, 'Pré-requisitos políticos e econômicos da integração', *Política Externa*, 1(2).

Pinheiro, A. C. and Giambiagi, F., 1997, 'Lucratividade, dividendos e investimentos das empresas estatais: uma contribuição para o debate sobre a privatização no Brasil' [Profitability, dividends and investment in state-owned enterprises: a contribution to the privatization debate in Brazil], in *Revista Brasileira de Economia*, 51(1), Jan–March: 93–132.

Petras, James, 1992, 'The retreat of the intellectuals', in James Petras and Morris Morley, *Latin America in the Time of the Cholera*, London: Routledge.

Porter, Michael E., 1993, *A vantagem Competitiva das Nações*, Rio de Janeiro: Campus.

PPB, [n.d.], Partido Progressista Brasileiro, *Manifesto Programa Estatuto do PPB*.

Prebisch, 1959, *El Mercado Comum Latioamericano*, México: Publicación de las Naciones Unidas.

Bibliography

———, 1968, *Dinâmica do Desenvolvimento Latino-Americano*, Rio de Janeiro: Fundo de Cultura.

Prevot-Schapira, Marie-France, 1992, 'Argentine: Fédéralismes et Territoires', *Cahiers des Amériques Latines*, No. 14.

PT, 1995, *Notas sobre o processo de integração do Mercosur*, São Paulo.

PT, 1993, Partido dos Trabalhadores, 'Carta de Curitiba', Curitiba: *Primeiro Seminário Nacional do PT sobre o Mercosur*, 25 September.

Puryear, Jeffrey, 1994, *Thinking Politics: Intellectuals and Democracy in Chile, 1973–1988*, Baltimore: Johns Hopkins University Press.

PTB, 1996, Partido Trabalhista brasileiro, *Programa e Estatuto do PTB*, Brasília.

Quermonne, Jean-Louis, 1995, 'La démocratisation du processus de décision communautaire depuis le Traité de Maastrischt', *Política Hoje*, No. 3, January–June.

Quesada, Ernesto, 1898, *La época de Rosas, su verdadero caráter histórico*, Buenos Aires: N. Moen.

Sartori, Giovanni, 1987, *Theory of Democracy Revisited*, 2 vols, Chatham: Chatham House.

Schmitter, Philippe C., 1998, *How to Democratize the European Union: Citizenship, Representation, Decision-making in the Emerging Euro-polity*, Florença: Instituto Universitario Europeo, mimeo.

Schumpeter, Joseph A., 1979, *Capitalism, Socialism and Democracy*, London: George Allen & Unwin.

Senado Federal, 2000, *Senadores*, www.senado.gov.br, Brasilia, February 2.

Silva, Patricio, 1999, 'The new political order in Latin America: towards technocratic democracies?', in Robert N. Gwynne and Cristobal Kay (eds), *Latin America Transformed, Globalization and Modernity*, London: Arnold.

Skocpol, T., Evans, P. and Rueschmeyer, D. (eds), 1989, *Bringing the State Back In*, New York: Cambridge University Press.

Starling, Sandra, 1995, 'Declaração de voto da Deputada Sandra Starling sobre o Parecer do relator Deputado André Franco Montoro sobre o Protocolo Adicional ao Tratado de Assunção sobre a estrutura institucional do Mercosur', Brasília: Comissão das Relações Exteriores da Câmara dos Deputados.

Stuart, Ana Maria, 1996, 'Um balanço político da reunião do Mercosur', *Carta Internacional*, São Paulo: Núcleo de Pesquisa em Relações Internacionais e Política Comparada.

Tavares, Maria da Conçeição and Melin, L. E., 1996, 'A Desordem Globalizada e a Nova Dependência', *Revista ANPEC*, No. 2: 11–30.

Thurow, Lester, 1993, *Cabeça a Cabeça. A batalha econômica entre Japão, Europa e Estados Unidos*, Rio de Janeiro: Rocca.

Tulchin, J. S., 1993, 'The enterprise for the Americas initiative', in Roy Green (ed.), *United States Trade Relations*, Boulder: Praeger.

Valls Pereira, Lia, 1991, 'Considerações preliminares sobre a Iniciativa para as Américas', in João Paulo Reis Velloso (org.), *O Brasil e o Plano Bush*, São Paulo: Nobel.
Verba, Sidney and Pye, Lucien, 1965, *Political Culture and Political Development*, Princeton: Princeton University Press.
Vigevani, Tullo (org.) *et al.*, 1996, *Processos de Integração Regional e a Sociedade. O Sindicalismo na Argentina, Brasil, México e Venezuela*, Sao Paulo: Paz e Terra.
——, 1998, *Mercosur: impactos para trabalhadores e sindicatos*, São Paulo: LTR; FAPESP; CEDEC.
Vilas, Carlos, 1996, 'Rhetoric and reality. The World Bank's new concern for the poor', *NACLA, Report on the Americas*, XXIX (6), May–June.
——, 1999, 'Estado, mercado y globalización', paper presented to the *I Interoceanic Congress of Latin American Studies*, National University of Cuyo, Mendoza, 10–12 March.
Von Hayek, Frederick, 1944, *The Road to Serfdom*, London: Routledge.
Weber, Max, 1974, 'Parlamentarismo e governo numa Alemanha Reconstruída', *Ensaios de Sociologia*, São Paulo: Abril Cultural.
Wendt, Alexander, 1994, 'Collective identity, formation and the international state', *American Political Science Review*, 88(2), June.
World Bank, 1994, *Paraguay: Poverty and the Social Sectors: a poverty assessment*, Washington DC.
——, 2001, Country Data Profile, http://devdata.worldbank.org
——, 2000, Country Brief, Washington DC.
——, 2001, World Development Indicators, Washington DC.

Other sources

ABC Color, 2001, Madrid, Spain, 5 March.
AmericasCanada.org, 2001, www.americascanada.org
Banco Central del Paraguay, Comercio Exterior, Estadísticas, Sector Externo.
——, http://www.cepal.org
——, 2000, http://www.bcp.gov.py
Câmara Dos Deputados, 2000, *Deputados*. www.camara.gov.br, Brasilia, 2 February.
Carneiro, Dirceu, 1994, Personal Interview by Tullo Vigevani, Brasília, 12 April.
Declaración De Iguazú, 30 November 1985, www2.uol.com.br/actasoft/actamercosul/espanhol/antecedentes.htm
Economist, The, London, UK
   1997, 'Pan-American Free Trade: Slow, but Ahead,' 24 May: 35.

Bibliography

1997, 'Partners or just neighbours?,' October 11: 63.
2000, 'Argentina's rocky finances', 11 November: 104.
2000, 'The World in 2000': 88.
2001, 'Another Blow to the Americas', 3 March: 67.
2001, 'Mercosur drifts off course', 31 March: 67.
2001, 'Argentina's economy', 21 July: 49.
2001, 'Democracy in Latin America', 28 July: 15.
2001, 'Argentina's economic crisis', 8 December: 62.
2002, 'Argentina's new new president', 5 January: 40–1.
2002, 'Uruguay's Argentine flu', 20 January: 50.
2002, 'Argentina's crisis', 26 January: 56
2002, 'Latin America and the European Union, 18 May: 62.

Financial Times, London, UK

Sally Bowen, 1998, 'Fujimori sidesteps re-election questions', 30 July: 3.
Geoff Dyer, 2000, 'Brazil's plan for a resurgent South America', 1 September: 17.

Folha de São Paulo, São Paulo, Brazil

Belluzzo, L. G., 1995, 'A crise do México e as forças do mercado', 8 January.
Mercadante, Aloizo, 2001, 'ALCA: mais de mesmo', *Caderno Folha Dinheiro*, 15 April: B-2.
Ricupero, Rubens, 2001, 'Equilibrando o jogo', *Caderno Folha Dinheiro*, 15 April: B-2.
Rossi, Clóvis, 2001, 'Cavallo recua e se derrete em elogios ao Brasil', *Caderno Folha Dinheiro,* 6 April,: B-4.
Silva, Carlos Eduardo Lins da, 1999, 'Mercosul pode ter o seu "Maastricht"', *Caderno Folha Dinheiro,* 8 June: 1-4.
——, 2001, 'Brasil não aceita mais negociar com Cavallo', 29 October: A-9.
Tavares, Maria da Conceição, 1993, 'A Realidade sobre o Nafta e o Mercosul', Caderno de Finanças, 28 November.
——, 1998, 'Acordos de Investimentos, privatização e cidadania', Lições Contemporâneas, Caderno Dinheiro, 1 March.
Zini, Álvaro, 1998, 'Rumo ao Impasse Fiscal', Caderno Dinheiro, 1 March.

Gazeta Mercantil, São Paulo, Brazil

1995, 'Sul: autonomia na integraçao', 23 October.
1997, 'Disputa pelo açúcar', 19 May.
1997, 'Argentina mantém proteção ao açúcar brasileiro', 27 May.
1997, 'Senado argentino imobiliza Menem na negociação do açúcar', 4 September.
1997, 'Lampreia lamenta decisão de parlamentares', 5 September.
1997, 'Em nota oficial, Itamaraty manifesta "séria preocupação"', 5 September.
1997, 'Câmara ameaça retaliação contra Argentina', 6 September.
1997, 'Menem pode apelar à Corte Suprema', 7 September.
1997, 'Menem reafirma posição contra proteção a açúcar', 8 September.

1997, 'ACM cobra reação', 9 September.
1997, 'Exportadores debatem crise do açúcar: reunião de brasileiros e argentinos avalia que solução para impasse ainda vai demorar', 17 September.
1997, 'Disputa pelo açúcar', 19 September.
1996, 'Amigos do presidente discutem neoliberalismo', 12 November,.
1996, 'Para Fishlow "Brasil está no caminho certo"', 13 November.
Gratius, Susanne, 2000, 'Las relaciones comerciales entre la Unión Europea y MERCOSUR en el actual contexto internacional', www.sela/docs/spstncmdi4-2000-1.htm, May.
——, 2000, 'Las relaciones comerciales entre la Unión Europea y MERCOSUR en el actual contexto internacional', www.sela/docs/spstncmdi4-2000-2.htm, May.
Mayobre, Eduardo, 2000, 'El sistema financiero internacional, su impacto sobre América Latina y el Caribe', www.lanic.utexas.edu/~sela/ponencias/ponen18.htm: 5, 12 May.
Mercosur Website www.americasnet.com/mercosur; www.mercosur.com
Mundo, El, 1999, Madrid, Spain, 19 August: 4.
PFL – Partido da Frente Liberal, 1998, *Programa do PFL*, www.pfl.org.br/programa.htm, 23 June.
PMDB – Partido do Movimento Democrático Brasileiro, 1998, *Programa do PMDB*, www.pmdb.org.br/progrm2.htm, 19 June.
PSDB – Partido da Social Democracia Brasileira, 1998, *Programa do PSDB*, www.psdb.org.br, 20 June.
PT – *Programa do Partido dos Trabalhadores*, 1998, www.pt.org.br/prog-pt.htm, 19 September.
Transparency International, http://www.transparency.de

About the Authors

Olivier Dabène is Professor of Political Science at the Institute of Political Studies (IEP) in Aix-en-Provence, where he is the director of the doctoral program, and at the Institute of Latin American Studies in Paris, France. Professor Dabène specialized in comparative politics and is the author of more than fifty articles and several books on Latin American politics, including: *Costa Rica: Juicio a la democracia* (1992), *L'Amérique latine au XXéme siècle* (fourth edition 2001), *La région Amérique latine. Interdépendance et changement politique* (1997), *Amérique latine, la démocratie dégradée* (1997). He lectures on a regular basis in several Latin American universities, including Universidad Externado in Colombia, Universidad de Buenos Aires in Argentina, Universidad de la República in Uruguay and Universidad de Costa Rica. Since September 2000, he has been cultural attaché for the French embassy in São Paulo, Brasil.

Francisco Domínguez is Head of Latin American Studies and Spanish and Director of the Centre for Brazilian Studies at Middlesex University, London, UK. He has published on Cuba's economic reform, economic integration in Latin America, NAFTA and Latin America's contemporary political economy. He has been visiting scholar at the Federal University of Rio Grande do Sul, Central and Los Andes Universities of Venezuela. He regularly gives interviews for the BBC on Latin American matters. Member of Executive Council of the Latin American Bureau, UK-based publisher, and of the Forum for the Study of Cuba, jointly run by Wolverhampton and Havana universities. Editor of *Identity and Discursive Practices: Spain and Latin America* (2000).

Marcelo Fernandes de Oliveira is a researcher at the Contemporary Culture Center of Studies (CEDEC) and Master from the University of the State of São Paulo (UNESP)

Karina Pasquariello Mariano is researcher at the Contemporary Culture Center of Studies (CEDEC) and PhD from the State University of Campinas (UNICAMP).

Marcos Aurelio Guedes de Oliveira is Professor of International Politics at Universidade Federal de Pernambuco and CNPq researcher in Brazil. He was Chair Simon Bolivar 2000 at the Institut des Hautes Études de l'Amerique latine at Sorbonne Universite, Paris III and Director of the Centre for Brazilian Studies at Middlesex University from 1999 to 2000. His latest book is *Mercosul e Politica* published in 2001 by LTR Editora, São Paulo, Brazil.

Peter Lambert is Senior Lecturer in Spanish and Latin American Studies at the University of Bath, UK. One of only a few experts on Paraguayan politics, he has published widely on Paraguay, principally on the issues of authoritarianism and democratisation. He lived in the country for 5 years in the 1980s working in the area of development and popular education.

Marcos Lima Costa is Professor at the Social Sciences Dept and Post-Graduate Program in Political Science – Federal University of Pernambuco since 1980. Maîtrise en Philosophie Politique, Université Paul Valéry – Montpellier – France; MSc in Sociology at UFPE; Dr in Social Sciences at UNICAMP-SP. Head of the Nucleus of Strategic Studies of UFPE. Member of the Latin American Studies Association and of the Brazilian Association of Political Science. Advisory Board of VOZES Publisher – *XXIth Century Collection*. Editor of *O Lugar da América do Sul na Nova Ordem Mundial* (2001); *O Mercosul no Limiar do Século XXI* (2000); *Processos de Integração Regional* (1999); *Planejamento Regional em Tempos de Globalização* (1999). Books Collaboration: *Los Rostros Del Mercosur* (2001); *Globalización, Integración, Mercosur y desarrollo local* (2000).

Marcelo de Almeida Medeiros, PhD in Political Science from the University of Grenoble, is Professor of Political Science at the Department of Social Sciences of the Federal University of Pernambuco (Recife/Brazil). He was Associated Professor of Political

Science at the Institut d'Etudes Politiques d'Aix-en-Provence (France, 2000–2001) and Visiting Scholar at the Université des Antilles et de la Guyane (Guadeloupe, May/June 1999). He is also Associated Researcher at the Centre de Recherches sur l'Amerique Latine et la Caraïbe of Marseille University. He has published *La genèse du Mercosud* (2000); 'A Hegemonia brasileira no Mercosul: o efeito samba e suas conseqüências no processo institucional de integração', in Costa Lima, Marcos (edit), *O Mercosul no Limiar do Século XXI* (2000); 'Brazil and Mercosur', in Grugel, Jean, Hout, Wil, (edits.), *The new regionalism and the developing world: states strategies in the semi-preiphery* (1999); 'Estratégias, atores e estrutura institucional da União Européia', in Almeida Medeiros Dantas and Costa Lima (orgs.), *Processos de Integração Regional: O Político, o Econômico e o Jurídico nas Relações Internacionais* (1999).

Suranjit Kumar Saha is a Senior Lecturer at the School of Social Sciences and International Development, University of Wales, Swansea, UK, has carried out a large number of research, consultancy and project management assignments in Brazil, India, Argentina, Bangladesh, Kenya and Ghana on behalf of UNDP, UNESCO, British Council, DFID and several national governments, worked as a Visiting Professor at the Federal University of Pará, Belém and written, co-authored and co-edited several books and journal articles on aspects of globalisation and sustainable development. Forthcoming: with David Parker (eds) *Globalisation and Sustainable Development in Latin America: Perspectives on the Economic Order*.

Tullo Vigevani is professor of Political Science and International Relations at the University of the State of São Paulo (UNESP) and researcher at the Contemporary Culture Center of Studies (CEDEC). Books: *O contencioso Brasil x Estados Unidos da Informática*, São Paulo: Alfa-Omega/Edusp, 1995; *Mercosul: impactos para trabalhadores e sindicatos*, São Paulo: LTR/FAPESP, 1998; and with Dupas, Gilberto, *O Brasil e as novas dimensões da segurança internacional*, São Paulo: Alfa-Omega/FAPESP, 1999. Member of Editorial Committee of Lua Nova, Contexto Internacional, Carta Internacional.

Carlos Thomaz G. Lopes

Brazil at a Crossroads

An Evaluation of the Economic, Political and Social Situation

Bern, Berlin, Bruxelles, Frankfurt am Main, New York, Oxford, Wien, 2002.
385 pp.
ISBN 3-906770-00-1 / US-ISBN 0-8204-5930-5 pb.
sFr. 94.– / €* 64.80 / €** 60.60 / £ 43.– / US-$ 72.95
* includes VAT – only valid for Germany and Austria   ** does not include VAT

This study presents a thorough assessment of Brazil's economy and society combining psychological, economic and sociological insights. Starting with a lucid description of Brazil's past and present social reality – including such essential aspects as health, education and cultural identity of the Brazilian population – the author outlines the main dilemmas which Brazil is facing today.

He then moves on to the practical agenda with special emphasis on the country's role in the global economy. The author's main objective is to introduce adequate instruments which support Brazil on its quest to greater stability and better education.

Contents: Combining the Economy, Society and the Individual – Elements of Economic Reality – Elements of Social Reality – Equality and Efficiency – The Economy: Theories and Vectors of Growth – Politics: Major Characteristics - Government – The Social Factor: A Profile of the Brazilian People – The Psychological Input – Stability – Education and Openness – Implementation.

The Author: Carlos Thomaz G. Lopes (born in 1942) has a law degree from the University of Minas Gerais (Brazil) and attended management courses at Harvard Business School (Boston, Mass). He has been a bank officer and worked in an investment company. The author lives in Rio de Janeiro and wrote two other books on corporate and state planning.

PETER LANG
Bern · Berlin · Bruxelles · Frankfurt am Main · New York · Oxford · Wien

Francisco Domínguez (ed.)

Identity and Discursive Practices

Spain and Latin America

Bern, Berlin, Bruxelles, Frankfurt am Main, New York, Oxford, Wien, 2000.
328 pp., num. tables
ISBN 3-906763-67-6 / US-ISBN 0-8204-4621-1 pb.
sFr. 83.– / €* 56.80 / €** 53.10 / £ 34.– / US-$ 63.95

* includes VAT – only valid for Germany and Austria   ** does not include VAT

Identity and Discursive Practices: Spain and Latin America focuses on contemporary mutual influences between Spain and Latin America. It examines discursive practices on both sides of the Atlantic specifically in the fields of political economy, identity, literature and gender. Although the Spanish influence is not obvious in all twelve contributions, it is an important component of the substratum from which Latin American culture and identity have both developed over the last five centuries and given rise to a variety of identities and discursive practices. With contributions by academics from Spain, Chile, Brazil, Guatemala and Britain, the book brings together scholarly expertise to examine issues such as masculinity, homosexuality, politics, culture, women's identity, nationalism, poetry, and the current economic influence of Spain in Latin America. Scholars and students of both Latin America and Spain will greatly benefit from *Identity and Discursive Practices*.

Contents: Francisco Domínguez: Latin America, Spain, the European Union and the United States – Marco Fonseca: Words of Change: The Guatemalan Peace Process and the International Community – Lila Haines: Spanish Investment in Cuba: A Second Coming – Clare Mar-Molinero: Conflicting and Competing Identities: Language and Nationalism in the Spanish-speaking World – Arnd Schneider: Discourses of Ethnic Distinctions in Contemporary Argentina – Geoffrey Kantaris: The Repressed Signifier: The Cinema of Alejandro Agresti and Eliseo Subiela – George Lambie: The Effect of the Spanish Civil War on the Politics and Poetry of César Vallejo – Márcia Hoppe Navarro: The Search for Identity in Latin American Women's Novels of the Eighties – Linda Craig: Decolonising the Mind: Rosario Ferré's «Cuando las mujeres quieren a los hombres» – Alberto Mira: Constructions of Masculinity in the Narratives of *Mundonovismo* – David Vilaseca: Enjoy Your Symptoms! AIDS as a Source of 'Enjoyment' in Reinaldo Arenas's «Antes que anochezca» – Stephen Wilkinson: Behind the Screen and into the Closet: Reading Homosexuality in the Cuban Revolution through «Conducta impropia», «Antes que anochezca», and «Fresa y chocolate».

 PETER LANG
Bern · Berlin · Bruxelles · Frankfurt am Main · New York · Oxford · Wien

Francesco Carlucci / Ferruccio Marzano (eds.)
Poverty, Growth and Welfare in the World Economy in the 21st Century
Bern, Berlin, Bruxelles, Frankfurt am Main, New York, Oxford, Wien, 2003.
524 pp., num. ill., tables and graphs
ISBN 3-906770-07-9 / US-ISBN 0-8204-5932-1 pb.
sFr. 104.– / €* 71.70 / €** 67.– / £ 43.– / US-$ 79.95

* includes VAT – only valid for Germany and Austria ** does not include VAT

This book includes the main papers presented at an International Conference on North-South Relationships in the 21st Century World Economy held at L'Aquila in Italy (September 2000). The underlying idea of the Conference was the «humanisation of the economy» and was destined to the study of the huge problems of underemployment, famine, disease and inequality, which tragically characterise very large sections of the world population.

Contents: F. Carlucci/F. Marzano: Preface – F. Marzano: Introduction – W. J. Baumol: Opening Paper. Endogenous Dissemination of Technology and North-South Divergence – S. Subramanian: Aspects of Global Deprivation and Disparity: A Child's Guide to Some Simple-Minded Arithmetic – F. Carlucci/S. Pisani: Well-Being in the World: A Stochastic Measure at the Turn of the Millennium – L. Frey: Labour, Human Development and Poverty – A. Barros de Castro: Re-evaluation of the Past and Discussion of the Future. A Perspective for the Brazilian Economy Centred on Growth – J. Vogel: Welfare Institutions and Inequality in the European Union: A Lesson for Developing Countries? – A. Franco/J. Sotelo/E. Carreras: The «State of Art» of the Welfare State – P. Utomi: Technical Aspects of Africa's Economic Development and the Challenge of Values and Ethics – S. Zamagni: From Migrants Integration Policies to a Policy that Acknowledges Diversities – V. Tanzi/C. Ke-Young: Foreign Debt and Fiscal Policy in Poor Countries in the 21st Century – M. Rossi: Harnessing Globalisation: The Role of the IMF – N. S. Ndungu: External Debt and its Impact on Fiscal Policy, Investment, and Growth in Sub-Saharan Africa – S. Fedeli/F. Forte: International Fiscal Policy and Economic Development – J. V. Massiá/M. L. Cabañes: Income - Labour - Leisure Analysis in the North-South Context M. Di Matteo: Capital Accumulation and Exports of the Labour Intensive Good: A North-South Trade Model – V. Monaldi: Globalisation and Underdevelopment: Which Way for LDC's? – O. Neves de Almeida/P. Ascani: Intellectual Property Rights, Biotechnology and Economic Development – A. Fazio: Closing Paper. Economic Development and the Reduction of Poverty.

PETER LANG
Bern · Berlin · Bruxelles · Frankfurt am Main · New York · Oxford · Wien